Competition Law in the ASEAN Countries

International Competition Law Series

VOLUME 73

Editor

In its series editor, Alastair Sutton, Kluwer is fortunate to engage and benefit from the experience and expertise of one of the world's outstanding authorities on European Union and international economic law.

Introduction

In their efforts to regulate competition in an increasingly complex business environment, competition authorities face a daunting task. The European Commission and Courts, as well as national courts and legislatures, policymakers, and regulators, are constantly proposing, enacting, reviewing, and enforcing new legal measures, often addressing novel situations. Every industry and service is affected.

Contents/Subjects

With many titles currently available and new ones appearing regularly, the series' coverage includes detailed analyses of relevant legislation and case law in major global trading jurisdictions, defences used in cases involving the digital network economy, state aid cases, enforcement methodologies and a great deal more.

Objective & Readership

The purpose of Kluwer's International Competition Law Series is to follow the ever-changing contours of this dynamic area of the law, keeping the practice in sharp focus so that practising lawyers (including in-house counsel) and academics can be assured of the most up-to-date guidance and sources, in the widest possible range of applications.

The titles published in this series are listed at the end of this volume.

Competition Law in the ASEAN Countries

Regional Law and National Systems

Ploykaew Porananond

Wolters Kluwer

Published by:
Kluwer Law International B.V.
PO Box 316
2400 AH Alphen aan den Rijn
The Netherlands
E-mail: international-sales@wolterskluwer.com
Website: lrus.wolterskluwer.com

Sold and distributed in North, Central and South America by:
Wolters Kluwer Legal & Regulatory U.S.
7201 McKinney Circle
Frederick, MD 21704
United States of America
Email: customer.service@wolterskluwer.com

Sold and distributed in all other countries by:
Air Business Subscriptions
Rockwood House
Haywards Heath
West Sussex
RH16 3DH
United Kingdom
Email: international-customerservice@wolterskluwer.com

ISBN 978-90-411-9102-1

e-Book: ISBN 978-90-411-9122-9
web-PDF: ISBN 978-90-411-9123-6

About the Author

Ploykaew Porananond is currently a lecturer at the Faculty of Law, Chiang Mai University, Thailand.

In her youth, she indulged in travelling the world perusing knowledge from different legal systems. She obtained her Licence and Masters in Law from Université Grenoble II and Université Toulouse I respectively, and her PhD in Law from the University of Glasgow. She is now settled in Chiang Mai University, Thailand and continues to work in the field of competition law in Southeast Asia.

Table of Contents

Acknowledgement

The topic of competition law in the ASEAN has long been of interest to me. While working on my Master's dissertation on the phenomenon of globalisation of competition law, I noticed the dearth of literature on the ASEAN's efforts regarding competition law and policy. Led by the sheer bravado of youth, I embarked on the journey to rectify this situation and attempt to contribute, however meagre, to the bibliography of the ASEAN's regional competition law in the form of a doctoral thesis. The present book is a revision and expansion of the aforementioned thesis with additional focus on the ASEAN Member States.

The present study incorporates analyses from different perspectives. Historical and legal economic methodologies are employed to help in the understanding of competition law in the ASEAN countries. While a comparison of different regimes is inevitable during the course of the study, the present book is not a comparative study in the strict sense and shall not engage in the theoretical rhetoric of comparative methodology. All the materials used in this book are stated as of January 2018.

I owe many intellectual debts to those who paved the way before me. I am inspired by the writings of Eleanor Fox, Michal Gal, Frédéric Jenny, Mark Williams, and Micheal J. Trebilcock. In particular, I remember the discussions shared with Professor Mark Furse whose ideas helped shaped the arguments present in this book. I would also like to extend my appreciation to Dr Akbar Rasulov, Professor Rosa Greaves, and Professor Ioannis Kokkoris. I would be remiss not to recognise the important work of the staff at Kluwer Law International. In particular, the completion of this manuscript would not be possible without the kind understanding and helpful encouragement of Simon Bellamy.

Finally, I owe my greatest debt to the support of my family and friends who chose to preserve their anonymity perhaps in the hope of a thriving career in reality television. The writing of this book was attempted during a particular difficult year of readjustment in Thailand, at times their support was the only thing holding me up and keeping the project moving.

Ploykaew Porananond
Chiang Mai, Thailand

List of Abbreviations

ABA	American Bar Association
AEC	ASEAN Economic Community
AEGC	ASEAN Expert Group on Competition
AFTA	ASEAN Free Trade Area
AMS	ASEAN Member State
APEC	Asia Pacific Economic Cooperation
APSC	ASEAN Political-Security Community
ASA	Association of Southeast Asia
ASCC	ASEAN Socio-Cultural Community
ASEAN	Association of Southeast Asian Nations
CARICOM	Caribbean Community and Common Market
CEPT	Agreement on the Common Effective Preferential Tariff Scheme
CJEU	Court of Justice of the European Union
COMESA	Common Market for Eastern and Southern Africa
DOJ	US Department of Justice's Antitrust Division
EAC	East African Community
ECJ	European Court of Justice
ECN	European Competition Network
ECOWAS	Economic Community of West African States
EEA	European Economic Area
EFTA	European Free Trade Association
EU	European Union
FTC	US Federal Trade Commission
GCEU	General Court of the European Union
GDP	Gross domestic product

GNI	Gross national income
ICN	International Competition Network
IMF	International Monetary Fund
MERCOSUR	Southern Common Market
NAFTA	North American Free Trade Agreement
OECD	The Organisation of Economic Cooperation and Development
PTA	ASEAN Preferential Trading Agreements
SACU	Southern Africa Customs Union
SADC	Southern African Development Community
SME	Small and Medium Enterprise
TFEU	Treaty on the Functioning of the European Union
UMOA	Monetary Union of West Africa
UNCTAD	United Nations Conference on Trade and Development
US	United States
WAUMU	West African Economic and Monetary Union
WTO	World Trade Organisation

CHAPTER 1
Overture

The twentieth century saw the sudden and abundant emergence of regional competition law agreements covering several continents around the globe and encompassing over sixty countries. This 'new wave of regionalism'[1] brought with it a new dynamic of a more ambitious and deeper level of regional integration that goes beyond traditional information sharing and comity mechanism. At the regional level, several trade arrangements have included competition laws and policies on an area-wide basis believing that competition law and policy is an integral part of effective economic integration in regional trade agreements.[2] More than fifty regional trading partners are now involved in regional competition law agreements.[3] As an illustration, there are the European Union (EU) in Europe; the Common Market for Eastern and Southern Africa (COMESA), the East African Community (EAC), the West African Economic and Monetary Union (WAEMU), the Southern African Development Community (SADC), and the Southern Africa Customs Union (SACU) in Africa; the Southern Common Market (MERCOSUR), the Andean Community, the Caribbean Community and Common Market (CARICOM), and the North American Free Trade Agreement (NAFTA) in the Americas and the Caribbean; and the Association of Southeast Asian Nations (ASEAN) in Asia. The phenomenon that is the proliferation of regional competition law now transcends geographical location, level of economic development, and socio-political ideology. It is important to note that regional competition law agreements are no longer reserved for developed economies but have extended to include developing economies, and in some instances are reserved exclusively for developing economies. What is striking about such agreements is the diversity of their institutional features,

1. Lucian Cernat, *Eager to Ink, But Ready to Act? RTA Proliferation and International Cooperation on Competition Policy, in Competition Provisions in Regional Trade Agreements: How to Assure Development Gains* (Philippe Brusick, et al. eds., UNCTAD/DITC/CLP/2005/1 2005).
2. O. Richard Cunningham & Anthony J LaRocca, *Harmonisation of Competition Policies in a Regional Economic Integration*, 27 Law & Pol'y Int'l Bus. (1995).
3. Luu Huong Ly, *Regional Harmonization of Competition Law and Policy: An ASEAN Approach*, 2 Asian J. Int. Law (2012).

varying provisions of substantive competition law, and different implementation success.[4]

The ASEAN is the latest to join the new wave of regionalism on the 31 December 2015 with the establishment of the ASEAN Economic Community (AEC), long regarded as an important pillar for the ASEAN Community. This new initiative is meant to transform the existing ASEAN into a regional single market with competition law and policy at the centre. The consequent ASEAN regional market forms the third largest market in the global economy, behind China and India, with over 622 million in population[5] amounting to 6% or 6.5 trillion dollars in Gross domestic product based (GDP) on purchasing-power-parity (PPP).[6] First announced at the thirty-ninth Meeting of the ASEAN Economic Ministers in 2007, the ASEAN initiative is deemed too slow and fraught with many difficulties due to political fragmentation, internal conflicts, and external pressures.[7] Others, however, asserted that the slowness was by design since the original conception for the ASEAN was a loosely formed cooperation in Southeast Asia.[8]

The ASEAN is distinguished from other regional organisations in that it regroups ten countries in the Southeast Asia region: Brunei Darussalam, Cambodia, Indonesia, Lao PDR, Malaysia, Myanmar, the Philippines, Thailand, Singapore, and Vietnam. The concept of 'Southeast Asia' is in itself an artificial construct having been referred to as such by the Western Allies in the aftermath of the World War II.[9] The ten ASEAN Member States (AMSs) represent the full spectrum of political, legal, and ideological diversity.[10]

§1.01 UNDERSTANDING THE ASEAN

Since its establishment in 1967,[11] the ASEAN has undergone numerous changes to preserve its survivability as the only regional organisation in Southeast Asia.

[A] The Formation of the ASEAN

The ASEAN was established by the *ASEAN Declaration of 1967*[12] as a regional intergovernmental organisation by five founding Member States: Indonesia, Malaysia,

4. Alberto Heimler & Frédéric Jenny, *Regional Agreements, in* Building New Competition Law Regimes (David Lewis ed. Edward Elgar Publishing 2013).
5. ASEAN Secretariat, *ASEAN Economic Community*, http://asean.org/asean-economic-community/ (accessed 5 Jan. 2018).
6. IMF, *World Economic Outlook Database* (April 2014).
7. Lin Chun Hung, *ASEAN Charter: Deeper Regional Integration under International Law?*, 9 Chinese J. of Int'l L 821 (2010).
8. Pearl Imada, et al., *A Free Trade Area: Implications for ASEAN* (ISEAS 1991).
9. Kevin Y.L. Tan, *The Making and Remaking of Constitutions in Southeast Asia: An Overview*, 6 Sing. J. Int'l & Comp. L. (2002).
10. Diane A. Desierto, *Postcolonial International Law Discourses on Regional Developments in South and Southeast Asia*, 36 Int'l J. Legal Info. (2008).
11. The ASEAN Declaration (1967) (alternatively known as the *Bangkok Declaration*).
12. *Ibid.*

the Philippines, Singapore, and Thailand.[13] It was created due to a combination of external threats and domestic challenges.[14] The *ASEAN Declaration* was drafted against a background of political discordance in the region fuelled by general apprehension over new territories arbitrarily acquired through colonial intervention.[15] At the time, Indonesia had a *Konfrontasi* (Borneo confrontation) with Malaysia, Singapore was ejected from the Federation of Malaysia, Malaysia and the Philippines shared an unresolved conflict over North Borneo, and Malaysia was distrustful of Thailand over the latter's lack of cooperation in combatting the Malayan Communist Party. Despite existing discordance, a degree of concordance emerged between the five states in their stance against communism and authoritarian regimes.[16] These issues are collectively referred to as 'common problems among countries of Southeast Asia' in the *ASEAN Declaration*.

The *ASEAN Declaration* is only a two-page document consisting of three articles describing the rationale for the establishment of the ASEAN and its ambitious objectives. It cites cooperation in various fields (including economic, social, cultural, technical, and educational), the promotion of regional peace and stability through abiding by the respect of justice and the rule of law, and adherence to the principles of the *United Nations Charter* as the organisation's aims and purposes.[17] Given the political climate of the region at the time, it is evident that the ASEAN's primary objective was to prevent regional conflicts, create mutual confidence, and promote regional stability and security by laying a regional foundation for the pursuit of economic development. However, the *ASEAN Declaration* refrains from giving any directions on how to achieve these expansive objectives. It was later suggested that economic cooperation was merely included as an afterthought to dispel suspicion over the ASEAN becoming a military alliance.[18] While the formulation of the *ASEAN Declaration* is laudable for its achievement despite regional political instability, its weakness lies in its lack of direction in pursuing the goals of the organisation. In its own words, the *ASEAN Declaration* represents the organisation's modus operandi of building on small voluntary steps and informal arrangements while moving towards more binding and institutionalised agreements.[19] As its name suggests, the ASEAN

---

13. Thanat Khoman, *ASEAN Conception and Evolution, in* The ASEAN Reader (K.S. Sandhu, et al. eds., ISEAS 1992).
14. Lin Chun Hung, *ASEAN Charter: Deeper Regional Integration under International Law?*, 9 Chinese J. of Int'l L 821 (2010).
15. For more in-depth information on the conflictual political climate surrounding Southeast Asia, *see*, Michael Leifer, *ASEAN and the Security of Southeast Asia* (Routledge 1989); Jürgen Haacke, *ASEAN's Diplomatic and Security Culture: Origins, Development and Prospects* (Routledge 2005); Christopher B. Roberts, *ASEAN Regionalism: Cooperation, Values and Institutionalisation* (Routledge 2012).
16. Christopher B. Roberts, *ASEAN Regionalism: Cooperation, Values and Institutionalisation*, 178 (Routledge 2012).
17. The ASEAN Declaration, Art. 2 (1967).
18. Siow Yue Chia & Michael G. Plummer, *ASEAN Economic Cooperation and Integration: Progress, Challenges and Future Directions*, 1 (Cambridge University Press 2015).
19. ASEAN, *ASEAN History*, http://www.asean.org/asean/about-asean/history (accessed 13 Nov. 2017).

membership is open to all states within the Southeast Asia region subscribing to its aims, principles, and purposes.[20]

It is noteworthy that while it is the largest in scope and membership, the ASEAN was not the first regional organisation in the Southeast Asia region. Previous regional organisations included the MAPHILINDO and the Association of Southeast Asia (ASA) which were both dismantled in the wake of the establishment of the much larger ASEAN. The MAPHILINDO, using the first syllable of its three-Member States, was composed of Malaysia, the Philippines, and Indonesia, thus regrouping the three Malay-based populations of the region who sought to resolve their conflicting territorial claims. The organisation ended prematurely because of the hostilities generated by Indonesia's *Konfrontasi* policy.[21] Another regional organisation was the ASA, composed of Malaysia, the Philippines, and Thailand, which emphasised cooperation in economic, social, cultural, scientific, and administrative matters. The ASA's life expectancy was cut prematurely because of the dispute between the Philippines and Malaysia over North Borneo.[22] North Borneo later became Sabah as part of the Malaysian Federation in 1963.

The ASEAN membership was expanded over time to finally include the entire Southeast Asia region, with the exception of Timor Leste, in accordance with the *ASEAN Declaration*. It was first joined by Brunei Darussalam in 1994 once it gained independence from the United Kingdom. Vietnam, Lao PDR, Myanmar, and Cambodia (often collectively referred to as the CLMV) entered the ASEAN during the period between 1995 and 1999. It was argued that the fear of perceived external threats, including the looming unified economic blocs of the EU and the NAFTA, played a role in the successful expansion of the ASEAN.[23] The increase in the number of the AMSs engendered new and challenging issues, in particular an increase in the existing diversity in the economic development between the AMSs.

[B] The Transformation of the ASEAN

From its humble origins, the ASEAN has undergone important fundamental changes in both ideology and structure. The ASEAN's transformation was deemed necessary for its survival[24] in order to maintain and gain political momentum through the organisation's new purpose.

20. The ASEAN Declaration, Art. 4 (1967).
21. Russel H. Fifield, *National and Regional Interests in ASEAN: Competition and Co-operation in International Politics*, 3 (ISEAS 1979).
22. Roger Irvine, *The Formative Years of ASEAN: 1967–1975, in* Understanding ASEAN 9 (Allison Broinowski ed. Macmillan 1982).
23. Deborah A. Haas, *Out of Others' Shadows: ASEAN Moves Toward Greater Regional Cooperation in the Face of the EC and NAFTA*, 9 Am. U. J. Int'l L. & Pol'y (1994); Christopher B. Roberts, *ASEAN Regionalism: Cooperation, Values and Institutionalisation* (Routledge 2012).
24. Lin Chun Hung, *ASEAN Charter: Deeper Regional Integration under International Law?*, 9 Chinese J. of Int'l L 821 (2010).

[1] Economic Cooperation

The expansion in membership accompanied by the perceived fear of the rapid growth of China and India[25] which led to the realisation that the ASEAN needed to be reinvented.[26] The adoption of the *Declaration of ASEAN Concord*[27] was an important cornerstone of the ASEAN's economic cooperation. It aimed to expand the ASEAN cooperation in economics, social, cultural, and political areas. Primarily, it provided the general framework of trade and industrial cooperation that led to the establishment of various programmes including the *ASEAN Preferential Trading Agreements (PTA)*,[28] the ASEAN Industrial Projects,[29] the ASEAN Industrial Complementation,[30] and the ASEAN Industrial Joint Venture Scheme.[31] None of these efforts would yield adequate results in the development of intra-regional trade and investment. It was described as a 'futile attempt'[32] largely because of the *PTA*'s flexibility which contributed to widespread abuse of exclusion lists that has weakened the *PTA* scheme.[33]

Concerned about the rapid proliferation of free trade areas and custom unions, such as the EU and the NAFTA, the leaders of the ASEAN sought to implement similar attempts to the ASEAN.[34] With the support of Thailand and Singapore, the ASEAN undertook another economic cooperation project.[35] Following the fourth ASEAN Summit in 1992, the ASEAN leaders established the ASEAN Free Trade Area (AFTA) through the adoption of a series of three important documents. The first document was the *Singapore Declaration*[36] describing the ASEAN's intention to forge closer political and economic cooperation. Regarding the economic cooperation, the document serves as an outline of economic measures to be taken in order to achieve the AFTA. The *Framework on Enhancing ASEAN Economic Cooperation*[37] provided the principles of the ASEAN economic cooperation and stressed that the AFTA was only one of the trade cooperation mechanisms in place. Finally, the primary vehicle of the AFTA was the

---

25. Simon S. C. Tay, *The ASEAN Charter: Between National Sovereignty and the Region's Constitutional Moment*, 12 SYBIL. (2008).
26. Simon S. C. Tay, et al., *Reinventing ASEAN* (ISEAS 2001).
27. Declaration of ASEAN Concord (1976) (ASEAN Concord I).
28. ASEAN Preferential Trading Agreements (1977).
29. Basic Agreement on ASEAN Industrial Projects (1980).
30. Basic Agreement on ASEAN Industrial Complementation (1981).
31. ASEAN Industrial Joint Venture Scheme (1983).
32. George O. III White, *From Snowplows to Siopao—Trying to compete in a Global Marketplace: The ASEAN Free Trade Area*, 8 Tulsa J. Comp. & Int'l L. (2000).
33. Many critics have ridiculed the inclusion of snowploughs and other Southeast Asian non-essentials in the exclusion list, *see*, Peter Kenevan & Andrew Winden, *Flexible Free Trade Area: The ASEAN Free Trade Area*, 34 Harv. Int'l L.J. (1993); White, *From Snowplows to Siopao—Trying to compete in a Global Marketplace: The ASEAN Free Trade Area*, 8 Tulsa J. Comp. & Int'l L. (2000).
34. Carolina Alberto Lopez & Jacint Soler Matutes, *Open Regionalism Versus Discriminatory Trading Agreements: Institutional and Empirical Analysis*, 14 ASEAN Econ. Bull. (1998); White, *From Snowplows to Siopao—Trying to compete in a Global Marketplace: The ASEAN Free Trade Area*, 8 Tulsa J. Comp. & Int'l L. (2000).
35. Paul J. Davidson, *ASEAN: The Evolving Legal Framework for Economic Cooperation*, 74 (Times Academic Press 2002).
36. Singapore Declaration (1992).
37. Framework on Enhancing ASEAN Economic Cooperation (1992).

Agreement on the Common Effective Preferential Tariff Scheme (CEPT).[38] The *CEPT* was an agreed effective tariff ranging from 0% to 5% applied to certain manufactured goods originating from the AMSs. It took precedence over the ASEAN Industrial Joint Venture Scheme and the goods covered in the *PTA* would be transferred to the *CEPT*.[39] To avoid a repetition of the *PTA*'s under-performance, the *CEPT* was drafted more precisely with less flexibility for the AMSs. What is striking about the *CEPT* is the lack of concrete mechanism for members' dispute resolution. While the AMSs can submit their unresolved issues to the AFTA Council – a ministerial-level council established by the *Singapore Declaration* to supervise, coordinate, and review the implementation of the AFTA[40]– the *CEPT* failed to proscribe the Council's role in dispute resolution. Ultimately, the AMSs were encouraged to resolve any disputes in a peaceful and amicable manner.[41]

It is possible that the AFTA true purpose was to provide a new political purpose to the ASEAN after the end of the US-Soviet confrontation and the Cambodian Crisis.[42] Indeed, studying the documents constituting the AFTA reveals that the AFTA was not created for trade liberalisation nor to increase of ASEAN intra-regional trade, but rather to attract foreign direct investment (FDI).[43]

[2] The ASEAN Community

The final transformation commenced at the ASEAN Summit in December 1997 with the publication of the *ASEAN Vision 2020*,[44] in which the ASEAN leaders envisioned a peaceful and stable region and planned to forge closer economic integration within the ASEAN by the year 2020. Thus, the *ASEAN Vision 2020* departed from the ASEAN's political and security intergovernmental origin and started steering in a new direction. It was argued that the ASEAN's morphology emerged more from perceptions of external threats, in particular the economic rise of China and India, than from an internal conviction of the benefits of stronger intra-regional integration.[45] Another impetus for the ASEAN's most important transformation was the effect of the aftermath of the Asian Financial Crisis in 1997 when the ASEAN's inability to react to crises was exposed and the necessity of better cooperation at the regional level was recognised.[46]

38. Agreement on the Common Effective Preferential Tariff (CEPT) Scheme for the ASEAN Free Trade Area (1992).
39. Davidson, *ASEAN: The Evolving Legal Framework for Economic Cooperation*, 75 (Times Academic Press 2002).
40. Singapore Declaration (1992).
41. Agreement on the Common Effective Preferential Tariff (CEPT) Scheme for the ASEAN Free Trade Area (1992).
42. Leszek Buszynski, *ASEAN's New Challenges*, 70 Pacific Affairs (1997).
43. Shaun Narine, *Explaining ASEAN: Regionalism in Southeast Asia*, 10 (Lynne Rienner Publishers 2002).
44. ASEAN Secretariat, *ASEAN Vision 2020*, http://www.asean.org/news/item/asean-vision-2020 (accessed 19 Nov. 2012).
45. Siow Yue Chia & Michael G. Plummer, *ASEAN Economic Cooperation and Integration: Progress, Challenges and Future Directions*, 3 (Cambridge University Press 2015).
46. Sanchita Basu Das, *The ASEAN Economic Community and Beyond: Myths and Realities*, 15–16 (ISEAS 2016).

Indeed, the ASEAN failed to present a united front to effectively resolve the 1997 crisis and instead left the AMSs to recover independently.[47]

Following the *ASEAN Vision 2020*, the ASEAN leaders decided, in the *Declaration of ASEAN Concord II*,[48] that the ASEAN Community would be supported by three pillars: the ASEAN Political-Security Community (APSC), the ASEAN Socio-Cultural Community (ASCC), and the ASEAN Economic Community (AEC). The choice of language ascertains that the ASEAN's transformation is modelled on the EU. The economic pillar is regarded as the most feasible of the three.[49] The AEC's goal is regional economic integration with free movement of goods, services, investment, skilled labour, and the freer flow of capital.[50] It envisages the following key characteristics: a single market and production base, a highly competitive economic region, a region of equitable economic development and a region fully integrated into the global economy. In 2007, the ASEAN leaders agreed by consensus to accelerate the establishment of the AEC, originally planned for 2020, to 2015.[51] The reason behind this unexpected acceleration was the ASEAN leaders' satisfaction with the progress towards narrowing the development gap within the region. They agreed that decreasing the deadline of the AEC would encourage a more enthusiastic attitude towards stronger regional integration.[52] Nonetheless, the formal establishment of the ASEAN Community comprising of the APSC, the ASCC, and the AEC was later delayed to 31 December 2015.[53]

The *ASEAN Charter*[54] was adopted to facilitate economic integration and enhance security cooperation among the AMSs. Its arrival was much anticipated with expectation that it could be the harbinger of the new ASEAN, one which focused on more meaningful regional integration and departed from the tradition of non-interference and mutual respect.[55] In reality, the *ASEAN Charter* did little more than grant the ASEAN a legal personality which is rather inconsequential in light of the its institutional capacity.[56] Furthermore, it was argued that the ASEAN had always had legal personality[57] although this had never been publicly acknowledged before the *ASEAN Charter*. While the *ASEAN Charter* failed to meet the expectations and the ASEAN's

47. Shaun Narine, *Explaining ASEAN: Regionalism in Southeast Asia*, 139 (Lynne Rienner Publishers 2002).
48. Declaration of ASEAN Concord II (2003) (ASEAN Concord II, also alternatively known as Bali Concord II).
49. Christopher B. Roberts, *ASEAN Regionalism: Cooperation, Values and Institutionalisation*, 187 (Routledge 2012).
50. ASEAN Secretariat, *ASEAN Economic Community*, http://www.asean.org/communities/asean-economic-community (accessed 19 Nov. 2012).
51. ASEAN Secretariat, *ASEAN Economic Community Blueprint* (2007).
52. *Ibid.*
53. Kuala Lumpur Declaration on the Establishment of the ASEAN Community (2015).
54. The ASEAN Charter (2007).
55. Lin Chun Hung, *ASEAN Charter: Deeper Regional Integration under International Law?*, 9 Chinese J. of Int'l L 821 (2010).
56. Lee Leviter, *The ASEAN Charter: ASEAN Failure or Member Failure?*, 43 NYU. J. Int'l L. & Pol. 159 (2010).
57. Simon Chesterman, *Does ASEAN Exist? The Association of Southeast Asian Nations as an International Legal Person*, 12 SYBIL. (2008). He inferred ASEAN's legal personality based on the principle laid down by the ICJ Advisory Opinion 11 Apr. 1949 *Reparations* Case that the Member

own ambitious goals, observers were quick to defend it.[58] What it did achieve was to steer the ASEAN towards an unprecedented direction; one that focuses on a rule-based approach and a more formal regional institution.

[C] The Genesis of the ASEAN Competition Law

At the thirty-ninth Meeting of the ASEAN Economic Ministers, the ASEAN leaders agreed to prioritise the ASEAN market integration as the main projected plan. The objective was to form a single regional market with competition law and policy as an important part of the mechanism.[59] It was the first time that competition law and policy had ever been mentioned within the ASEAN. There is no public record that suggests the ASEAN's interest in competition law and policy derives from external or internal pressures. At the time, only four AMSs had introduced and implemented competition law: Thailand,[60] Indonesia,[61] Singapore,[62] and Vietnam.[63] There is considerable variance in the range and depth of the national competition regulations in these four regimes and questions may arise as to the effectiveness of the enforcement of these competition laws. For the four AMSs, the emphasis would be on how to harmonise and make their existing national competition laws more effective within the regional common framework. For other AMSs without comprehensive competition law, the focus would be on how best to introduce national competition law. Therefore, it is reasonable to deduce that the AMSs' experiences were not sufficiently established to influence the organisation's decision to adopt a regional competition law regime. The only plausible justification regarding the origin of the ASEAN competition law is the organisation's internal conviction that there was a natural correlation between trade liberalisation, a single regional market, and a competition policy. Once the ASEAN leaders had fixed their sights on the establishment of a regional economic community with a single regional market, it was only natural they would want to introduce competition law and policy.

The management and development of the ASEAN competition law and policy was placed under the authority of the Sectoral Bodies and under the purview of the ASEAN Economic Ministers. Moreover, the ASEAN Expert Group on Competition (AEGC) was also established in order to promote the exchange of information,

States intended ASEAN to have the necessary authority to exercise its functions and fulfil its purpose as specified or implied in the treaty.

58. *See*, e.g., Simon S. C. Tay, *The ASEAN Charter: Between National Sovereignty and the Region's Constitutional Moment*, 12 SYBIL. (2008); Desierto, *Postcolonial International Law Discourses on Regional Developments in South and Southeast Asia*, 36 Int'l J. Legal Info. (2008); Asian Development Bank, *Institutions for Regional Integration: Toward an Asian Economic Community*, 123 (2010).
59. ASEAN Secretariat, *The Thirty-Ninth ASEAN Economic Ministers Meeting Makati City*, http://www.asean.org/news/item/the-thirty-ninth-asean-economic-ministers-aem-meeting-makati-city-philippines-24-august-2007 (accessed 13 Nov. 2017).
60. Thailand Trade Competition Act (1999).
61. Law of the Republic of Indonesia Number 5 Year 1999 Concerning Prohibition of Monopolistic Practices and Unfair Business Competition (1999).
62. Singapore Competition Act of 2004 (Cap. 50B) revised on 30 Jan. 2006 (2004).
63. Vietnam Law on Competition of 2004, No. 27/2004/QH11 (2004).

experience, and cooperation on competition law and policy within the region.[64] The AEGC does not have the status of a competition authority in that it is not charged with any enforcement responsibilities. It merely functions as a regional network forum to help coordinate and encourage the introduction of national competition laws. Since its conception, the AEGC has been working consistently on capacity-building in respect of national competition laws with the AMSs' national authorities.[65]

Finally, at the thirteenth ASEAN Summit on 20 November 2007,[66] the AMSs adopted the *AEC Blueprint (Blueprint)*[67] to serve as a master plan to facilitate and ensure the coherence of the AEC. The *Blueprint* is significant in that it represents a shift from a style of operation that depended solely on leaders' declarations, to one that is more methodical and relies on a collectively endorsed set of objectives.[68] According to the *Blueprint*, each AMS is committed to implement national competition law by the arrival of the AEC in 2015. By admitting that the main objective of the competition law is to 'foster a culture of fair competition,'[69] the *Blueprint* immediately calls attention to competition advocacy. The emphasis on advocacy is reflected in the *Blueprint*'s first action plan regarding competition policy which aims to introduce competition law in all AMSs by the AEC deadline of 2015 through the aides of capacity-building programmes and regional guidelines. The AMSs' commitment to the implementation of competition policy is to 'ensure a level playing field and incubate a culture of fair business competition for enhanced regional economic performance in the long run'.[70] The ASEAN's reluctance to push beyond competition advocacy is understandable in light of the AMSs' significant variances in economic and social structures. Moreover, it was claimed that a 'uniform system would only be equitable when countries enjoy the same levels of economic development, research and development capability, infrastructure and technological prowess'.[71] Put differently, a unified regional competition law appears too ambitious for the ASEAN's state of diversity. Moreover, since the

64. ASEAN Secretariat, *The Thirty-Ninth ASEAN Economic Ministers Meeting Makati City*, http://www.asean.org/news/item/the-thirty-ninth-asean-economic-ministers-aem-meeting-makati-city-philippines-24-august-2007 (accessed 13 Nov. 2017).
65. ASEAN, *Activities & Archived Activities, in Competition Policy*, http://www.asean.org/communities/asean-economic-community/category/competition-policy (accessed 13 Nov. 2017).
66. ASEAN Secretariat, *Chairman Statement of the 13th ASEAN Summit, One ASEAN at the Heart of Dynamic Asia*, http://www.asean.org/news/item/chairman-s-statement-of-the-13th-asean-summit-one-asean-at-the-heart-of-dynamic-asia-singapore-20-november-2007 (accessed 19 Nov. 2012).
67. ASEAN Secretariat, *ASEAN Economic Community Blueprint* (2007).
68. Simon S. C. Tay, *The ASEAN Charter: Between National Sovereignty and the Region's Constitutional Moment*, 12 SYBIL. (2008).
69. ASEAN Secretariat, *ASEAN Economic Community Blueprint* (2007).
70. Anthony Amunategui Abad, *Competition Law and Policy in the Framework of ASEAN in Competition Policy and Regional Integration, in* Competition Policy and Regional Integration in Developing Countries (Josef Drexl, et al. eds., Edward Elgar Publishing 2012).
71. Lawan Thanadsillapakul, *The Harmonization of ASEAN: Competition Laws and Policy from an Economic Integration Perspective, in* Competition Policy and Regional Integration in Developing Countries (Josef Drexl, et al. eds., Edward Elgar 2012).

ASEAN is not a supranational organisation,[72] it neither has a regional institution nor a judicial organ to implement and enforce competition law.

Due to the lack of a central institution capable of developing competition law, the *Blueprint* sets out to establish 'a network of authorities or agencies responsible for competition policy to serve as a forum for discussing and coordinating competition policies'.[73] The 'network of authorities or agencies' mentioned in the *Blueprint* is in reality the already established AEGC because both share similar characteristics as a regional discussion and cooperation platform. The AEGC held its first meeting in 2008[74] whence the experts agreed to focus on building up competition law capabilities and best practices in the member countries within the following three to five years. Following the goal specified in the *Blueprint*, the AEGC released the *ASEAN Regional Guidelines on Competition Policy (Guidelines I)*,[75] a self-proclaimed 'pioneering attempt'[76] to achieve a highly competitive economic region. The *Guidelines I* are based on the experiences of both the AMSs and the wider international community and have as their aim the harmonisation of the AMSs' competition rules. They were later complemented by the *Guidelines on Developing Core Competencies in Competition Policy and Law for ASEAN (Guidelines II)*[77] which concentrate more on the development of competition law enforcement mechanisms. The AEGC hopes that both *Guidelines* will raise the awareness of competition law and policy, stimulate the development of best practice in competition law, and enhance cooperation between the AMSs. *An ASEAN Competition Action Plan (2016–2025)* was later published in 2016 detailing strategic goals and continued measures regarding the ASEAN competition law after the entrance of the AEC. To date, these are the only competition law specific documents established by the ASEAN in pursuit of a regional competition law and policy framework.

§1.02 THE ASEAN PARTICULARITIES

Amongst other regional organisations, the ASEAN stands out due to the considerable diversity among the AMSs ranging from their respective economic and politics heritage, governance systems, legal institutions, stages of economic development, and exposure to or reliance on foreign trade and investments. While diversity among Member States is also present in other regional organisations, what differentiates the AMSs from others is the diversified level of disparity exhibited in the region.

72. ASEAN Secretariat, *The ASEAN Charter*, http://www.asean.org/archive/publications/ASEAN-Charter.pdf (accessed 15 Oct. 2012).
73. ASEAN Secretariat, *ASEAN Economic Community Blueprint*, Art. 41 (2007).
74. ASEAN, *Activities & Archived Activities, in Competition Policy*, http://www.asean.org/communities/asean-economic-community/category/competition-policy (accessed 13 Nov. 2017).
75. ASEAN Secretariat, *ASEAN Regional Guidelines on Competition Policy* (ASEAN Secretariat August 2010) (The Guidelines I).
76. *Ibid.*, Foreword at i.
77. ASEAN Secretariat, *Guidelines on Developing Core Competencies in Competition Policy and Law for ASEAN* (2012) (the Guidelines II).

In terms of population within the region, the ASEAN's overall population places third after China and India at 621 million, with Indonesia holding the largest population within the region at 252 million, whereas Brunei Darussalam has a population of only 0.4 million.[78] The legal systems of the AMSs also vary considerably, ranging from common to civil law systems, or a hybrid of both.[79] Brunei Darussalam, Malaysia, and Singapore have common law systems; the Philippines and Thailand use a hybrid of civil and common legal systems; Indonesia has a civil law system; Vietnam inherited the French civil law system but this is located in communist legal theory; Lao PDR, Myanmar, and Cambodia are still in the process of finding a legal identity. In terms of population within the region, the ASEAN's overall population places it third after China and India at 621 million, with Indonesia holding the largest population within the region at 252 million. Brunei Darussalam has a population of only 0.4 million.[80] The legal systems of the AMSs also vary considerably, ranging from common to civil law systems or a hybrid of both.[81] Brunei Darussalam, Malaysia, and Singapore have common law systems; the Philippines and Thailand use a hybrid of civil and common legal systems; Indonesia has a civil law system; Vietnam inherited the French civil law system but this is located in communist legal theory; Laos, Myanmar, and Cambodia are still struggling to find a legal identity.

This deep level of diversity contributes to the divergence in the AMSs' competition law enforcement and therefore could potentially render the regional harmonisation process of competition law more challenging to accomplish. Eventually, this level of diversity could delay or impede the ASEAN's development of regional competition law. In recognition of the serious impact of the eco-political context on competition law, this section will focus on the diversity in political system and economic development in South East Asia.

[A] The Political Regimes

It is undeniable that political traits such as the type of political regime, the electoral system, and the quality of governance have a significance impact on the enactment and enforcement of competition law. However, scholars struggle to agree on the extent of such an impact on competition law. Some scholars claim countries with a functioning democratic political regime and a stable rule of law are more inclined to enact national competition law.[82] Functioning democracy refers to a political system which encompasses a usable legislative instrument, competent and impartial administration of the law, and the ability to enforce. This notion tentatively goes beyond the inclusion of

78. IMF, *World Economic Outlook Database* (April 2014).
79. Haas, *Out of Others' Shadows: ASEAN Moves Toward Greater Regional Cooperation in the Face of the EC and NAFTA*, 9 Am. U. J. Int'l L. & Pol'y (1994).
80. IMF, *World Economic Outlook Database* (April 2014).
81. Haas, *Out of Others' Shadows: ASEAN Moves Toward Greater Regional Cooperation in the Face of the EC and NAFTA*, 9 Am. U. J. Int'l L. & Pol'y (1994).
82. Raju Parakkal, *Political Characteristics and Competition Law Enactment: A Cross-Country Empirical Analysis*, 56 The Antitrust Bulletin (2011); Mark Williams, *Competition Law in Thailand: Seeds of Success or Fated to Fail?*, 27 World Competition (2004).

democracy in a country's Constitution. However, the type of competition law experience, in particular regarding political restraint, that a state encountered is independent of that state's chosen political regime.[83]

The range of political regimes represented among the AMSs is wide, from democracy to monarchy. Cambodia,[84] Malaysia,[85] and Thailand[86] pride themselves on their constitutional monarchy, while Brunei Darussalam has a system of Malay Islamic monarchy.[87] Singapore is a parliamentary republic.[88] The Philippines, Indonesia,[89] and most recently, Myanmar[90] are presidential republics. The political reform undergone by Myanmar seems to indicate the emergence of a liberal democracy but the reform could not erase the omnipresence of the military in the government despite the self-abolition of the military junta. Lao PDR[91] and Vietnam[92] are the two remaining socialist states in the region. Despite having enshrined the principle of democracy in their Constitution, the AMSs' state of democracy appears illusory and is marred by frequent political instability. For example, the legitimacy of the Myanmarian elections of 2010 was called into question.[93] Thailand has continuously suffered from political instability. To date, it has enacted nineteen Constitutions and has intermittently reverted to a military junta – its current political state.

Yet, it is not the diversity in political forms that critics fear could mar the ASEAN attempt in regional competition law; it is the lack of good governance and rule-based system.[94] Corruption is widely recognised as attributing to the distortion of market efficiency and preventing the market from functioning properly.[95] The issue of corruption is a global one which can be found in both developing economies and developed economies. The EU highlights corruption as a serious issue affection

83. Maher M. Dabbah, *Competition Law and Policy in Developing Countries: A Critical Assessment of the Challenges to Establishing an Effective Competition Law Regime*, 33 World Competition (2010).
84. The Constitution of the Kingdom of Cambodia, Art. 1 (1993).
85. The Federal Constitution of Malaysia, Art. 1 (1957). Malaysia is a federal constitutional monarchy in which the head of State is the Yang di - Pertuan Agong and the head of government is the Prime Minister. The Yang di - Pertuan Agong is elected for a five-year term by and from the rulers of the nine states in Peninsular Malaysia which have retained their hereditary Malay royal family.
86. The Constitution of the Kingdom of Thailand, Art. 2 (2007).
87. The Constitution of Brunei Darussalam, Art. 4 (1959).
88. The Constitution of the Republic of Singapore, Art. 3 (1965).
89. The Constitution of the Republic of Indonesia, Art. 4 (1945).
90. The Constitution of the Republic of the Union of Myanmar, Art. 16 (2008).
91. The Constitution of the Lao People's Democratic Republic, Art. 2 (1991).
92. The Constitution of the Socialist Republic of Vietnam, Art. 4 (1992).
93. Neil Macfarquhar, *U.N. Doubts Fairness of Election in Myanmar*, The New York Times, 21 Oct. 2010.
94. *See*, generally, Lawan Thanadsillapakul, *The Harmonization of ASEAN: Competition Laws and Policy from an Economic Integration Perspective, in* Competition Policy and Regional Integration in Developing Countries (Josef Drexl, et al. eds., Edward Elgar 2012); Williams, *Competition Law in Thailand: Seeds of Success or Fated to Fail?*, 27 World Competition (2004).
95. *See*, generally, Eleanor M. Fox, *Economic Development, Poverty and Antitrust: The Other Path*, 13 Sw. J. L. & Trade Am. (2007). (The OECD has also organised a Global Forum on Competition focusing on fighting corruption and promoting competition on 27–28 Feb. 2014.)

competition law which needs to be addressed at both the EU and the Member State level.[96]

The political diversity within the Southeast Asian region is aggravated by the issue of corruption which in these countries is usually deeply embedded within the administrative system and becomes a major obstacle to any change or reform. It is common in Southeast Asia to have a strong relationship between the business and government sectors.[97] This system is described as one of patronage where political leaders or the patrons serve the interest of their financial supporters or the clients.[98] This system is attributed to the historical situation whereby many businessmen in this area are of Chinese descent. To avoid resentment of their cultural differences in a foreign land that would obstruct their business, they turned to indirect political influence to smooth their business endeavours.[99] In this climate of cronyism, the government is inevitably implicated in the management of its local economy. Unquestionably, it is possible that the government may willingly participate in the market without the encouragement of a third party. Historically, the Singaporean government invested through government-linked companies in numerous sectors that the private sector was unwilling or unable to enter.[100] These companies later grew considerably and consequently contribute to anticompetition problems in Singapore's economy. It is necessary that the role of the government in the local economy be curbed[101] regardless of how difficult the task may be as many governmental interventions have become part of a cultural practice. Governmental interventions can impede the emergence of a viable private sector in the local economy which rests on, among other things, competition. At the same time, the government may exhibit anticompetition behaviour by favouring the participation of certain foreign firms in the local economy. Furthermore, there could be direct participation of the government in an area where privatisation has emerged, thus the government is in direct competition with the private sector.

Transparency International rates countries and territories according to how corrupt their public sector is perceived to be, using the Corruption Perceptions Index. Singapore ranks sixth worldwide and is the best ranked country in the region while

96. OECD, *Fighting Corruption and Promoting Competition: Contribution from the European Union* (DAF/COMP/GF/WD(2014)40 2014). As such, the fight against corruption is regarded as an integral part of the EU. However, in the field of the EU competition policy, no specific policy initiatives have been developed in order to target this particular issue.
97. Sakda Thanitcul & R. Ian McEwin, *Thailand, in* The Political Economy of Competition Law in Asia (Mark Williams ed., Edward Elgar Publishing 2013).
98. S. N. Eisenstadt & Louis Roniger, *Patron-Client Relations as a Model of Structuring Social Exchange*, 22 Comparative Studies in Society and History (1980).
99. Sakda Thanitcul & R. Ian McEwin, *Thailand, in* The Political Economy of Competition Law in Asia (Mark Williams ed., Edward Elgar Publishing 2013).
100. OECD, *Fighting Corruption and Promoting Competition: Contribution from Singapore* (DAF/COMP/GF/WD(2014)6 2014).
101. Maher M. Dabbah, *Competition Law and Policy in Developing Countries: A Critical Assessment of the Challenges to Establishing an Effective Competition Law Regime*, 33 World Competition (2010).

Cambodia is the worst scorer.[102] The data suggest slight improvements in some countries, such as Singapore and Indonesia, amidst stagnation the combat against corruption in the in other AMSs.

Conscious of the corruption problem, many AMSs adopted an ambitious law and/or enforcement agency in an attempt to tackle this issue directly. For instance, Vietnam adopted a comprehensive anti-corruption law in 2009 which established the Anti-Corruption Agency while Indonesia appointed the Indonesian Anti-Corruption Commission (Komisi Pemberantasan Korupsi).[103] Despite these efforts, corruption remains a concern,[104] suggesting that more concrete actions are needed in order to obtain the intended effect of the law.

[B] Diversity in Economic Conditions

'As far as market structure and market culture are concerned, ASEAN is ten-tiered, not two.'[105] Identifying the economic conditions of the AMSs is made more complicated by the fact that there is no single agreed upon evaluation criterion. Some systems use GDP per capita while others prefer gross national income (GNI). The reported GDP per capita of the AMSs demonstrates significant diversity.[106] Singapore is the only country with a reported GDP per capita of above USD 40,000 followed at a distance by Brunei Darussalam at USD 30,994 while Myanmar ranks the lowest among the AMSs at USD 1,147. Applying this International Monetary Fund (IMF) classification, Singapore is the only advanced economy in the region whereas the majority of the AMSs are classified as developing economies. Among these developing economies, Cambodia, Lao PDR, Myanmar, and Vietnam are considered low-income developing countries.[107] On the other hand, the World Bank categorises economic development based on the GNI per capita.[108] In applying the World Bank criteria, Cambodia, Indonesia, Lao PDR, Myanmar, the Philippines, and Vietnam are lower-middle-income economies. Malaysia and Thailand are upper-middle-income economies while Brunei Darussalam and Singapore are high-income economies. According to the United Nations (UN) classification intended to reflect basic economic situation, all of the AMSs are regarded as developing economies.[109] Yet, in the same document, Cambodia, Lao PDR, and Myanmar also appear among least developed countries when categorising using the

---

102. Transparency International, *Corruption Perception Index 2017*, https://www.transparency.org/news/feature/corruption_perceptions_index_2017 (accessed 6 Feb. 2018).
103. Natasya Sirait Ningrum, *Indonesia, in* The Political Economy of Competition Law in Asia (Mark Williams ed. Edward Elgar Publishing 2013).
104. May Fong Cheong, *Competition Policy and Law and ASEAN's Economic Integration Agenda*, http://www.clmr.unsw.edu.au/article/risk/competition-policy-and-law-and-aseans-economic-integration-agenda (accessed 13 Nov. 2017).
105. Khin Ohn Thant, *Competition Policy and Economic Growth in ASEAN Countries: A Myanmar's Perspective* (The ASEAN Conference on Fair Competition Law and Policy 2003).
106. IMF, *World Economic Outlook Database* (April 2014).
107. IMF, *World Economic Outlook Database*, 147–152 (April 2015). IMF, *World Economic Outlook: Seeking Sustainable Growth: Short-Term Recovery, Long-Term Challenges*, 224 (October 2017).
108. World Bank, *Country and Lending Groups*, http://data.worldbank.org/about/country-and-lending-groups (accessed 13 Nov. 2017).
109. UN, *World Economic Situation and Prospects*, 142 (2018).

GNI data.[110] In the end, the sole shared trait among the AMSs seems to be their geographical proximity.

Generally, small and developing economic markets tend to limit competition.[111] This is inherent in their natural condition where monopolies or oligopolies can easily emerge. This situation contributes to the need to regulate the conduct of players within these economies. However, even in monopolistic or oligopolistic markets, competition law can 'significantly improve market performance by reducing the opportunities and incentives for firms to abuse their market power'.[112]

There are also differences in the economic structures among the AMSs. The nature of the economy in Vietnam, as defined by its Constitution, is a socialist-oriented market economy.[113] It is the country's 'attempt to balance its communist heritage of centralised planning with increasing private participation'.[114] Brunei is a small energy-rich country, while most of the AMSs are heavily dependent on imported energy and commodity exports.[115] The economic structure of Thailand, Indonesia, and the Philippines is a mixture of agricultural, industrial, and commercial activities. Singapore, with its restriction on natural resources, focuses more on its commercial economy. Furthermore, there is more economic competition among the AMSs than complementary trade since geographical and technological similarities lead to similar exports of natural resources, and labour-intensive manufacturing.[116] The AMSs are in competition for the extra-ASEAN markets. The governments of the AMSs are also renowned for interfering in the economy of the country. The governments of both Malaysia and Singapore, in particular, play a significant role in the management of the economy, whether fully or partially, through state-owned enterprises and unofficial government-linked companies.[117] In Myanmar, the military government has the majority stakeholder positions in all of the major industrial corporations of the country. An oligarchic structure is prominent in countries such as the Philippines[118] and Thailand[119] where the majority of businesses are controlled by conglomerates with strong ties to politicians. The oligarchs in these countries seem to be protected and sustained by imperfect regulations.

Because of the governmental intervention in the economy and the lack of effective and efficient corruption-free regulatory and juridical infrastructure, it was

110. *Ibid.*, at 145.
111. Michal S. Gal, *Competition Policy for Small Market Economies* (Harvard University Press 2003).
112. *Ibid.*
113. The Constitution of the Socialist Republic of Vietnam Art. 15 (1992).
114. David Fruitman, *Vietnam, in* The Political Economy of Competition Law in Asia (Mark Williams ed. Edward Elgar Publishing 2013).
115. Stefano Inama & Edmund W. Sim, *The Foundation of the ASEAN Economic Community: An Institutional and Legal Profile*, 21 (Cambridge University Press 2015).
116. Siow Yue Chia & Michael G. Plummer, *ASEAN Economic Cooperation and Integration: Progress, Challenges and Future Directions* (Cambridge University Press 2015).
117. May Fong Cheong & Yin Harn Lee, *Malaysia and Singapore, in* The Political Economy of Competition Law in Asia (Mark Williams ed. Edward Elgar Publishing 2013).
118. Mark Williams & Ruby Ann S. Jalit, *The Philippines, in* The Political Economy of Competition Law in Asia (Mark Williams ed. Edward Elgar Publishing 2013).
119. Sakda Thanitcul & R. Ian McEwin, *Thailand, in* The Political Economy of Competition Law in Asia (Williams ed. Edward Elgar Publishing 2013).

predicted that the existing competition laws and those being planned in the Asia Pacific Economic Cooperation (APEC) countries are 'almost certain to fail'.[120] Instead of promoting and protecting competition, these competition laws are regarded as mere regulatory tools that are more likely to be manipulated in favour of politically involved firms and industries. Consequently, competition laws enacted under these economic situations are poised to create even more regulatory barriers to the entry to market.

Regardless of the diversified economic conditions of the AMSs, the implementation of a regional competition law does not necessarily require identical level of economic development in the participating states.[121] Admittedly, similar level of development could lead to an easier adoption of a common competition law, but the actual application of competition law to the individual cases is more important.

[C] The ASEAN Way

Admittedly, the diversity among the AMSs can be resolved through the willingness to commit to the ASEAN's cause. However, the much-needed political will is deflected by the ASEAN's traditional mode of dispute resolution, often referred to as the ASEAN Way. It is the fundamental ethos of the ASEAN and has its origin from the very beginning when the idea of a loosely connected organisation was first conceived. The ASEAN's origin would explain the AMSs' traditional obsession with sovereignty and a strong predilection for decentralised decision-making.[122] Former ASEAN Secretary General Ong Keng Yong explained that 'the ASEAN founding fathers wanted the ASEAN to be an organisation with minimal legal institutionalisation because to them, ASEAN was first and foremost a diplomatic instrument for confidence-building in a time when member countries' common concern was containing communist China'.[123] The fact that the ASEAN Secretariat was not created until 1976 exemplifies the informal ASEAN Way that was deliberately embraced from its beginning.[124]

The ASEAN Way is described as the method employed when dealing with situations of conflict within the region. This ideal consists of:

(a) Mutual respect for the independence, sovereignty, equality, territorial integrity and national identity of all nations.

120. John O. Haley, *Competition Law for the Asia-Pacific Economic Cooperation Community: Designing Shoes for Many Sizes*, 1 Wash. U. Global Stud. L. Rev. (2002).
121. Josef Drexl, *Economic Integration and Competition Law in Developing Countries, in* Competition Policy and Regional Integration in Developing Countries (Josef Drexl, et al. eds., Edward Elgar Publishing 2012).
122. Christopher B. Roberts, *ASEAN Regionalism: Cooperation, Values and Institutionalisation*, 178 (Routledge 2012).
123. Keng Yong Ong, *ASEAN and the 3 L's: Leaders, Laymen and Lawyers*, http://www.asean.org/resources/2012-02-10-08-47-56/speeches-statements-of-the-former-secretaries-general-of-asean/item/asean-and-the-3-l-s-leaders-laymen-and-lawyers-by-he-ong-keng-yong-secretary-general-of-asean (accessed 13 Nov. 2017).
124. Inama & Sim, *The Foundation of the ASEAN Economic Community: An Institutional and Legal Profile*, 19 (Cambridge University Press 2015).

(b) The right of every State to lead its national existence free from external interference, subversion or coercion.
(c) Non-interference in the internal affairs of one another.
(d) Settlement of differences or disputes by peaceful means.
(e) Renunciation of the threat or use of force.
(f) Effective cooperation among themselves.[125]

A recent trend in legalisation has emerged within the ASEAN. The organisation has subsequently evolved from a loose political organisation based solely on the ASEAN Way to a more legalistic framework based on regulations and a dispute settlement mechanism.[126] Economic integration combined with the desire to better attract foreign investment are the principal reasons transforming the ASEAN into a more legalised organisation.[127] Legalisation has become even more urgent when the ASEAN aims at building a single market. Nonetheless, some doubts have arisen about whether the current 'weak legalisation'[128] in the ASEAN is the right platform from which to launch a regional integration project. Another reason in support of the replacement of the traditional ASEAN Way with a legalised approach comes from the need for market regulation. The 1997 financial crisis convinced East Asian countries to move away from a relationship-based approach to conducting business and creating wealth to one that is more rule-based and market oriented.[129] The same mentality resurfaced during the global economic crisis of 2007–2008 where there were calls for better regulation of the market.[130] In the ASEAN's context the transformation towards a more legalised organisation is of particular importance for the organisation's survivability and viability. The future of the regional organisation depends on how the ASEAN and the AMSs manage the economic challenges posed by intra-regional growth and globalisation.[131]

The ASEAN legalisation development continued with the *ASEAN Charter*. The *ASEAN Charter* serves as a firm foundation for the ASEAN Community by conferring a legal personality to the ASEAN for the first time and providing it with an institutional framework. It also codifies the ASEAN norms and values while at the same time setting clear objectives for the organisation. The *ASEAN Charter* is therefore a legally binding agreement between the ten AMSs. The principle of the ASEAN Way is, however, reaffirmed in the *ASEAN Charter* which now includes reliance on peaceful settlement of disputes, non-interference in the internal affairs of the AMSs, and enhanced

125. Treaty of Amity and Cooperation in Southeast Asia, Art. 2 (1976).
126. Paul J. Davidson, *The ASEAN Way and the Role of Law in ASEAN Economic Cooperation*, 8 SYBIL. (2004).
127. *Ibid.*
128. Michael Ewing-Chow, *Culture Club or Chameleon: Should ASEAN Adopt Legalization for Economic Integration?*, 12 SYBIL. (2008).
129. ASEAN Secretariat, *Reforms and Integration in East Asia Could Strengthen Regional Stability*, http://www.asean.org/archive/newdata/content1.txt (accessed 13 Nov. 2017).
130. Ioannis Kokkoris & Rodrigo Olivares-Caminal, *Antitrust Law amidst Financial Crises*, 19 (Cambridge University Press 2010).
131. Shaun Narine, *Explaining ASEAN: Regionalism in Southeast Asia* (Lynne Rienner Publishers 2002).

consultation on matters seriously affecting the common interest of the ASEAN.[132] With regard to the language used in the *ASEAN Charter*, the ASEAN Way resembles the process of regional interactions and cooperation based on discreteness, informality, consensus building and non-confrontational bargaining styles that contrast with the adversarial posturing, majority vote and other legalistic decision-making procedures in other regional organisations.[133] It appears that the harbinger of the new ASEAN[134] has not lived up to the expectation. The *ASEAN Charter* reaffirmed that the ASEAN is simply an intergovernmental organisation, founded on the principles of equal sovereignty of all the AMSs and non-interference in the AMSs' internal affairs.[135] Through the *ASEAN Charter*, the ASEAN was officially conferred an international legal personality but not much else; the document failed to confer 'the legally important elements of rule-making, monitoring and enforcement for [the] ASEAN'.[136] Although the *ASEAN Charter* envisages a committee of permanent representatives based in Jakarta, Indonesia, who would be appointed to the ASEAN and hold the rank of an Ambassador, this committee will not be the primary decision-making body. Instead, the ASEAN Summit continues as the main forum for decision-making. Decisions at all levels within the organisation will continue to be made by consultation and consensus,[137] thus continuing the organisation's adherence to the ASEAN Way. This low level of legalisation is, nonetheless, not a unique attribute of the ASEAN but rather a shared feature common in the larger Asia Pacific region.[138] Nevertheless, the ASEAN Secretary General and the ASEAN Secretariat still managed to gain greater responsibility to monitor compliance and facilitate the implementation of the AEC.[139]

There have been several calls to replace the traditional ASEAN Way with a more formal form of cooperation to better adjust to the new goal of economic integration.[140] The current ASEAN Way has been criticised for its non-resolution of disputes.[141] Strong partnerships or formal links between national competition agencies through various cooperation channels such as the AEGC, the International Competition Network (ICN) or the Organisation for Economic Co-operation and Development (OECD) were

132. The ASEAN Charter, Art. 2.2 (2007).
133. Amitav Acharya, *Europe and Asia: Reflections on a Tale of Two Regionalisms, in* Regional Integration in East Asia and Europe: Convergence or Divergence? (Bertrand Fort & Douglas Webber eds., Routledge 2006).
134. Lin Chun Hung, *ASEAN Charter: Deeper Regional Integration under International Law?*, 9 Chinese J. of Int'l L 821 (2010).
135. The ASEAN Charter, Arts 2.2. & 3 (2007).
136. Ewing-Chow, *Culture Club or Chameleon: Should ASEAN Adopt Legalization for Economic Integration?*, 12 SYBIL. (2008).
137. The ASEAN Charter, Arts 7, 12 & 20 (2007).
138. Miles Kahler, *Legalization as Strategy: The Asia-Pacific Case*, 54 International Organization (2000).
139. The ASEAN Charter Art. 11 (2007).
140. *See*, for example, Megan R. Williams, *ASEAN: Do Progress and Effectiveness Require a Judiciary?*, 30 Suffolk Transnat'l L. Rev. 433 (2007); Mark Beeson, *ASEAN's Ways: Still Fit for Purpose?*, 22 Cambridge Review of International Affairs (2009).
141. Megan R.Williams, *ASEAN: Do Progress and Effectiveness Require a Judiciary?*, 30 Suffolk Transnat'l L. Rev. 433 (2007).

proposed, particularly in the area of merger review and transnational cartel investigation[142] but the ASEAN Way has been defended because of its significant past contribution to regional security and economic development. It represents a necessary foundation for the ASEAN's past *modus operandi* due to the strategic, political, economic, and socio-cultural diversity of the countries in Southeast Asia.[143] Admittedly, the ASEAN Way did not achieve such feats alone. It was argued that the primary contributing factor was the economic growth and the associated performance legitimacy[144] such growth delivers that represented the key foundation to the security of both the region and its governments.[145]

Some commentators have remained hopeful about the future of the ASEAN Way. 'The measures taken by the *Charter* may not go as far as some critics would like. But on the whole, the *Charter* helps ASEAN move from an almost purely political relationship towards relationships in which there are legitimate expectations that arise from repeated interactions, shared principles and purposes, and norms, as well as stronger regional processes and institutions that will foster compliance by the member countries to their promises and obligations.'[146] It is believed that, over time, as the ASEAN moves towards further legalisation, the ASEAN Way will no longer be a constraint in adopting a binding agreement on competition policy in the region.[147] These optimistic views are not shared by those who are convinced that the creation of a set of uniform rules is not feasible and that, given the political, legal, and economic diversity in the region, it is too simplistic to assume a common market and common rules will emerge naturally.[148] Therefore, further regulations and mechanisms reflecting deeper integration within the organisation need to be in place first to ensure their forced emergence.

In reality, a transformation of the ASEAN Way is unlikely to occur in the near future since the principle is embedded in the *ASEAN Charter* as early as in Article 2. Its placement articulates the importance of the ASEAN Way doctrine to the organisation. In its own way, the ASEAN Way is the stumbling block preventing the ASEAN from moving forward with fruitful cooperation in order to attain the desired ambition of regional integration.

142. Global Competition Review, *ACCC's Sims Pushes for More Regional Cooperation*, http://www.globalcompetitionreview.com/news/article/31471/acccs-sims-pushes-regional-cooperation (accessed 13 Nov. 2017).
143. Christopher B. Roberts, *ASEAN Regionalism: Cooperation, Values and Institutionalisation*, 70 (Routledge 2012).
144. Amitav Acharya, *Transnational Production and Security: Southeast Asia's 'Growth Triangles'*, 17 Contemporary Southeast Asia (1995) (coined the term *performance legitimacy*).
145. Christopher B. Roberts, *ASEAN Regionalism: Cooperation, Values and Institutionalisation*, 70 (Routledge 2012).
146. Simon S. C. Tay, *The ASEAN Charter: Between National Sovereignty and the Region's Constitutional Moment*, 12 SYBIL. (2008).
147. Luu Huong Ly, *Regional Harmonization of Competition Law and Policy: An ASEAN Approach*, 2 Asian J. Int. Law (2012).
148. George T. L. Shenoy, *The Emergence of a Legal Framework for Economic Policy in ASEAN*, 29 Malaya Law Review (1987).

§1.03 UNDERSTANDING HARMONISATION

Harmonisation of competition laws and policy is considered an integral part of effective economic integration in regional trade agreements,[149] yet little is known of the term *harmonisation*. The terms *harmonisation* and *convergence* are often confused and used interchangeably. Gerber referred to convergence as being independent choices made by the states while harmonisation refers to decisions resulting from international agreements.[150] Harmonisation implies that the states are bound by the agreements and have no choice but to comply or face sanction. Within the harmonisation process, there is a distinction between *hard harmonisation* and *soft harmonisation*. Hard harmonisation is used to describe binding multilateralism.[151] Binding multilateralism in the field of competition law can take on the form of legally binding multilateral agreements, international competition law codes or international competition law regimes, with an international institution capable of handling international competition cases.[152] Interest in multilateral competition law was shown as early as the 1920s with the creation of the World Economic Conference.[153] The project was abruptly dropped due to political and economic problems. The proposal was re-considered and abandoned on several further occasions.

Non-binding multilateralism is known as soft harmonisation.[154] Soft harmonisation revolves around recommendations, best practices and guidelines and can cover both substantive and procedural issues. Soft harmonisation resorts to the power of persuasion rather than hard binding obligations. Legally, this means that countries are neither obliged to subscribe to nor implement the recommendations, guidelines or best practices resulting from the non-binding multilateralism into their domestic legislations. In this respect, soft harmonisation is similar to the term *convergence* which describes the transformation from a state of difference to increasing similarity without binding obligations from a multilateral source.[155]

Soft harmonisation was an instant success because countries are more accepting and show less reticence towards it. Despite not having binding legal force, it gained a foothold in the field of competition law. In contrast to hard harmonisation, countries appear more willing to establish common understandings in the field of competition

149. O. Richard Cunningham & Anthony J. LaRocca, *Harmonisation of Competition Policies in a Regional Economic Integration*, 27 Law & Pol'y Int'l Bus. (1995).
150. David J. Gerber, *The Extraterritorial Application of German Antitrust Law*, 77 American Journal of International Law (1983).
151. Diane P. Wood, *International Harmonization of Antitrust Law: The Tortoise or the Hare*, 3 Chi. J. Int'l L. (2002).
152. David J. Gerber, *The Extraterritorial Application of German Antitrust Law*, 77 American Journal of International Law (1983).
153. League of Nations, *Report and Proceedings of the World Economic Conference*, 146–148 (CEI 46 II: League of Nations Pub 1927).
154. Diane P. Wood, *International Harmonization of Antitrust Law: The Tortoise or the Hare*, 3 Chi. J. Int'l L. (2002).
155. David J. Gerber, *The Extraterritorial Application of German Antitrust Law*, 77 American Journal of International Law (1983).

law through consultation and cooperation than through binding obligations.[156] Admittedly, non-binding multilateralism is more flexible and more practical than binding commitments. It is less time-consuming and does not suffer from the long and arduous negotiations that are often linked to binding multilateralism. Consequently, it is also easier to amend and update non-binding commitments. Because of its non-binding character, soft harmonisation does not pose a threat to nations' sovereignty. It appears that soft harmonisation responds well to new competition law jurisdictions' requirement of accepted up-to-date best practices in the field accompanied by a large margin of discretion that national competition authorities could enjoy.[157] It was suggested that the fact that the United States (US) fully supported this alternative favoured its chance of success.[158] Nonetheless, soft harmonisation also has its disadvantages. Ironically, its shortcomings are inherent in its principal characteristic which is the lack of binding obligations. Non-binding multilateralism could translate into uncertainty. Soft harmonisation has been justifiably criticised for leaving too much to the discretion of national authorities.[159] Furthermore, the language used in the recommendations, guidelines, and best practices appears too general and does not provide sufficient guidance on how best to implement the commitments within domestic competition law regime.[160]

Harmonisation of competition laws can occur at three distinct levels: substantive law, procedural requirements, and enforcement practices.[161] The harmonisation of substantive law rests on the assumption that economic integration can only occur after Member States have adopted competition laws and policies that are generally consistent. It can either be a part of a regional trade agreement or a conditional clause for regional economic formation. An example of a direct and explicit linkage between harmonisation of general competition law standards and economic integration is the EU. In this regard, market integration and competition law harmonisation exist on a relatively parallel track. The structural reorganisation of regional markets is a major objective of regional integration and regional arrangements are aimed at and have resulted in increased cross-border investment. Accordingly, an obvious target for harmonisation of procedural requirements is in the area of merger control. This can be harmonised by creating parallel procedures, establishing direct enforcement cooperation, or creating a single merger system. Harmonising enforcement practices means coordinating the enforcement of existing competition laws by related national authorities. Enforcement coordination is a necessary complement for substantive law harmonisation in the sense that it could bring about more tangible benefits. The most

156. Diane P. Wood, *International Harmonization of Antitrust Law: The Tortoise or the Hare*, 3 Chi. J. Int'l L. (2002).
157. Thomas K. Cheng, *Convergence and Its Discontents: A Reconsideration of the Merits of Convergence of Global Competition Law*, 12 Chi. J. Int'l L 433 (2012).
158. Eleanor M. Fox & Daniel A. Crane, *Global Issues in Antitrust and Competition Law*, 505 (West 2010).
159. Diane P. Wood, *International Harmonization of Antitrust Law: The Tortoise or the Hare*, 3 Chi. J. Int'l L. (2002).
160. *Ibid.*
161. O. Richard Cunningham & Anthony J LaRocca, *Harmonisation of Competition Policies in a Regional Economic Integration*, 27 Law & Pol'y Int'l Bus. (1995).

obvious example of this is the EU's creation of a supranational enforcement authority. The harmonisation of enforcement practices is also attempted in a more limited capacity under cooperation agreements which typically contain four types of cooperation:[162]

1. exchanging information and data that might be relevant to the other country's enforcement activities;[163]
2. notifying other authorities and consulting with them about areas where enforcement conduct in one country is likely to create friction with another country;[164]
3. assisting other enforcement agencies with investigations that those agencies are carrying out in their own territory;[165]
4. coordinating parallel investigations into similar conduct.[166]

§1.04 SCOPE AND NATURE OF THE BOOK

The ASEAN's initiative in establishing a regional competition law is often overlooked by the literature even when the discussion is about global competition law or regional competition laws. It is plausible that this is due to the ASEAN's relatively recent interest in competition law and the region's moderate impact on the global market. In light of the arrival of the AEC where competition policy occupies an important place, there is a pressing need to examine the ASEAN's competition law. This book aims to bridge the gap in the literature by providing a detailed analysis of competition law in the ASEAN countries. In doing so, the book offers a contribution to the expansion of the literature of the ASEAN competition law. While the subject of the present study is specifically the ASEAN, the contents of this book could contribute to a better understanding of competition law regimes in developing economies and contribute to the more general literature on global competition law. Another purpose of this book is to expand the discourse on the issues surrounding developing economies' endeavours in establishing and enforcing competition law both at national and regional level.

As the title would suggest, this book is essentially an analysis of competition law in the ASEAN countries. It attempts to answer whether the harmonisation approach undertaken by the ASEAN regarding competition law could contribute to a meaningful economic integration of the AEC. Moreover, it seeks to unveil the relationship between the ASEAN regional competition law and the AMSs national competition laws in order

162. *Ibid.*
163. Agreement between the Government of the United States of America and the Commission of the European Community Regarding the Application of Their Competition Law, Art. 3(2) (1991).
164. Agreement between the United States of America and Canada Regarding the Application of Their Competition and Deceptive Marketing Practices Laws, Art. II(I) (1997).
165. Agreement between the Government of the United States of America and the Commission of the European Community Regarding the Application of Their Competition Law, Art. 4(1) (1991).
166. Agreement between the United States of America and Canada Regarding the Application of Their Competition and Deceptive Marketing Practices Laws, Art. IV(1) (1997).

to better understand the harmonisation dynamic of the ASEAN competition law. To answer these questions, the book must first identify and locate the ASEAN competition law among other regional competition laws. This attempt would lead to an examination of important regional competition law regimes in the world, including and especially the experiences of developing economies. However essential the experiments of other regional organisations may be, they are not the primary subject of this study and thus are only examined to the extent that they aid in the understanding of the ASEAN's initiative. The book will then make an in-depth inquiry into the ASEAN's pursuit of regional competition law both substantive and institutional. Lastly, an investigation into the inter-relationship between the ASEAN and the AMSs' competition laws is necessary to ascertain the reception of the AEC's regional economic integration.

The book is organised as follows: Chapter 2 begins with a review of the current landscape of regional approaches to competition law. Chapter 3 examines the goals of the ASEAN competition law as determining them is considered a precondition to developing a body of coherent competition law rules. Chapter 4 analyses the substantive approach taken by the ASEAN in pursuance of the previously announced goals. Chapter 5 considers the ASEAN reliance on the AMSs national systems to enforce competition law. Chapter 6 then scrutinises the inter-relationship between the ASEAN regional competition law and the AMSs domestic competition law regime. Lastly, the analysis of the ASEAN competition law concludes with a finale and an encore in Chapter 7.

CHAPTER 2

The Regionalisations of Competition Law

> Harmonisation of competition laws and policy is an integral part of effective economic integration in regional trade agreements. Nations committed to trade liberalisation will not allow inconsistent or discriminatory application of competition laws to nullify the benefits gained from dismantling formal trade barriers, competition law harmonisation, however does not follow a single model.[1]

Economic integration is rarely achieved without a promise of competition and welfare improvement.[2] However, economic integration can also be the source of anticompetitive conducts.[3] For instance, when trade barriers between countries are reduced, so do trade costs in all areas including international collusion, thus making cartels attractive.[4] Economic integration could also create more opportunity for new collusions, prolong existing cartels' stability, or expanding the reach of existing cartels. To preserve the promised benefits of economic integration, competition law must be actively enforced especially when economies are becoming increasingly open.[5] Economic integration alone can never be a substitute of competition law.

---

1. O. Richard Cunningham & Anthony J LaRocca, *Harmonisation of Competition Policies in a Regional Economic Integration*, 27 Law & Pol'y Int'l Bus. (1995).
2. Chris Allen, et al., *The Competition Effects of the Single Market in Europe*, 13 Economic Policy 441 (1998); David Cox & Richard Harris, *Trade Liberalisation and Industrial Organisation: Some Estimates for Canada*, 93 Journal of Political Economy 115 (1985); Alasdair Smith & Anthony J. Venables, *Completing the Internal Market in the European Community: Some Industry Simulations*, 32 European Economic Review 1501 (1988).
3. Philipp J. H. Schroder, *Cartel Stability and Economic Integration*, 15(2) Review of International Economics 313 (2007).
4. Carl Davidson, *Cartel Stability and Tariff Policy*, 17 Journal of International Economics 219 (1984); K. C. Fung, *Economic Integration as Competitive Discipline*, 33 International Economic Review 837 (1992); Kjell Erik Lommerud & Lars Sorgard, *Trade Liberalization and Cartel Stability*, 9 Review of International Economics 343 (2001).
5. K. C. Fung, *Economic Integration as Competitive Discipline*, 33 International Economic Review 837 (1992).

During the past decades, competition law and policy framework have been among the most common features in the ongoing process of regionalisation.[6] There are a number of reasons for the proliferation of regional competition law.[7] The most obvious of these lies in the fact that competition law is regarded as a necessary complement to trade policy, and especially to regional trade liberalisation and market integration within specific geographical regions.[8] Furthermore, regional competition agreement makes it easier to detect and regulate anticompetitive conduct with trans-border dimensions, thus enhancing the ability of a single national competition authority confined within the scope of its territory to act against such practices.[9]

Regional competition agreements are often entered into by neighbouring countries. They appear in various configurations in both the scope of the arrangement and the institutional features. This chapter offers a review of different regional approaches to competition law. The experiences of these regional arrangements will provide a helpful guidance to locating the ASEAN's own approach to competition law. It was once noted that 'looking at different regional communities established around the world, it is clear that there has been too much borrowing from the EU experience and at the same time extremely little - if any - consultation on the experience of other regions in the field of competition law'.[10] In response to this observation, this chapter will focus more on developing economies' experiences with regional competition law.

In this chapter, regional agreements shall be arranged according to their degree of harmonisation. The least developed regional agreements are limited to broad and non-binding language with no realistic intention of disciplining anticompetitive conduct. The NAFTA is the best-known agreement in this category. At the opposite end of the spectrum are region-wide common competition regimes that not only impose substantive rules directly on participating states and private undertakings but also establish a supranational authority to enforce those rules. Except for the EU, which still offers an exemplary model, it is rare to find a region with such an advanced regime. Therefore, most regional cooperation falls somewhere between these two extremes.[11]

6. Pradeep S. Mehta & Nitya Nanda, *The Role of Civil Society in Promoting Competition Culture at the Regional Level, in* Competition Provisions in Regional Trade Agreements: How to Assure Development Gains (Philippe Brusick, et al. eds., UNCTAD/DITC/CLP/2005/1 2005).
7. *See*, Eleanor M. Fox, *Competition, Development and Regional Integration: In Search of a Competition Law Fit for Developing Countries, in* Competition Policy and Regional Integration in Developing Countries (Josef Drexl, et al. eds., Edward Elgar Publishing 2012); George K. Lipimile, *The COMESA Regional Competition Regulations, in* Competition Policy and Regional Integration in Developing Countries (Josef Drexl, et al. eds., Edward Elgar Publishing 2012). Have described the benefits of regionalisation of competition laws in great detail.
8. Robert Z. Lawrence & Robert E. Litan, *Saving Free Trade: A Pragmatic Approach* (Brookings Institution 1986); Simon J. Evenett, *What Can We Really Learn from the Competition Provision of RTAs?, in* Competition Provisions in Regional Trade Agreements: How to Assure Development Gains (Philippe Brusick, et al. eds., UNCTAD/DITC/CLP/2005/1 2005).
9. Frédéric Jenny, *Competition Enforcement in Testing Times: Beyond National Level* (2009).
10. Maher M. Dabbah, *International and Comparative Competition Law*, 412 (Cambridge University Press 2010).
11. Melaku Geboye Desta, *Exemptions from Competition Law in Regional Trade Agreements: A Study Based on Experiences in the Agriculture and Energy Sectors, in* Competition Provisions in Regional Trade Agreements: How to Assure Development Gains (Philippe Brusick, et al. eds., UNCTAD/DITC/CLP/2005/1 2005).

The EU and the NAFTA, despite being at opposite ends of the spectrum, both enjoy successful harmonisation and convergence within the regional framework. However, developing economies' efforts at regionalisation do not yield the same results. This method in categorisation also coincides with the OECD report in which regional trade agreements are divided into two families: the North American style that focuses more on coordination and cooperation provisions, and the European-style agreements that are oriented towards more substantive rules.[12] The experience of developing economies in regional harmonisation warrant special attention due the disparity between the proposed goal for harmonisation and the actual approach taken to achieve it.

§2.01 TRADITIONAL MODELS OF REGIONAL COMPETITION LAW

Traditionally, there are two referential regional competition law models, standing at the opposite spectrum of regional organisation from each other are the regional trade agreements and regional integration model.

[A] Regional Trade Agreements

Regional trade agreements seek to reduce obstacles to trade within a specific geographical region.[13] Typically, competition law only plays a marginal role in these regional agreements since there is little evidence that competition provisions have been an important focus of negotiations leading to such agreements insofar that they appear not to have played a major role in implementation.[14]

[1] The NAFTA

One of the most influential regional trade agreement is the NAFTA, a trade bloc comprising the US, Canada and Mexico. The NAFTA requires each party to adopt or maintain measures to proscribe anticompetitive activity and take appropriate measures against it.[15] Following this requirement, Mexico enacted a comprehensive competition law statute in 1993.[16] The NAFTA does not contain any substantive rules whether general or specific regarding the field of competition nor does it establish a supranational authority in charge of enforcing competition regulations. It does, on the other hand, contain provisions on cooperation and coordination among national competition

12. Oliver Solano & Andreas Sennekamp, *Competition Provisions in Regional Trade Agreements* (OECD, COM/DAF/TD(2005)3/FINAL 2006).
13. David J. Gerber, *Global Competition: Law, Markets and Globalisation*, 110 (Oxford University Press 2010).
14. On regional trade agreements and their values, *See*, Francisco Marcos, *Downloading Competition Law from a Regional Trade Agreement: A Strategy to Introduce Competition Law in Bolivia and Ecuador, in* Competition Law and Policy in Latin America (Eleanor M. Fox & D. Daniel Sokol eds., Hart Publishing 2009).
15. North American Free Trade Agreement Art. 1501(1) (8 Dec. 1993).
16. Ley Federal de Competencia Económica [LFCE.] [Competition Law], as amended, Diario Oficial de la Federación [DO.] (Mex.) (1992).

authorities.[17] The NAFTA's choice reflects the US's preference for a global competition law institution without imposing common competition rules nor a centralised regional competition authority. This vision relies on a more practical approach based on cooperation in the enforcement of domestic competition laws between countries with similar economic, political, and legal backgrounds. The NAFTA has established a Working Group specifically to oversee convergence in participating states.

The NAFTA is primarily a free trade area, market integration has never been its aim. Therefore, a supranational institution to ensure enforcement of competition law would not fit within this purposeful narrative. The NAFTA opts for a more appropriate solution which is a consensual-based consultation on the effectiveness of members' national competition laws and cooperation in the enforcement of national laws through mutual legal assistance, notification, consultation, and the exchange of information.[18] What is interesting in the case of the NAFTA is that despite having a dispute settlement mechanism involving multilateral panels, the competition provisions are expressly excluded from the dispute settlement procedures.[19] This is clearly a unique feature of competition law provisions in regional trade area agreements.[20] Consequently, disputes on competition policy between participating parties are settled by informal cooperation[21] or, in rare occurrences, taken to the World Trade Organisation (WTO).[22] It is precisely this absence of dispute resolution mechanism for competition law matters that contributes to the NAFTA's limited effectiveness. Yet, in spite of their non-binding nature, countries still include competition chapters in regional trade agreements. It is possible that this particular feature contains symbolic value which contain the possibility to lead to a natural improvement in cooperation between national authorities.[23]

It should be noted that the NAFTA countries' experience in the field of competition law differs from other regional groups. By the time the Agreement came into force, all three members had already enacted national competition laws.[24] Thus the NAFTA only serves to coordinate existing competition law regimes and is not concerned with implementing competition law. Admittedly, the three regimes do diverge in some respects. The Mexican law leans more towards economic efficiency and producer welfare; the US law favours consumer welfare while the Canadian law falls somewhere

17. North American Free Trade Agreement Art. 1501(2) (8 Dec. 1993).
18. *Ibid.*, at Art. 1501.
19. *Ibid.*, at Art. 1501(3).
20. D. Daniel Sokol, *Order Without (Enforceable) Law: Why Countries Enter into Non-enforceable Competition Policy Chapters in Free Trade Agreements*, 83 Chi.-Kent L. Rev. (2008).
21. Jones Clifford, *Competition Dimensions of NAFTA and the European Union: Semi-Common Competition Policy, Uncommon Rules, and No Common Institutions* (2006).
22. WTO Panel Report, *Mexico-Measures Affecting Telecommunications Services* (2004). Clifford, *Competition Dimensions of NAFTA and the European Union: Semi-Common Competition Policy, Uncommon Rules, and No Common Institutions* (2006).
23. D. Daniel Sokol, *Order Without (Enforceable) Law: Why Countries Enter into Non-enforceable Competition Policy Chapters in Free Trade Agreements*, 83 Chi.-Kent L. Rev. (2008).
24. Janet D. Steiger, *Harmonization of the United States and Mexican Antitrust Law under NAFTA* (1995).

in between.[25] Nonetheless, this divergence is not considered significant and does not warrant serious consideration; there are more similarities between the three countries than differences.[26] The NAFTA experience demonstrates that national competition laws of participating states need not be identical in order to guarantee a successfully functional regional trade agreement.

[2] The European Free Trade Association

Another notable example of regional trade agreement is the European Free Trade Association (EFTA) which was established as a free trade zone by the *Stockholm Convention*[27] in 1960 and was later revised by the *Vaduz Convention*.[28] The original signatory states were Austria, Denmark, Norway, Portugal, Sweden, Switzerland, and the United Kingdom. The EFTA was created in direct response to the EU's progressive move towards integration.[29] It was established as an alternative route for states which disagreed with the integration approach or simply did not wish to join the EU.[30] Its purpose is to pursue economic objectives notably the operation of free trade between members in industrial products. The *EFTA Convention* contains competition law related provisions, namely, the prohibition of anticompetitive agreement, the prohibition of abuse of dominant position,[31] and state aid.[32] The EFTA has undergone various alterations in membership: Finland joined as an associate member in 1961 before fully joined in 1981, Iceland joined in 1970, and Lichtenstein in 1991. There have been some withdrawals as well: Denmark and the UK withdrew in 1973, Portugal in 1986, and finally Austria, Finland, and Sweden in 1995. Current members of the EFTA are Iceland, Liechtenstein, Norway, and Switzerland.

In 1992, the *Agreement on the European Economic Area (EEA)* was signed and came into force on 1 January 1994 uniting the EU members with the EFTA members[33] with a view to form the EEA. Most of the EFTA members had already applied to the EU membership by the time the *EEA Agreement* came into effect.[34] Today, the EFTA states party to the *EEA Agreement* are Iceland, Lichtenstein, and Norway. Switzerland, while

25. ABA Section of Antitrust Law, *Report of the Task Force of the ABA Section of Antitrust Law on The Competition Dimension of NAFTA*, 17 (1994).
26. Janet D. Steiger, *Harmonization of the United States and Mexican Antitrust Law under NAFTA* (1995).
27. Convention Establishing the European Free Trade Association (1960).
28. Convention Establishing the European Free Trade Association (Consolidated version) (2013) (the EFTA Convention).
29. Martin J. Dedman, *The Origins and Development of the European Union 1945–2008*, 110 (2nd ed., Routledge 2009).
30. Thérèse Blanchet, et al., *The Agreement on the European Economic Area (EEA): A Guide to the Free Movement of Goods and Competition Rules*, 1 (Clarendon Press 1994).
31. Convention Establishing the European Free Trade Association (Consolidated version), Art. 18 (2013).
32. *Ibid.*, at Art. 16.
33. Agreement on the European Economic Area OJ L1/3 (1994) (the EEA Agreement).
34. Jarrod Tudor, *A Comparison of the Jurisprudence of the ECJ and the EFTA Court on the Free Movement of Goods in the EEA: Is There an Intolerable Separation of Article 34 of the TFEU and Art. 11 of the EEA?*, 17 San Diego Int'l L.J. 75 (2015).

not part of the EEA, concluded a separate bilateral agreement with the EU. The *EEA Agreement* is a hybrid between a free trade area and an economic integration community.[35] For many of the members, the EFTA was a stepping stone to the membership of the EU and they thus supported the creation of the EEA.[36] The EEA objective is a continuous economic relationship aided by the development of a common set of rules for trade and competition. More specifically, its economic objective is to extend the EU's internal market rules to the EFTA states which are part of the EEA with the exception of the custom union and common policies in taxation, agriculture, and fishery.[37] The *EEA Agreement* has accepted the EU legislation almost in its entirety in relevant domain including the jurisprudence of the Court of Justice of the European Union (CJEU). Through this document, the process of soft harmonisation between the EU and the EFTA rules is ensured.

Competition rules are considered essential to the successful creation of the EEA[38] and have accordingly been included in the *EEA Agreement*. The *EEA Agreement* contains the prohibition of anticompetitive agreements[39] which mirrors Article 101 of the *TFEU*.[40] Its prohibition of abuse of dominant position[41] reflects Article 102 of the *TFEU*. Together with *Protocol 24*,[42] the *EEA Agreement*[43] extend the reach of the EU merger control regime[44] throughout the EEA. Finally, the *EEA Agreement* also contains the control of state aid.[45] The EEA rules apply only when a conduct or agreement is likely to have an effect on trade between the EEA contracting parties[46] or merger realised in the territory of the EFTA states.[47]

A number of new institutions were created as a result of the *EEA Agreement*. Of particular importance to the competition law domain is the creation of the EFTA Surveillance Authority (ESA) and the EFTA Court.[48] Both supranational institutions are modelled after the EU institutions namely the EU Commission and the CJEU. The ESA is responsible for the investigation and the enforcement of the competition rules in its

35. Jeremy Brown & Gavin Robert, *The European Economic Area: How Important Is It?*, 14 E.I.P.R. 379 (1992).
36. Martin J. Dedman, *The Origins and Development of the European Union 1945–2008*, 118 (2nd ed., Routledge 2009).
37. Even though the *EEA Agreement* contains provisions on trade in agricultural and fishery products.
38. Jeremy Brown & Gavin Robert, *The European Economic Area: How Important Is It?*, 14 E.I.P.R. 379 (1992).
39. Agreement on the European Economic Area, Art. 53 (1994).
40. Treaty on the Functioning of the European Union (2008) (TFEU).
41. Agreement on the European Economic Area, Art. 54 (1994).
42. Protocol 24 to the EEA Agreement on Cooperation in the Field of Control of Concentrations OJ L 1, 3.1. (1994).
43. Agreement on the European Economic Area, Art. 57 (1994).
44. Council Regulation (EC) No. 4064/89 on the Control of Concentrations between Undertakings (1989).
45. Agreement on the European Economic Area, Art. 61 (1994).
46. *Ibid.*, at Arts 53(1) & 54(1).
47. *Ibid.*, at Art. 57(2).
48. *Ibid.*, at Art. 108. Read in light of Agreement between the EFTA States on the Establishment of a Surveillance Authority and a Court of Justice, 3 OJ L344 (1994).

area with similar powers to the EU Commission.[49] The decisions of the ESA are subject to the judicial review handled by the EFTA Court. The Court, composed of seven judges, is capable of handling disputes between the ESA and Member States, hearing appeal concerning decisions of the ESA in the field of competition, the settlement of disputes between EFTA states, and giving advisory opinions on the interpretation of the *EEA Agreement*.

'A two-pillar system' [50] was conceived to enforce the EEA competition rules in which the EU institutions are kept separated from those of the EFTA yet both institutions have the responsibility of maintaining the EEA system. This mechanism is implemented in pursuance of the promotion of the harmonisation of the EEA and the EU law. In this regard, both the EU Commission and the ESA function as competition enforcement bodies of the *EEA Agreement*. This two-pillar system was chosen due to the belief that effective implementation of the substantive EEA competition rules had to be ensured in the whole of the territory covered by the *EEA Agreement*.[51] The two-pillar system is approved by the CJEU[52] and later by the EFTA Court.[53]

The *EEA Agreement* provides certain mechanisms to ascertain harmonisation between contracting EFTA states and the EU internal market structure. Firstly, the EU Commission and the ESA are under obligation to cooperate.[54] Secondly, there is a certain regard of supremacy benefitting the CJEU since the ESA and the EFTA Court must decide in accordance with the rulings of the CJEU.[55] If disputes were to arise between the EFTA Court and the CJEU relative to the interpretation of the *EEA Agreement*, the EEA Joint Committee, which is responsible of the management of the *Agreement*, will intervene in attempt to reach an agreement.[56] Ultimately, if an agreement cannot be reached after three months, the CJEU can give a ruling at the request of the contracting parties to the dispute. In practice, the EFTA Court generally follows the CJEU decisions.[57] Lastly, in the case of disparity between national laws and the EEA rules, the latter would prevail.[58] This particular mechanism is in place to guarantee homogeneity of the EEA since the *EEA Agreement* lacks legislative power and its provisions cannot be directly applied but must be transposed into national law by contracting members. The harmonisation mechanism is complemented by the EFTA

49. Protocol 21 to the EEA Agreement on the Implementation of Competition Rules Applicable to Undertakings OJ L 1, 3.1. (1994).
50. Andreas Diem, *EEA Competition Law*, 15 E.C.L.R. 268 (1994).
51. Christine Federlin, *Enforcement of the European Economic Area Competition Rules (EEA): Division of Competence and Co-operation between the European Commission*, 4 Int'l Bus. L.J. (1994).
52. Opinion Pursuant to the Second Subparagraph of Art. 228(1) of the EEC Treaty (Opinion 1/92), para. 3 ECR I-2821 (1992).
53. *L'Oréal Norge AS v. Aarskog Per AS and Others and Smart Club Norge*, Cases E-9/07 and E-10/07, para. 28 (EFTA Ct. Rep. 258 2008).
54. Protocol 24 to the EEA Agreement on Cooperation in the Field of Control of Concentrations, Art. 1(2) (1994).
55. Agreement between the EFTA States on the Establishment of a Surveillance Authority and a Court of Justice, Art. 3(2) (1994).
56. Agreement on the European Economic Area, Art. 111 (1994).
57. *Directorate-General for Internal Policies, Internal Market beyond the EU: EEA and Switzerland*, 30 (IP/A/IMCO/NT/2009-13 2009).
58. Protocol 35 to the EEA Agreement on the implementation of EEA Rules (1994).

states' eagerness to incorporate EU internal market legislation into their national regimes.[59]

Both the mechanisms and the members' eagerness contribute to a sufficient level of effectiveness attained by the EEA. However, there have been concerns that the EEA's harmonisation approach only assists countries in improving their legal qualifications to the accession to the EU while doing little to improve the economic qualifications.[60] It inevitably calls into question the level of harmonisation actually achieved through the EEA alone. The EFTA's standing as a stand-alone free trade area is also ambiguous since its effectiveness is entirely dependent to that of the EU as a result of the *EEA Agreement*. In this regard, the EFTA wears an appearance of a precursor to the full membership of the EU.[61] Historically, many members left the EFTA to join the EU: UK, Denmark, Portugal, Austria, Sweden, and Finland. Nonetheless, it is undeniable that the *EEA Agreement* introduced important changes to the EFTA states considering that at the time of its conclusion many countries did not have national comprehensive competition law, or it was rarely implemented.[62] In this regard, the *EEA Agreement*'s usefulness and effectiveness regarding harmonisation should not be ignored.

[B] The Integration Model

The EU model stands at the most advanced end of regional competition law spectrum with its region-wide common substantive and procedural competition rules accompanied by a supranational competition authority enforcing those rules. This high degree of harmonisation corresponds with a high level of economic integration.[63] The EU's origin dates back to the *Treaty Establishing the European Coal and Steel Community*[64] followed by the establishment of the European Economic Community in 1957.[65] The initial denomination of the European Economic Community was later replaced by the European Community by the *Treaty on European Union* in 1992[66] which in turn was incorporated into the EU by the *Treaty of Lisbon* in 2009.[67] The *Treaty of Lisbon* then renamed the *Treaty of Rome* as the *Treaty on the Functioning of the European Union (TFEU)*. One of the principal objectives of the formation of the EU was the establishment of an internal market with the free movement of goods, capital, services and

59. EFTA Surveillance Authority, *36th Internal Market Scoreboard of the EFTA States of the European Economic Area* (2015). (The latest average transposition deficit of the three EFTA States is only 1.1%. In comparison, the average transposition deficit of the EU members is 0.7%.)
60. Andrew Evans, *Voluntary Harmonisation in Integration between the European Community and Eastern Europe*, 22 EL. Rev. 201 (1997).
61. Jeremy Brown & Gavin Robert, *The European Economic Area: How Important Is It?*, 14 E.I.P.R. 379 (1992).
62. *EEA Competition Law*, 14 E.C.L.R. Supp. 1 (1993).
63. O. Richard Cunningham & Anthony J LaRocca, *Harmonisation of Competition Policies in a Regional Economic Integration*, 27 Law & Pol'y Int'l Bus. (1995).
64. Treaty Establishing the European Coal and Steel Community (1951). (It expired on 23 Jul. 2002.)
65. Treaty Establishing the European Economic Community (1957) (Treaty of Rome).
66. Treaty on European Union (1992) (Treaty of Maastricht).
67. Treaty of Lisbon amending the Treaty on European Union and the Treaty establishing the European Community (2007) (Treaty of Lisbon).

people.[68] It follows that the principle of free competition was established early[69] to assist with the unification of a competitive single economic area.[70] Competition law was recognised as fundamental to the goal of regional integration.[71] It is undeniable that competition law has a pivotal role in the process of integration and in turn it is the integration aspect that has made the EU competition law special.[72]

The EU has a comprehensive body of substantive provisions regarding competition rules. The principal EU competition rules can now be found in Articles 101 and 102 of the *TFEU*[73] prohibiting anticompetitive agreements which have as their object or effect the prevention, restriction, or distortion of competition within the Internal Market and abuse of dominant position.[74] The competition rules are affirmed as essential for the accomplishment of the task entrusted to the EU and in particular, the functioning of the Internal Market.[75] The provisions of merger control were not included in the Treaty but instead were introduced by the EC *Regulation 4064/89*,[76] the current merger regulation is *Regulation 139/2004*.[77]

The substantive provisions are complemented by regional and national institutions in the enforcement of the regional competition rules. Given the novelty and almost revolutionary concept of the EU competition law, the creation of a new supranational institution was considered unavoidable in order to establish a proper culture of competition.[78] The EU has exclusive competence in the establishment of the competition rules necessary for the functioning of the Internal Market.[79] Accordingly, the initial responsibility of the enforcement of competition rules is shouldered by the European Commission.[80] The Commission is equipped with extensive powers from investigating to imposing penalties on relevant undertakings or Member States.[81] It appears that a centralised institution is in the best position to establish uniform regional

68. Originally the Common Market before the change to Internal Market in 1992 with the adoption of the Treaty on European Union (1992).
69. Treaty Establishing the European Economic Community Art. 2 (1957).
70. Barry J. Rodger, *Competition Law and Policy in the EC and UK*, 20 (3rd ed., Cavendish 2004).
71. Lee McGowan & Stephen Wilks, *The First Supranational Policy in the European Union: Competition Policy*, 28 European Journal of Political Research (1995).
72. David J. Gerber, *Law and Competition in Twentieth-Century Europe: Protecting Prometheus*, 334 (Oxford University Press 2001).
73. First enacted as Arts 85 and 86 of the Treaty Establishing the European Economic Community (1957).
74. Treaty on the Functioning of the European Union (2008).
75. *Eco Swiss China Time Ltd v. Benetton International NV*, para. 36 (2000).
76. Council Regulation (EC) No. 4064/89 on the Control of Concentrations between Undertakings (1989).
77. Council Regulation (EC) No. 139/2004 on the Control of Concentrations between Undertakings (2004) (EUMR).
78. Ian Forrester & Christopher Norall, *The Laicization of Community Law: Self-Help and the Rule of Reason: How Competition Law Is and Could Be Applied*, 21 Common Market L. Rev. (1984).
79. Treaty on the Functioning of the European Union 3(1)(b) (2008).
80. Council Regulation (EEC) No. 17/62 First Regulation implementing Arts 85 and 86 of the Treaty (1962).
81. *Ibid.*

competition law among Member States as well as ensure market integration.[82] Moreover, the Commission is not restrained by a myopic state-centric vision. The principle of subsidiarity only allows the EU to act in so far as the objectives of the proposed action cannot be sufficiently achieved by the Member States in areas which do not fall within its exclusive competence.[83] In accordance with this principle, a decisive change was later introduced when *Regulation 1/2003* empowered national competition authorities and national courts with the direct application of the EU competition rules.[84] The Commission's competence, consequently, is limited to serious competition issues with an intra-regional dimension.

Since the *Treaty of Nice*[85] the judicial review body of first instance of the Commission decisions in competition cases is the General Court of the European Union (GCEU). Its role is the assessment of the legality of the decision in light of the *TFEU*. The CJEU,[86] in turn, hears appeals of the GCEU decisions strictly on points of law[87] and preliminary rulings concerning the interpretation of the Treaties and the validity and interpretation of acts of the institutions, bodies, offices, or agencies of the Union from national courts.[88] The European Competition Network (ECN), established by *Regulation 1/2003*,[89] further strengthens the enforcement of EU competition law by offering a forum where the Commission and national competition authorities meet to discuss their common interests, coordinate their enforcement efforts as well as ensure an efficient allocation of resources. The *Commission Notice of 2004* helps regulate the issue of case allocation between members and the Commission or among members.[90] The ECN is a valuable platform of coordination and cooperation that considers all of the twenty-eight-Member States.[91] It has systems of competition law that are largely modelled after the EU competition law.[92]

The EU competition law was boldly claimed as the most important and influential of all the European ideas within the EU and internationally.[93] Indeed, it is likely that the effectiveness of the EU competition law regime within its jurisdiction helps support the recognition of its distinctiveness beyond the EU. The EU competition law owes its effectiveness to the robust substantive provisions coupled with effective enforcement

82. Maher M. Dabbah, *International and Comparative Competition Law*, 169–170 (Cambridge University Press 2010).
83. Treaty on the Functioning of the European Union 5(3) (2008).
84. Council Regulation (EC) No. 1/2003 on the Implementation of the Rules on Competition Laid Down in Arts 81 and 82 of the Treaty (2003).
85. Treaty of Nice Amending the Treaty on European Union (2001).
86. Informally known as the ECJ.
87. *See*, in particular, *John Deere v. Commission*, paras. 17–22 (1998); *General Motors BV v. Commission*, paras 50–51 (2006).
88. Treaty on the Functioning of the European Union Art. 267 (2008).
89. Council Regulation (EC) No. 1/2003, OJ. L. 1, 15 (2003).
90. Commission Notice on Cooperation within the Network of Competition Authorities (2004).
91. European Union, *EU Member Countries*, http://europa.eu/about-eu/countries/member-countries/ (accessed 13 Nov. 2017).
92. Richard Whish & David Bailey, *Competition Law*, 75 (7th ed., Oxford University Press 2012).
93. Maher M. Dabbah, *International and Comparative Competition Law*, 160 (Cambridge University Press 2010).

attempts by both national and regional competition authorities. Moreover, its continued enforcement differentiates it from other regional competition law regimes. It is thus not surprising that the EU is considered to be the laboratory of regional competition law.[94] The EU's success has inspired policymakers from developing economies to seek insight and guidance from the EU when deciding to adopt or adapt existing competition laws.[95] In this respect, the EU's influence can be felt when other legislatures and competition authorities use the EU model as a reference for the enactment and interpretation of national competition laws. Furthermore, the EU is actively seeking to establish the EU model on the global stage.[96] Such was the case of the Economic Partnership with the CARICOM[97] which resulted in the establishment of the CARICOM Competition Commission.[98] It is possible that the EU's active involvement is motivated by the belief that regional competition law in developing economies is a necessity for the promotion of sustainable development.[99] The EU also plays an active role in many international organisations such as the United Nations Conference on Trade and Development (UNCTAD), the OECD, and the ICN.[100] For instance, *The United Nations Set of Principles and Rules on Competition* is ostensibly influenced by the EU model.[101]

The task of promoting the EU model comes with its own challenges, primarily because the unique characteristic of the EU competition law is its integration of the regional organisation. In this respect, competition law is simply another means, regardless of how pivotal, of eliminating the barriers between Member States and helping to establish the Internal Market. Regardless of this specificity, the EU continues to actively export its competition law model through its network of bilateral trade and association agreements.[102]

94. Eleanor M. Fox & Daniel A. Crane, *Global Issues in Antitrust and Competition Law* (West 2010).
95. Michal S. Gal, *Antitrust in a Globalized Economy: The Unique Enforcement Challenges Faced by Small and Developing Jurisdictions*, 33 Fordham Int'l L.J. (2009).
96. Marco Botta, *Competition Policy: The EU and Global Networks*, *in* EU Policies in a Global Perspective: Shaping or Taking International Regimes? (Gerda Falkner & Patrick Müller eds., Routledge 2014).
97. The Caribbean Community and Common Market (CARICOM) consists largely of the former British West Indian colonies and regroups sixteen Caribbean nations. It was established by the Revised Treaty of Chaguaramas Establishing the Caribbean Community Including the CARICOM Single Market and Economy (2001).
98. Economic Partnership Agreement between the CARICOM States and the European Community and its Member States Art. 125(1) (30 Sept. 2008).
99. Josef Drexl, *Economic Integration and Competition Law in Developing Countries*, *in* Competition Policy and Regional Integration in Developing Countries (Josef Drexl, et al. eds., Edward Elgar Publishing 2012).
100. Marco Botta, *Competition Policy: The EU and Global Networks*, *in* EU Policies in a Global Perspective: Shaping or Taking International Regimes? (Falkner & Müller eds., Routledge 2014).
101. UNCTAD, *The United Nations Set of Principles and Rules on Competition* (2000). (The anticompetitive conducts are defined in a manner which resemble the terms used in the EU competition law).
102. Marco Botta, *Competition Policy: The EU and Global Networks*, *in* EU Policies in a Global Perspective: Shaping or Taking International Regimes? (Falkner & Müller eds., Routledge 2014).

§2.02 MODERN APPROACHES TO REGIONAL COMPETITION LAW

Small and developing economies could gain special benefits from the harmonisation efforts of competition laws.[103] Because of scarce resources and little experience in competition law, small and developing economies are rarely in a position to make credible threats to deter the anticompetitive conduct of foreign companies. A possible solution is to pool their resources at regional level. Regional cooperation could also enlarge the scope of competence of competition authorities in the enforcement of competition law since restraints on competition would no longer be restricted to a single region but would expand across borders. Furthermore, regional cooperation could serve as a forum for small and developing economies to analyse traditional approaches of reginal competition law and assess the merits of these models. It is essential that small and developing economies first take into account their distinctive considerations in their development of competition law before making the choice of adopting or adapting established regional competition law model.

In recognition of its potential, there have been many attempts to regionalise small and developing economies. Although there are many possible configurations, three modern approaches to regional competition law could be identified: a centralised approach, a convergence/soft harmonisation approach, and a download approach.[104]

[A] Distinctive Considerations for Developing Jurisdiction

Developing jurisdictions often face unique issues in enforcing competition law due to their natural inclination for accommodating anticompetitive practices.[105] Their low level of economic development, often accompanied by institutional design problems and complex government regulation and bureaucracy, aggravate the difficulties facing developing countries.[106] Developing economies' regional efforts in the field of competition law have had limited success despite initial potential, reinforcing the belief that regional competition law for developing economies is premature.[107] Nonetheless, a premature regional effort can still serve as added motivation for developing economies to further commit to introducing competition law.

Admittedly, each regional organisation is unique, yet despite this idiosyncrasy some common issues emerge. While there are many reasons behind the limited success of developing jurisdictions' regional competition law, this section highlights only the

103. Michal S. Gal, *Antitrust in a Globalized Economy: The Unique Enforcement Challenges Faced by Small and Developing Jurisdictions*, 33 Fordham Int'l L.J. (2009).
104. Josef Drexl, *Economic Integration and Competition Law in Developing Countries*, *in* Competition Policy and Regional Integration in Developing Countries (Josef Drexl, et al. eds., Edward Elgar Publishing 2012).
105. Alberto Heimler & Frédéric Jenny, *Regional Agreements*, *in* Building New Competition Law Regimes (David Lewis ed., Edward Elgar Publishing 2013).
106. Michal S. Gal, *The Ecology of Antitrust: Precondition of Competition Law Enforcement in Developing Countries*, *in* Competition, Competitiveness and Development: Lessons from Developing Countries (Unctad ed., UNCTAD/DITC/CLP/2004/1 2004).
107. Maher M. Dabbah, *International and Comparative Competition Law* (Cambridge University Press 2010).

two most impactful considerations in the development of developing economy's competition law.

[1] Resources Restriction

'Possibly the main enforcement obstacle faced by developing and small jurisdictions involves enforcement resource constraints – both financial and human.'[108] Resource scarcity is not limited to financial affairs but extends to that of human capabilities. In order to effectively enforce competition law, jurisdictions need qualified personnel, preferably with some experience. Plagued by restricted resources, many countries cannot justify the investment required to commence their own competition law regime. It is seemingly more logical to create communal enforcement at a regional level by pooling resources with neighbours. The benefits of this method seem apparent: '[j]oining forces to create some form of participatory governance, jurisdictions can reduce, *inter alia*, limitations resulting from scarce enforcement resources, political economy constraints, and limited ability to create credible enforcement threats'.[109] Furthermore, it is argued that regional competition law is 'the optimal solution'[110] for resource-constrained countries to achieve the goal of regional competition law.

The vision of pooling resources in the administrative design and enforcement of regional competition law is not, however, universally shared. '[T]o the extent that a regional arrangement is an agreement for a community-wide competition law, and especially one with centralised enforcement, all of the problems that undermine successful national enforcement, other than lack of economies of scale, recur'.[111] Regionalising competition law does not provide immunity from the problems of resource restriction. Furthermore, there are few incentives to conceding precious financial and human resources to a regional organisation when the same resources are needed in the national jurisdiction. The WAEMU serves as an exemplary tale of persisting resource starvation at regional level. In 2012, the WAEMU Competition Commission only recorded three ex-officio members of staff.[112] It would seem that despite the effort of gathering the resources, the problem still exists and simply manifests itself differently. It should not be forgotten that creating a regional competition law regime, especially when using a centralised approach, involves the direct

108. Michal S. Gal & Inbal Faibish Wassmer, *Regional Agreements of Developing Jurisdictions: Unleashing the Potential, in* Competition Policy and Regional Integration in Developing Countries (Josef Drexl, et al. eds., Edward Elgar Publishing 2012).
109. Michal S. Gal, *Regional Competition Law Agreements: An Important Step for Antitrust Enforcement*, 60 U. Toronto L.J. (2010).
110. Delroy S. Beckford, *Implementing Effective Competition Policy through Regional Trade Agreements: the Case of CARICOM, in* Competition Policy and Regional Integration in Developing Countries (Josef Drexl, et al. eds., Edward Elgar Publishing 2012).
111. Eleanor M. Fox, *Competition, Development and Regional Integration: In Search of a Competition Law Fit for Developing Countries, in* Competition Policy and Regional Integration in Developing Countries (Josef Drexl, et al. eds., Edward Elgar Publishing 2012).
112. Mor Bakhoum & Julia Molestina, *Institutional Coherence and Effectiveness of a Regional Competition Policy: the Case of the West African Economic and Monetary Union (WAEMU), in* Competition Policy and Regional Integration in Developing Countries (Josef Drexl, et al. eds., Edward Elgar Publishing 2012).

costs of building a new institution (or institutions) and the resources for its operation.[113] Such costs can be burdensome, especially for countries whose resources are already scarce. Moreover, the cost of complying with the obligations of the regional arrangement, especially the effective enforcement of domestic competition law, for a state with inadequate institutional and regulatory capacity can be too costly for that state.[114] It is apparent now that regionalisation does not automatically solve the problem of restricted resources. Only with clear communal resolve and some sacrifice can participating states overcome this particular challenge.[115]

[2] The Nature of Member States

The nature of participating members in regional integration directly influences the level of integration, in particular the allocation of competence between members and regional regulatory body. In theory, smaller groups of countries with similar political and economic backgrounds and levels of development would be best suited to the centralised approach, the deepest form of integration. In contrast, larger groups of countries with diverse economic characteristics and differing levels of development cannot afford to adopt the centralised approach.[116] Earlier in this chapter the case of the WAEMU was analysed, and it was noted that over-centralisation halted the progress of Senegal's competition law regime as well as stifled other new jurisdictions in the nascent state. The MERCOSUR members also faced internal political and economic divisions on the importance of a free market which resulted in the slow implementation of its regulations.[117]

On the other hand, it was once argued that 'the implementation of common competition policy does not require a similar level of economic development of the participating states. What matters more is the concrete application of the rules to the individual cases'. [118] The focus, here, is on the willingness to commit on the part of members as it is believed that commitment could overcome local contextual obstacles. Nonetheless, commitment to regional obligations is not absolute and may waver when

113. Michal S. Gal & Inbal Faibish Wassmer, *Regional Agreements of Developing Jurisdictions: Unleashing the Potential, in* Competition Policy and Regional Integration in Developing Countries (Josef Drexl, et al. eds., Edward Elgar Publishing 2012).
114. Michal S. Gal, *Regional Competition Law Agreements: An Important Step for Antitrust Enforcement,* 60 U. Toronto L.J. (2010).
115. O. Richard Cunningham & Anthony J LaRocca, *Harmonisation of Competition Policies in a Regional Economic Integration,* 27 Law & Pol'y Int'l Bus. (1995).
116. Mor Bakhoum & Julia Molestina, *Institutional Coherence and Effectiveness of a Regional Competition Policy: the Case of the West African Economic and Monetary Union (WAEMU), in* Competition Policy and Regional Integration in Developing Countries (Josef Drexl, et al. eds., Edward Elgar Publishing 2012).
117. Frédéric Jenny & Pierre M. Horna, *Modernization of the European System of Competition Law Enforcement: Lessons for Other Regional Groupings, in* Competition Provisions in Regional Trade Agreements: How to Assure Development Gains (Philippe Brusick, et al. eds., UNCTAD/DITC/CLP/2005/1 2005).
118. Josef Drexl, *Economic Integration and Competition Law in Developing Countries, in* Competition Policy and Regional Integration in Developing Countries (Josef Drexl, et al. eds., Edward Elgar Publishing 2012).

faced with political and financial instability. If sufficient numbers of Member States find themselves in such predicaments, this would in turn reduce the potential benefits that other members could gain from regional organisation. Such was the case with the COMESA when it prompted some members to leave and join a smaller and more stable regional agreement.[119]

Theoretically, the incentive for states to join a regional arrangement is the potential benefits to be gained in relation to the costs and burden in the form of requirements resulting from the arrangement. The benefits, in this case, are not restricted to competition law, especially if the regional competition agreement is merely part of a wider trade agreement. It is a challenge to convince states to abandon their sovereignty in favour of the regional organisation. The unwillingness to join is not reserved exclusively for developing economies with elementary experience in competition law enforcement. Indeed, 'the greater the ability of a country to solve its anticompetitive issues on its own, the lower its incentive to cede sovereignty'.[120] This is principally because '[n]ations normally have myopic vision and bounded concern'.[121] Developing regional institutions must carefully package their product as politically acceptable for participating countries. One way to convince them of the regional competition authority's usefulness is to introduce an institutional feature that favours the participation of national authorities in the decision-making process at the central level.[122] Furthermore, it must be clarified that members would preserve their sovereignty over competition cases which do not raise regional competition issues. Responding to this concern, the EU's principle of subsidiarity seems appropriate.

It should be noted that the difficulty in negotiating the allocation of competence between Member States and regional institution is more pronounced the deeper the integration approach is. In this regard, the negotiation is most demanding for an institution with a centralised orientation. Among other forms of regionalisation, the negotiation of the allocation of competence continues even within the framework of mere collaboration. An effective cooperation and coordination mechanism between members and between members and the regional authority is crucial in order to avoid the risk of overlapping competences. Weak collaboration between members and the community could still occur even in looser forms of regional harmonisation.[123]

119. Michal S. Gal & Inbal Faibish Wassmer, *Regional Agreements of Developing Jurisdictions: Unleashing the Potential, in* Competition Policy and Regional Integration in Developing Countries (Josef Drexl, et al. eds., Edward Elgar Publishing 2012).
120. *Ibid. See also*, Andrew T. Guzman, *Is International Antitrust Possible?*, 73 NYUL. Rev. 1501 (1998).
121. Eleanor M. Fox, et al., *The Past and Future of International Antitrust: Gaps, Overlaps and the Institutional Challenge, in* Building New Competition Law Regime (David Lewis ed., Edward Elgar 2012).
122. Alberto Heimler & Frédéric Jenny, *Regional Agreements, in* Building New Competition Law Regimes (David Lewis ed., Edward Elgar Publishing 2013).
123. Mor Bakhoum & Julia Molestina, *Institutional Coherence and Effectiveness of a Regional Competition Policy: The Case of the West African Economic and Monetary Union (WAEMU), in* Competition Policy and Regional Integration in Developing Countries (Josef Drexl, et al. eds., Edward Elgar Publishing 2012).

[B] The Centralised Approach

[1] The WAEMU

The WAEMU could serve as a cautionary tale for overly ambitious attempts at regional integration.[124] Its integration process began with the adoption of a common currency, the CFA franc, under the auspices of the Monetary Union of West Africa (UMOA)[125] and signed in 1994 by seven West African countries: Benin, Burkina Faso, Côte d'Ivoire, Mali, Niger, Senegal, and Togo. Guinea-Bissau was the last to join in 1997. The *Treaty of Dakar*[126] would later be introduced to transform the existing monetary union into full economic integration with the creation of a common market under the auspice of the WAEMU.

The *Treaty of Dakar* institutes common competition law: the prohibition of anticompetitive agreements with the object or effect of restraining or distorting competition within the Union, abuse of dominant position in the common market or in a significant party of the common market, and state aid.[127] The WAEMU Council of Ministers, a political organ with national representatives, has exclusive competence to legislate on these matters[128] consequently reducing Member States' competence to merger control and unfair competition. The *Treaty of Dakar* also established a supranational enforcement organ called the WAEMU Competition Commission with a mandate to enforce regional competition law and cooperate with Member States in the enforcement of the law.[129] The Commission can conduct independent investigations into alleged anticompetitive conduct without a request from member countries or affected undertakings. The *Treaty of Dakar* established the principle of direct applicability and supremacy of the Union's regulations.[130] In addition, the WAEMU Court of Justice ambitiously stated that the WAEMU competition law had supremacy over Member States' competition laws since the WAEMU's law purports to be centralising.[131] The Court of Justice further refrained from identifying the limit of the applicability of regional competition law, thus suggesting that regional competition law applies even when there is only a small element of intra-community market and is not limited to the effect on trade between Member States. It follows that the Commission's exclusive enforcement power is extended accordingly. It is not surprising that the Court's opinion was heavily criticised for its deviation from the Treaty's intent. It was argued that the *Treaty of Dakar* merely created common substantive rules and entrusted the Council of Ministers to direct the Commission in its competition-related

124. Daniel P. Weick, *Competition Law and Policy in Senegal: A Cautionary Tale for Regional Integration?*, 33 World Competition (2010).
125. Traité de l'Union Monétaire Ouest-Africaine (14 Nov. 1973).
126. Traité Modifié de l'Union Économique et Monétaire Ouest Africaine (2003).
127. *Ibid.*, at Art. 88.
128. *Ibid.*, at Art. 89.
129. *Ibid.*, at Art. 90.
130. *Ibid.*, at Art. 43.
131. *Advisory Opinion No. 003/2000* (27 Jun. 2000).

enforcement.[132] It did not create an exclusive community regulatory authority that would supplant the national authority. In light of the Court's interpretation, Senegal, a member country with the most experience in competition law enforcement,[133] was forced to withdraw enforcement of its own competition law to make room for the WAEMU even though the latter's credibility and efficiency had not been affirmed.[134] Also of concern is the well-documented fact that the Commission's resources are extremely limited.[135] Not only has the Court succeeded in alienating an important member with a reliable competition regime but local problems would not be addressed if the national authority had to defer to and await the enforcement of a supranational body.[136] Regardless of the criticism and discontent expressed, the interpretation of the Court has been upheld by members who have refrained from implementing their domestic competition laws in favour of referring cases to the WAEMU Commission.[137] National competition authorities' competence is thus limited to unfair competition, price regulation and merger control. Consequently, national authorities have creatively enlarged the scope of application of those provisions.[138] However, Member States may still participate in the regional decision-making process through the Advisory Committee on Competition, which is based on the ECN that can give opinions on pending cases. While the Advisory Committee's opinion is not binding, it has been observed that the Commission generally follows it.[139]

Despite gaining recognition as 'the most successful of all the regional agreements [in developing jurisdictions] in terms of enforcement,'[140] in reality the WAEMU's competition law regime's effectiveness is limited by its over-centralised enforcement as previously demonstrated. The *UNCTAD Peer Review Report* suggested a reallocation of competence whereby national competition authorities can conduct the initial investigation, leaving the Commission to make the final decision.[141] Such restructuring, while not ideal since the principle of subsidiarity comparable to that of the EU would be more

132. Daniel P. Weick, *Competition Law and Policy in Senegal: A Cautionary Tale for Regional Integration?*, 33 World Competition (2010).
133. Senegal has begun its competition law enforcement since the enactment of its competition law in 1994, *see*, Loi n° 94-63 du 22 août 1994 sur les Prix, la Concurrence et le Contentieux Economique.
134. Eleanor M. Fox & Daniel A. Crane, *Global Issues in Antitrust and Competition Law* (West 2010).
135. Mor Bakhoum & Julia Molestina, *Institutional Coherence and Effectiveness of a Regional Competition Policy: the Case of the West African Economic and Monetary Union (WAEMU), in* Competition Policy and Regional Integration in Developing Countries (Josef Drexl, et al. eds., Edward Elgar Publishing 2012).
136. Eleanor M. Fox, *Competition, Development and Regional Integration: In Search of a Competition Law Fit for Developing Countries, in* Competition Policy and Regional Integration in Developing Countries (Josef Drexl, et al. eds., Edward Elgar Publishing 2012).
137. Daniel P. Weick, *Competition Law and Policy in Senegal: A Cautionary Tale for Regional Integration?*, 33 World Competition (2010).
138. UNCTAD, *Voluntary Peer Review of Competition Policies of WAEMU, Benin and Senegal* (2007).
139. Mor Bakhoum & Julia Molestina, *Institutional Coherence and Effectiveness of a Regional Competition Policy: the Case of the West African Economic and Monetary Union (WAEMU), in* Competition Policy and Regional Integration in Developing Countries (Josef Drexl, et al. eds., Edward Elgar Publishing 2012).
140. Alberto Heimler & Frédéric Jenny, *Regional Agreements, in* Building New Competition Law Regimes (David Lewis ed., Edward Elgar Publishing 2013).
141. UNCTAD, *Voluntary Peer Review of Competition Policies of WAEMU, Benin and Senegal* (2007).

appropriate, would undoubtedly reconnect national competition authorities in the regional structure as well as help the WAEMU gain from the experiences of more established national authorities.

[2] The COMESA

'To date, the COMESA remains one of the most successful regional economic cooperation and integration groups in Africa.'[142] In comparison to the experience of the WAEMU, the COMESA experience with regional competition law appears to be more measured.

In 1993, the *COMESA Treaty*[143] was signed to replace the *Preferential Trade Area Treaty*.[144] This subregional organisation has a large membership comprising of a block of the EAC and the SADC. The COMESA was designed to provide economic integration at community level with competition law as one of the core economic tools. The *COMESA Treaty* provides some elements of competition law, namely prohibitions of collusion and state aid control.[145] At the same time, the Treaty also encourages Member States to adopt and enforce their own domestic competition laws. When the Treaty was adopted, some Member States had already enacted national competition laws, but the laws were deemed inadequate.[146] In this regard, regional competition law is necessary in order to assure harmonisation and consistency in the enforcement of the law.

The *COMESA Competition Regulations* would later come to complement regional competition law inaugurated by the *COMESA Treaty*. They prohibit anticompetitive agreements, abuse of dominant position, cartel arrangements, and merger control.[147] They also establish the COMESA Competition Commission as a corporate body capable of enforcing regional competition law.[148] The Commission has the power to monitor and investigate anticompetitive behaviours, mediate disputes between Member States concerning anticompetitive conduct and coordinate with national competition authorities in the enforcement of regional competition law within the regional block.[149] It can only intervene when there is an effect on trade between Member States. The Commission can also initiate an investigation on its own without waiting for notification or a request from Member States. The decisions of the Commission can be appealed to the

142. George K. Lipimile & Elizabeth Gachuiri, *Allocation of Competences Between National and Regional Competition Authorities: The Case of COMESA*, *in* Competition Provisions in Regional Trade Agreements: How to Assure Development Gains (Philippe Brusick, et al. eds., UNCTAD/DITC/CLP/2005/1 2005).
143. Treaty Establishing the Common Market for Eastern and Southern Africa (1993) (COMESA Treaty).
144. The Treaty Establishing the Preferential Trade Area for Eastern and Southern Africa (1981).
145. Treaty Establishing the Common Market for Eastern and Southern Africa Arts 51 and 52 (1993).
146. Lipimile, *The COMESA Regional Competition Regulations*, *in* Competition Policy and Regional Integration in Developing Countries (Josef Drexl, et al. eds., Edward Elgar Publishing 2012).
147. COMESA Competition Regulations [2004], Arts 16, 18, 19 and 24 (*hereinafter* COMESA Regulations).
148. *Ibid.*, at Art. 6.
149. *Ibid.*, at Art. 7.

Board of Commissioners.[150] In turn, the latter's decision can be heard by the COMESA Court of Justice that can conduct a judicial review of the acts of all COMESA institutions.[151]

Unlike the WAEMU and more like the experience of the EU, the principle of subsidiarity applies in this case. The COMESA Commission shares jurisdiction of regional competition law with national competition authorities with the Commission having supremacy in case of conflicts.[152] Members are required to create conditions conducive to achieving the aims of the common market and the implementation of the *COMESA Treaty* and to refrain from undermining these aims. With a comprehensive substantive provision complemented by enforcement by both national and regional competition authorities, the COMESA's attempt at regional competition law has all the necessary elements to achieve effectiveness.

[C] The Harmonisation Approach

The MERCOSUR was founded in 1991 by the *Treaty of Asunción*.[153] It consists of four sovereign countries: Argentina, Brazil, Paraguay, Venezuela and Uruguay. Bolivia, Chile, Columbia, Ecuador and Peru are Associate Member States. The MERCOSUR's main objective is to promote free trade and free movement of people, goods and currency.[154] In light of this objective, it is necessary for Member States 'to harmonise their legislation in the relevant areas in order to strengthen the integration process'.[155] The field of competition law was regarded as a necessary step towards regional integration and attempts were made to harmonise members' different domestic competition laws and policies. However, it was not until 1996 when the *Fortaleza Protocol*[156] was signed that an ambitious set of guidelines to establish a harmonised competition policy was adopted. Among other institutional innovations, the *Fortaleza Protocol* requires all members to establish national competition laws that apply to all sectors of the economy, and an autonomous competition agency capable of its enforcement. For the purpose of creating a common competition policy, the *Fortaleza Protocol* advocates greater harmonisation of domestic competition laws in the area of anticompetitive conduct and merger controls. This measure was of crucial importance in light of Member States' frequent adoption of anti-dumping measures against each other which consequently impeded trade within the community.[157]

---

150. *Ibid.*, at Art. 12.
151. *Ibid.*, at Art. 19.
152. Treaty Establishing the Common Market for Eastern and Southern Africa, Art. 5(2) (1993).
153. Treaty Establishing a Common Market Between the Argentine Republic, the Federative Republic of Brazil, the Republic of Paraguay and the Eastern Republic of Uruguay (MERCOSUR) (1991) (*hereinafter* Treaty of Asunción).
154. *Ibid.*, at Art. 1.
155. *Ibid.*
156. The Protocolo de Defesa da Concorrência no Mercosul, Decision 18/96 (1996) (the Fortaleza Protocol).
157. Frédéric Jenny & Pierre M. Horna, *Modernization of the European System of Competition Law Enforcement: Lessons for Other Regional Groupings*, *in* Competition Provisions in Regional

The MERCOSUR Trade Commission, composed of four members and four alternates from each Member State[158] and the Committee for the Defence of Competition, consisted of national competition authorities, are the two organs in charge of monitoring the enforcement of the *Fortaleza Protocol.*[159] Both organs are not supranational but intergovernmental bodies. The Committee for the Defence of Competition handles the investigation of cross-border competition cases at the request of Member States in cooperation with the national competition authorities of the state in which the infringing party is domiciled.[160] In contrast, competition issues with no regional element fall exclusively within the jurisdiction of Member States.[161] The Committee recommends sanctions or any other appropriate measures to the Trade Commission if the infringement has MERCOSUR implications.[162] It cannot impose sanctions or measures by its own. The Trade Commission then, taking into account the recommendation of the Committee, adopts a Directive applying sanctions or other enforcement measures.[163] The national authorities of the defendant's domicile are under obligation to apply this Directive. In this regard, the Trade Commission is the sole organ with adjudicating power relative to cross-border competition issues among Member States. However, its power is only indirectly since it requires actual enforcement from national authorities. While it is true that both the Trade Commission and the Committee for the Defence of Competition are composed of representative from the Member States, the former is awarded a better status since it is an intergovernmental organ with decision-making power within the MERCOSUR[164] and can thus be entrusted with adopting Directives applying enforcement measures.

Following the MERCOSUR philosophy, the *Fortaleza Protocol* did not create any supranational institution. Consequently, the effectiveness of the regional competition regime relies solely on the national competition authorities' power of enforcement.[165] In theory, the absence of a centralised institution does not necessary translate to ineffectiveness in competition law regime provided that national competition authorities are capable of fulfilling in the role of regional enforcement. Nonetheless, this is not the case for the MERCOSUR.[166] Consequently, the MERCOSUR's ambitious policy of economic integration has had limited success. Another contributing factor to this limitation is the economic instability of Member States.[167] The unequal development of

Trade Agreements: How to Assure Development Gains (Philippe Brusick, et al. eds., UNCTAD/DITC/CLP/2005/1 2005).

158. Additional Protocol to the Treaty of Asunción on the Institutional Structure of MERCOSUR, Art. 17 (1994) (Protocol of Ouro Preto).
159. The Protocolo de Defesa da Concorrência no Mercosul, Decision 18/96, Art. 8 (1996).
160. *Ibid.*, at Art. 10.
161. *Ibid.*, at Art. 3.
162. *Ibid.*, at Art. 19.
163. *Ibid.*, at Art. 20.
164. *Ibid.*, at Art. 2.
165. José Tavares De Araújo, Jr. & Louis Tineo, *Harmonization of Competition Policies among MERCOSUR Countries*, 24 Brook. J. Int'l L. (1998).
166. Anestis S. Papadopoulos, *The International Dimension of EU Competition Law and Policy*, 197 (Cambridge University Press 2010).
167. André Filipe Zago De Azevedo, *MERCOSUR: Ambitious Policies, Poor Practices*, 24 Brazilian J. of Pol. Econ. (2004).

members is also an important factor. Some members, namely Paraguay and Uruguay, lack experience and expertise in the field of competition law enforcement.[168] Moreover, members are also resistant to anti-dumping and state aid control provisions in a perceived reaction to Brazil's trade dominance in the region.[169]

[D] Download Approach

The term *download approach* refers to the process of transferring supranational rules from a regional institution directly into national norms. This feature is unique to the Andean Community.

The Andean Community was created in 1969 by the *Cartagena Agreement*[170] originally as a free trade area, a custom union with common external tariffs and trade policy. The Andean Community achieved the elimination of tariffs in 1993.[171] It has undergone some changes in membership, and the current members are Bolivia, Columbia, Ecuador, and Peru.[172] The *Cartagena Agreement* simply mandates Member States to adopt regulations dealing with restrictive business practices without any explicit competition provisions. It was *Decision 285*[173] that established substantive regulations and supranational authority in the field of competition law in intra-regional cases. It includes provisions on collusion and the abuse of dominant position. The Board of Commission, established by the *Cartagena Agreement*, is in charge of overseeing the enforcement of *Decision 285*. At the request of member countries or affected private parties, the Board will conduct investigations and authorise countries to impose corrective measures. It cannot impose sanctions directly on undertakings. Due to the restriction on the power of the competition authority, no anticompetitive practices were detected nor sanctioned under this rule.[174] It was not until 2005, with the introduction of *Decision 608*,[175] that the Andean Community gained a more effective regional competition regime. *Decision 608* forbids agreements and collusion

168. Frédéric Jenny & Pierre M. Horna, *Modernization of the European System of Competition Law Enforcement: Lessons for Other Regional Groupings*, *in* Competition Provisions in Regional Trade Agreements: How to Assure Development Gains (Philippe Brusick, et al. eds., UNCTAD/DITC/CLP/2005/1 2005).
169. *Ibid.*
170. Andean Subregional Integration Agreement (1969) (*hereinafter* Cartagena Agreement).
171. Gesner Oliveira, *Competition Policy in Brazil and MERCOSUR: Aspect of the Recent Experience*, 24 Brook. J. Int'l L. (1998).
172. For general information on the Andean Community, *See*, Andean Community, *What Is CAN?*, http://www.comunidadandina.org/Seccion.aspx?id = 189&tipo = QU&title = somos-comunidad-andina (accessed 13 Nov. 2017).
173. *Decision 285 Concerning Rules and Regulations for Preventing or Correcting Distortions in Competition Caused by Practices that Restrict Free Competition* (Commission of the Cartagena Agreement 1991).
174. Francisco Marcos, *Downloading Competition Law from a Regional Trade Agreement: A Strategy to Introduce Competition Law in Bolivia and Ecuador*, *in* Competition Law and Policy in Latin America (Eleanor M. Fox & D. Daniel Sokol eds., Hart Publishing 2009).
175. *Decision 608 Concerning Regulations for the Protection and Promotion of Competition in the Andean Community* (Commission of the Cartagena Agreement 2005).

that restrict competition as well as the abuse of dominant position by undertakings that may affect trade among Member States. It directly addresses the weakness of *Decision 285* by, among others, giving enforcement power to the General Secretariat in cross-border cases as well as the power to directly impose sanctions on undertakings. Addressing the issue of absence of comprehensive competition law in certain Member States, it allows members to directly apply the Community's competition law regime – hence the denomination *download approach*. Member States are to refrain from adopting rules that contradict the aims or the Community law.[176] Furthermore, the Andean Community has also established an Advisory Committee for the Protection of Competition, composed of representatives of national authorities, to facilitate the exchange of information between Member States.

The justification of the download approach is to allow states without national competition law to provisionally use supranational rules until the adoption of comprehensive domestic competition law. This method should help circumvent traditional challenges, namely resource restrictions and political and institutional obstacles, when adopting new competition rules and building a competition culture. On the other hand, by avoiding addressing these challenges, the download approach would inevitably lead to the implementation of supranational rules without the necessary support of the local context. Another difficulty resides in the interpretation of *Decision 608* because its language is unclear regarding the extent of the flexibility given to members when downloading the Andean Community's competition rules. It follows that the interesting download approach to regional harmonisation may only obtain minimal effectiveness in the long run since it only allows temporary solution to use regional competition rules without aiding the actual harmonisation process within members' regimes.

§2.03 CONCLUSION

This chapter explores a variety of regional competition law models which ranges from the loosely connected form of regional trade agreements to fully integrated systems. The experiences demonstrated in this chapter have shown that an ideal model suitable for all states does not exist. Each configuration must navigate both the particular and shared challenges of regional competition law.

The three modern experiences of developing economies, namely the centralised approach, the harmonisation approach, and the download approach, are of particular interest to the ASEAN. Despite their differences, they all offer a valuable lesson to the ASEAN, namely, the local context of both the Member States and the region will be ignored at its peril. There is no shortage of examples in this regard: the WAEMU disregarded the advantages of national competition authorities in favour of its over-regionalisation approach to competition law. The result has been an unsatisfactory enforcement of regional competition law. The COMESA ignored some Member States'

176. *Ibid.*, at Art. 15.

inability to fulfil their regional obligations due to national political and economic instability, leading to a reduction in gains from the arrangement and the eventual departure of some of the Member States. The MERCOSUR underestimated the importance of unequal development levels and differences in even a basic understanding of the philosophy underlying competition policy.

CHAPTER 3

The ASEAN Competition Law Goals

When the ASEAN leaders agreed to prioritise the ASEAN single market integration as the main project and endorsed the creation of the AEGC, this decision sets the stage for the formation of a regional single market with competition law as an important part of the mechanism. Following the example of the EU model, the ASEAN leaders placed competition law at the centre of the AEC's structure. Since inventing a new path can be difficult and costly, there is nothing wrong with travelling down a path well-travelled. However, developing economies deserve a competition law regime that fits the facts of their market and responds to their conditions and needs.[1] A competition law that is so designed and characterised is imperative in order to obtain greater legitimacy and acceptance from national vested interests, as well as resulting in better implementation. Consequently, the ASEAN, whose Member States are mainly developing economies, also needs to take into consideration the reality of its own market and conditions when considering regional competition law in this region.

Determining the goals of competition law is a precondition to building a body of coherent competition rules.[2] Furthermore, unveiling the goals of competition law is linked to revealing the identity of competition law itself.[3] The objectives of competition law will directly influence how competition law is shaped and enforced.[4] Consequently, it is essential to carefully and clearly specify the objectives of competition law while bearing in mind the practical realities of business. Unclear goals will leave margins of interpretation in the hands of competition authorities and may divert competition enforcement from its original purposes: '[w]hat [competition law] aims for must accord with what is economically feasible'.[5] In reality, it is impossible to define

1. Eleanor M. Fox, *Economic Development, Poverty and Antitrust: The Other Path*, 13 Sw. J. L. & Trade Am. (2007).
2. Robert H. Bork, *The Antitrust Paradox: A Policy at War with Itself*, 50 (Free Press 1978).
3. *Ibid.*
4. Maurice E. Stucke, *Reconsidering Antitrust's Goals*, 53 B.C. L. Rev. (2012).
5. David K. Round & Alec Zuo, *The Welfare Goal of Antitrust Laws in Asia: For Whom Should the Law Toil?*, 22 Asian-Pacific Economic Literature 2 (2008).

with absolute specificity any economic regulation since the economy changes almost constantly. Nonetheless, competition law should have enough flexibility and discretional room for interpretation by authorities while not hindering the ultimate goal or goals set in the legislation.

Defining the objectives of competition law serves two general purposes. First, the objectives inform the enforcement and application of the law.[6] They can alert policy makers and decision makers to any discrepancies between actual and desired outcomes from current enforcement and assist in aligning the outcomes to the stated objectives.[7] Second, the objectives can elevate the accountability of competition authorities through increasing transparency in order to 'facilitate reasoned debate to the extent that they make explicit the rationale for decisions in individual cases.'[8] In order to reveal the goals of competition law, one has to first look into the language of the statute.[9] However, in the field of competition law the language used in the statutes may be too vague and malleable for this approach.[10] It was also recommended that the legislative history be looked into, but unfortunately this approach is not always useful either.[11] As a result, the ambiguous language used in the statutes has led to too many academic debates over the true legislative intent behind the enactment of competition law. The search for the goals of competition law should not be strictly confined to legislative intent since competition law is capable of having wider overriding goals.[12] Restricting debate to legislative intent could lead to a great restriction of viewpoint.[13] Competition law is believed to belong to an order where different disciplines, factors and interests are interwoven and evolve constantly according to changes related to the relevant time period.[14]

There is no doubt that searching for the goals beyond legislative intent is not an easy task. In this regard, the debate on the goals of competition law is ongoing and there is still no consensus on this matter.[15] It is plausible that the absence of a unanimous answer, despite various academic writings and competition authorities' enforcement, is the major factor behind the persistent debate on the most appropriate goals of competition law. Moreover, this debate has branched out beyond national

6. ABA, *Report on Antitrust Policy Objectives 1* (2013).
7. Maurice E. Stucke, *Reconsidering Antitrust's Goals*, 53 B.C. L. Rev. (2012).
8. ABA, *Report on Antitrust Policy Objectives 1* (2013).
9. Michael C. Dorf, *Legal Indeterminacy and Institutional Design*, 78 NYUL. Rev. (2003). (Scalia's crusade against use of legislative history is designed to combat interest group power by forcing them to get desired goals enacted into explicit statutory language).
10. Herbert Hovenkamp, *Federal Antitrust Policy: The Law of Competition and Its Practices*, 49 (Thomson West 2005).
11. *Ibid.*
12. Maher M. Dabbah, *The Internationalisation of Antitrust Policy*, 49 (Cambridge University Press 2003).
13. John J. Flynn, *The Raegan Administration's Antitrust Policy, 'Original Intent' and the Legislative History of the Sherman Act*, 33 Antitrust Bull. (1988).
14. ABA Sections of Antitrust Law and International Law and Practice, *The Internationalization of Competition Law Rules: Coordination and Convergence* (1999).
15. Maher M. Dabbah, *International and Comparative Competition Law*, 36 (Cambridge University Press 2010).

level to regional and international level.[16] The possibilities range from economic to socio-political goals.

Determining the goals of competition law is also 'the focal point of the convergence strategy'.[17] If all competition law systems move towards the same set goal, convergence is the expected outcome generating an increasingly uniform normative framework for global competition. However, this hypothesis rests upon the assumption that the stated goals and the goals actually pursued by competition officials or national governments are identical. It has been noted before that the two are often dissimilar.[18] It is true that the lack of consensus on the goals of competition law may not matter much as long as it is universally believed that competition is *good* and should be encouraged and that anticompetitive restriction is *bad* and should be condemned.[19] Yet, in light of the regionalisation of competition policy, consensus on the goals of competition law does matter. It is vital to address the issue of the goals of competition law from the very beginning.

Many goals have been advocated under competition law, but no exhaustive list has been drawn up.[20] The difficulty in unveiling the identity of the goals of competition law lies in the fluid nature of competition law itself. Economic factors do not remain static and the understanding of competition law has to adapt accordingly.[21] As competition law systems develop, there will inevitably be changes in the focus accorded various policy objectives within the same jurisdiction. The goals of competition law also vary according to the jurisdiction since they are related to each country's definition of competition.[22] Because competition law is likely to be influenced by a country's social and historical context, it is to be expected that countries may respond to different objectives.[23] In general, the identity of competition law remains veiled[24] and there is little awareness of how they have developed, why they were created and the extent to which the systems have achieved their intended goals.[25] This lack of awareness leads to the question of whether it is possible to overcome this difficulty or

16. Claus Dieter Ehlermann & Laraine L. Laudati, *Panel Discussion: Competition Policy Objectives*, *in* European Competition Law Annual 1997: Objectives of Compeittion Policy (Claus Dieter Ehlermann & Laraine L. Laudati eds., Hart Publishing 1998).
17. David J. Gerber, *Asia and Global Competition Law Convergence*, *in* Asian Capitalism and the Regulation of Competition (Michael W. Dowdle, et al. eds., Cambridge University Press 2013).
18. *Ibid.*
19. G. Bruce Doern & Stephen Wilks, *Comparative Competition Policy: National Institutions in a Global Market* (Oxford University Press 1996).
20. *See*, for example, WTO, *Annual Report* (1997); ICN, *Advocacy and Competition Policy Report* (2002); ICN, *Report on the Objectives of Unilateral Conduct Laws, Assessment of Dominance/Substantial Market Power, and State-Created Monopolies* (the 6th Annual Conference of the ICN, Russia 2007) (have all tried to identify competition policy objectives, many of which do not coincide).
21. Whish & Bailey, *Competition Law*, 23 (7th ed.,Oxford University Press 2012).
22. Maurice E. Stucke, *Reconsidering Competition*, 81 Miss. L.J. (2011).
23. Massimo Motta, *Competition Policy: Theory and Practice*, 1 (Cambridge University Press 2004).
24. Robert H. Bork, *The Tempting of America*, 33 (Touchstone 1990).
25. David J. Gerber, *Law and Competition in the Twentieth Century Europe*, 22 (Oxford University Press 1998).

whether it is at all desirable to do so[26] given the potential conflicts this question would inevitably unleash.

This chapter attempts to unveil the identity of the ASEAN's competition law goals. Establishing an understanding of the goals of different competition law systems is crucial for a better understanding of the ASEAN's experience in the same field. This chapter will start with a general overview of the goals of competition law before moving towards the specific goals. The goals of the EU competition law are selected here since the EU is regarded as the reference model for regional competition law. The US model, frequently regarded as another referential model, will not be examined in this section since it does not encompass the experience from a regional organisation's point of view.[27] Special attention is paid to other developing economies' experiences in order to better appreciate how other developing economies adapt the established models to their local situations. The chapter ends with a study into the challenges faced by the ASEAN in achieving these goals.

§3.01 GENERAL GOALS IN COMPETITION LAW

Generally, the goals discussed can be classified into three categories: economic, social and political. The social and political goals are sometimes referred to as non-economic goals, extra-competition policies, or non-competition law proper policies.[28] The wording of the latter in particular suggests that competition policy should not be concerned with them and that some degree of discretion is required in their implementation, thus, reducing the legal certainties expected from having identifiable goals. Some doubts have been cast on whether these non-economic goals are simply reflexes or have beneficial side effects.[29] It can be argued that they are achievable through other trade policies.[30]

1. The Economic Goals: This category includes economic efficiency, promotion of trade, economic liberalization, and enhancing the development of a market economy. It is implemented by proscribing and preventing occurrences of

26. Maher M. Dabbah, *International and Comparative Competition Law*, 37 (Cambridge University Press 2010).
27. The dominant doctrine states that the purpose of the antitrust law is to enhance economic efficiency and maximise welfare. *See*, in particular, Robert H. Bork, *Legislative Intent and the Policy of Sherman Act*, 9 J. of L. & Eco. (1966). While others argue that the aim of antitrust law is to protect small or medium firms, justice and fairness in business. *See*, for example, Christopher Bellamy, *Some Reflections on Competition Law in the Global Market*, 34 New Eng. L. Rev. (1999); Louis B. Schwartz, *'Justice' and Other non-Economic Goals of Antitrust*, 127 U. Pa. L. Rev. (1979).
28. Rodger, *Competition Law and Policy in the EC and UK*, 16 (3rd ed.,Cavendish 2004).
29. Andreas Fuchs, *Characteristic Aspects of Competition and Their Consequences for the Objectives of Competition Law – Comment on Stucke*, *in* The Goals of Competition Law (Daniel Zimmer ed., Edward Elgar Publishing 2012).
30. D. G. Goyder, et al., *Goyder's EC Competition Law*, 10 (5th ed., Oxford University Press 2009); Andreas Fuchs, *Characteristic Aspects of Competition and Their Consequences for the Objectives of Competition Law – Comment on Stucke*, *in* The Goals of Competition Law (Daniel Zimmer ed., Edward Elgar Publishing 2012).

pricing above the marginal cost of production. This goal is widely considered to be the primary aim of modern competition law.[31] However, there is no shortage of scholars arguing that economic efficiency should not be considered as the only goal of competition law since it completely overlooks the issue of income distribution among consumer and producers.[32]

2. The Social Goals: Under this category, competition law is seen as a safeguard to social values. It covers the idea of safeguarding the consumer from undue exercise of market power and the dispersion of socioeconomic power of large firms, safe guarding the interest of small and medium-sized firms, protecting democratic values and principles, protecting public interest and ensuring market fairness and equity.[33] In other words, the social goals are motivated by the risks of private power, the principles of justice and economic equity in market democracy.[34] This category is sometimes criticised for it populist nature.[35]
3. The Political Goals: This category relates to wide political aims such as regional market integration, prevention of the concentration of economic power, promotion of national interests, global enhancement of the international competitiveness of domestic firms and industries, national economic developments, financial stability and reducing unemployment.[36] It is undeniable that there is a political aspect inherent in the nature of competition law.

Admittedly, these three categories could conflict with each other.[37] They sometimes are designed to not coincide.[38] It is therefore hard to imagine such diverse expectations being consistent with one another.[39] A lack of consensus in this area may lead to important hurdles in achieving regional harmonisation, a goal that the ASEAN wishes to reach. However, it seems that these concerns are not particularly problematic because it is enough to have commonalities in certain core principles of competition

31. A. E. Rodriguez & Ashok Menon, *The Limits of Competition Policy: The Shortcomings of Antitrust in Developing and Reforming Economies*, 83 (Wolters Kluwer 2010).
32. *See*, for example, Kenneth G. Elzinga, *The Goals of Antitrust: Other Than Competition and Efficiency, What Else Counts?*, 125 U. Pa. L. Rev. (1977); Lawrence A. Sullivan, *Economics and More Humanistic Disciplines: What Are the Sources of Wisdom for Antitrust*, 125 U. Pa. L. Rev. (1977); Joseph F. Brodley, *The Economic Goals of Antitrust: Efficiency, Consumer Welfare, and Technological Progress*, 60 NYUL. Rev. (1987); Eleanor M. Fox & Lawrence A. Sullivan, *Antitrust – Retrospective and Prospective: Where Are We Coming From? Where Are We Going?*, 62 NYUL. Rev. (1987).
33. Giuliano Amato, *Antitrust and the Bounds of Power*, 2 (Hart Publishing 1997); Whish & Bailey, *Competition Law*, 13 (7th ed.,Oxford University Press 2012).
34. Maher M. Dabbah, *International and Comparative Competition Law*, *supra* n. 15, 53.
35. Alison Jones & Brenda Sufrin, *EU Competition Law: Text, Cases, and Materials*, 17 (4th ed.,Oxford University Press 2011).
36. Amato, *Antitrust and the Bounds of Power*, 2–3 (Hart Publishing 1997).
37. Ernst-Ulrich Petersmann, *Legal, Economic and Political Objectives of National and International Competition Policies: Constitutional Functions of WTO, 'Linking Principles' for Trade and Competition*, 34 New Eng. L. Rev. (1999).
38. Mary L. Azcuenaga, *The Evolution of International Competition Policy: a Federal Trade Commission Perspective* (1992).
39. WTO, *Annual Report*, 39 (1997).

law. Accordingly, convergence is to be expected as countries increasingly look to other experiences for lessons and as increasing numbers of countries seek to become partners in the global trading system.[40] It is also argued that convergence in this area cannot be achieved since competition law is dynamic and constantly evolving.[41] Other criticisms are that certain goals adopted by strong countries will prevail over other goals advocated by weaker countries.[42]

There is also an ongoing debate on whether competition law should have single or multiple goals. Leading advocates for a single goal believe that efficiency is the ultimate goal of competition law while competition is only an interim goal that will often be close enough to the ultimate goal to allow the judiciary to look no further.[43] Focusing on one well-defined concept of competition law has the advantage of simplicity in ensuring coherence throughout the system of competition law resulting in legal certainties for the subjects of the law, most notably the firms. However, it has been argued that different competition scenarios require different concepts of what competition is.[44] These different concepts are in turn connected to different objectives of competition law and, hence, the establishment of a single well-defined objective is simply impossible. There was strong opposition to his theory since different competition scenarios do not necessarily require different objectives of competition law. Instead, what is needed is a different approach in order to deal with varying competition problems.[45] If a state or a region acknowledges multiple goals of competition law, these various goals need to be balanced against each other when competition law is applied in order to avoid conflicts between them.[46]

On one hand, competition law needs to serve multiple goals and must be flexible in order to serve different societal needs at different times. On the other hand, competition law needs to be clear, transparent, and predictable in order to ensure legal certainty. 'Managing with multiple goals is obviously complicated'[47] and often conflicting. A legitimate social goal in the competition policy could have the effect of distorting prices away from the prices associated with economic optimality. A state may offer special conditions and incentives that could limit, restrict, or reduce national competition in order to attract foreign investment. Poverty reduction initiatives may favour small, inefficient enterprises at the expense of more efficient ones. It was argued

40. OECD, *Interim Report on Convergence of Competition Policies*, 64 (OECD 1994); Federal Trade Commission, *Anticipating the 21st Century: Competition Policy in the New High-Tech Global Marketplace* (1996); UNCTAD, *Draft Commentaries to Possible Elements for Articles of a Model Law of Laws* (1995). (the latter gives examples of countries; Canada & Norway, who have adopted 'core' goals of competition law).
41. Maher M. Dabbah, *The Internationalisation of Antitrust Policy*, 55 (Cambridge University Press 2003).
42. Guzman, *Is International Antitrust Possible?*, 73 NYUL. Rev. 1501 (1998).
43. Richard A. Posner, *Antitrust Law*, 29 (2nd ed.,University of Chicago Press 2001).
44. Maurice E. Stucke, *Reconsidering Antitrust's Goals*, 53 B.C. L. Rev. (2012).
45. Andreas Fuchs, *Characteristic Aspects of Competition and Their Consequences for the Objectives of Competition Law – Comment on Stucke, in* The Goals of Competition Law (Daniel Zimmer ed., Edward Elgar Publishing 2012).
46. *Ibid.*
47. A. E. Rodriguez & Ashok Menon, *The Limits of Competition Policy: The Shortcomings of Antitrust in Developing and Reforming Economies*, 84 (Kluwer Law International 2010).

that in some instances, the pursuit of non-economic goals may not be damaging provided that economic welfare considerations were taken into account.[48] The neglect of economic considerations may reduce competition or be in direct conflict with the maximisation of economic welfare. The EU competition law, and its political goal of market integration, serves as an example for this scenario. Frequently, the aims overlook economic welfare for the benefit of enabling cross-border trade and stimulating competition in the region.

§3.02 SPECIFIC GOALS IN COMPETITION LAW

[A] European Union

There is little awareness of how European systems of competition law have developed, why they were created and the extent to which the systems have achieved their intended goals.[49] The lack of discussion is due to the possibility of revealing major differences of opinion that might lead to division. European academics have long realised that substantive and institutional problems that have arisen in connection with the EU competition law are due to an implicit divergence of the objectives of EU competition policy.[50]

Despite being called competition law, competition is not an aim in itself.[51] The law is often used to pursue other goals.[52] These include economic welfare and the strengthening of the single market; protection of small business, economic freedom and ensuring fairness; social, political and environmental goals; and industrial or trade policy to herald national industrial champions or to prevent them from coming under foreign ownership. In the EU, competition law has one dominant objective: to further market integration. However, consumer welfare and economic efficiency are also increasing in importance.

[1] The Integration Goal

The promotion of market integration is the dominant objective of the EU competition law.[53] The competition rules laid down in Articles 101[54] and 102 *TFEU*[55] were the necessary compliments to the ultimate (the establishment of a common market)[56] and

---

48. D. G. Goyder, et al., *Goyder's EC Competition Law*, 10 (5th ed., Oxford University Press 2009).
49. David J. Gerber, *Law and Competition in Twentieth-Century Europe: Protecting Prometheus*, 2 (Oxford University Press 2001).
50. Ehlermann & Laudati, *Panel Discussion: Competition Policy Objectives, in* European Competition Law Annual 1997: Objectives of Competition Policy vii, (Ehlermann & Laudati eds., Hart Publishing 1998).
51. D. G. Goyder, et al., *Goyder's EC Competition Law*, 10 (5th ed., Oxford University Press 2009).
52. A detailed summary of all the goals could be find in Massimo Motta, *Competition Policy: Theory and Practice*, 17 (Cambridge University Press 2004).
53. Treaty Establishing the European Community OJ C 325 Art. 2 (2002).
54. Treaty on the Functioning of the European Union Art. 101 (2008).
55. *Ibid.*, at Art. 102.
56. Treaty Establishing the European Community, Art. 2 (2002).

intermediate goals[57] of the Community since agreement or abusive conduct and state measures can create an obstacle to trade between Member States.

Most commentators[58] have accepted that market integration has traditionally been the unifying aim of the EU competition policy:

> A genuine single market cannot be brought about except through free competition. If the market were to remain subject to the arbitrary decisions of the cartels or to the restrictive practices of monopolies, then the benefits of the single market would soon be offset by the effects of price-fixing and production quotas.[59]

This is understandable since competition law serves as part of an overall policy to promote the regional as well as national economy.[60] The aim in this case is to break down barriers to cross-border trade within the EU. This feature was said to be unique to the EU competition law.[61] The existence of the market integration goal explains the Commission's hostility to agreements or business practices that prevent or hinder cross-border trade.[62] It is seen most clearly in cases where companies allocate different national territories, either among themselves (in a horizontal-market sharing cartel), or to different distributors (in vertical distribution arrangements.)[63]

There may be a conflict between the objective of market integration and economic welfare. Using the example of forbidding price discrimination across national borders, there is generally no economic rationale for forbidding such practice.[64] However, even though this is considered to be the primary goal of European competition law, it does not stand alone and economic considerations need to be taken into account.[65] Ignoring economic efficiency in favour of market integration could lead to contrary outcomes; instead of promoting integration, the Commission could be retarding it.[66] In *GlaxoSmithKline*, if the Commission were to win its case to restrict parallel importing, the company would cease trading in Spain and Greece. This would be detrimental to consumers in these countries. A similar case took place in 1998[67] and

57. *Ibid.*, at Art. 3.
58. D. G. Goyder, et al., *Goyder's EC Competition Law*, 11 (5th ed., Oxford University Press 2009).
59. High Authority, *Memorandum on the Anti-Trust Policy of the High Authority* (European Coal and Steel Community 1964).
60. Laura Perret, *The Multiple Personalities of EU Competition Law: Time for a Comprehensive Debate on Its Objectives, in* The Goals of Competition Law (Daniel Zimmer ed., Edward Elgar Publishing 2012).
61. D. G. Goyder, et al., *Goyder's EC Competition Law*, 11 (5th ed., Oxford University Press 2009).
62. Simon Bishop & Mike Walker, *The Economics of EC Competition Law: Concepts, Application and Measurement*, 5 (3rd ed.,Sweet & Maxwell 2010).
63. *Établissements Consten S.à.R.L. and Grundig-Verkaufs-GmbH v. Commission*, Cases 56/64, 58/64 (ECR 299 1966) (serves as an early example).
64. Massimo Motta, *Competition Policy: Theory and Practice*, 23 (Cambridge University Press 2004).
65. Simon Bishop & Mike Walker, *The Economics of EC Competition Law: Concepts, Application and Measurement*, 7 (3rd ed., Sweet & Maxwell 2010).
66. Opinion of Advocate Jacobs in *Synetairismos Farmakopoion Aitolias & Akarnanias and Others v. GlaxoSmithKline plc and GlaxoSmithKline AEVES* Case 53/03 (ECR I-4609 2005); *GlaxoSmith-Kline Services Unlimited v. Commission*, Cases 501/06 P, 513/06 P, 515/06 P, 519/06 P, I-09291 (4 CMLR 2 2009).
67. *Silhouette International Schmied GmbH & Co. KG v. Hartlauer Handelsgesellschaft mbH* (ECR I-4799 1998).

1983.[68] The result of the *United Distillers'* case was an increase in the price of some brands in the UK and the subsequent withdrawal from trade of Johnny Walker Red Label in the UK with an obvious reduction in consumer welfare. This marked an apparent difference between the brand promoted in the UK and in continental Europe.[69] It should be noted that this conflict only arose at Community level.

The integration goal seems to have declined in importance in EU competition law, coinciding with the rising in prominence of the consumer welfare goal. Nonetheless, it was argued that the objective of market integration still remained relevant in EU competition law.[70]

[2] Consumer Welfare

The goal of consumer welfare is not a recent concept and was present during the formative years of the competition rules in the EU.[71] While it is true that the first decisions of the Commission and the CJEU refer to the generic benefits of competition, such as lower prices and technological advances,[72] there is a strong belief that the market integration ideal assumes the interest of consumers.[73] The interest in consumer welfare also appears in the Commission's *Report on Competition Policy*.[74] Furthermore, Article 101 *TFEU* explicitly mentions consumer welfare.[75]

There is a need to reconcile the objective of market integration with the objective of consumer welfare.[76] A consumer-focused approach that protects weaker consumers or certain groups could potentially conflict with an approach that focuses more on the economic aspects of competition law. The latter approach would lead to more aggressive competition law enforcement.

---

68. *Distillers Company Plc. (Red Label)* (CMLR 173, OJ C245/3 1983).
69. Simon Bishop & Mike Walker, *The Economics of EC Competition Law: Concepts, Application and Measurement*, 8 (3rd ed., Sweet & Maxwell 2010).
70. Laura Perret, *The Multiple Personalities of EU Competition Law: Time for a Comprehensive Debate on Its Objectives, in* The Goals of Competition Law (Daniel Zimmer ed., Edward Elgar Publishing 2012) (citing *GlaxoSmithKline Services Unlimited v. Commission; Synetairismos Farmakopoion Aitolias & Akarnanias and Others v. GlaxoSmithKline plc and GlaxoSmithKline AEVES; Sot Lélos kia Sia EE and Others v. GlaxoSmithKline AEVE Farmakeftikon Proïonton*, Cases 468/06 to 478/06 (ECR I-07139 2008).
71. Laura Perret, *The Multiple Personalities of EU Competition Law: Time for a Comprehensive Debate on Its Objectives, in* The Goals of Competition Law (Daniel Zimmer ed., Edward Elgar Publishing 2012).
72. *Établissements Consten S.à.R.L. and Grundig-Verkaufs-GmbH v. Commission.*
73. Laura Perret, *The Multiple Personalities of EU Competition Law: Time for a Comprehensive Debate on Its Objectives, in* The Goals of Competition Law (Daniel Zimmer ed., Edward Elgar Publishing 2012).
74. D. G. Goyder, Competition European Commission, *Report on Competition Policy*, 9 (1976). '[The] aim is to ensure that business operates along competitive lines, while protecting the consumer by making goods and services available on the most favourable terms possible.'
75. Treaty on the Functioning of the European Union, Art. 101 (2008).
76. Laura Perret, *The Multiple Personalities of EU Competition Law: Time for a Comprehensive Debate on Its Objectives, in* The Goals of Competition Law (Daniel Zimmer ed., Edward Elgar Publishing 2012).

[3] *Economic Efficiency*

Many scholars still steadfastly hold that economic efficiency is the primary goal of competition law.[77] Others consider economic efficiency to be a fairly new objective that was not part of older decisions.[78] The notion of economic efficiency is increasingly present in merger control and in the discussion surrounding the enforcement of Article 102 *TFEU*[79] but with a different meaning, namely, the arguments that a dominant undertaking presents to the authority to justify its behaviour.[80]

The efficiency and integration goals of the EU competition law are potentially conflicting.[81] For example, some manufacturers may seek to confine the activities of retailers to certain territories. This behaviour could be considered economically efficient, yet it might be an infringement of the European market's integration goal. In EU law, economic welfare and consumer welfare are often closely associated[82] making it difficult to distinguish between the two goals. Moreover, American commentators often criticised the EU competition policy for protecting the competitors rather than protecting the process of competition. The latter would happen with an economic approach. This comment is less true today.[83]

[B] Developing Jurisdictions

It is generally acknowledged that 'the enactment of competition legislation has become a global phenomenon'.[84] In a short period of time, the ICN saw its membership soar from 14 jurisdictions at its launch in October 2001 to 123 competition agencies from over 108 jurisdictions in 2012.[85] The enactment of competition law in an emerging economy was once likened to 'giving a silk tie to a starving man'[86] by Godek. Now, competition law is no longer a luxury but has become necessary if a country wants to join an exclusive club of countries who have competition law. Enacting competition legislation has been compared to having a proper dress to enter members of an elite

77. D. G. Goyder, et al., *Goyder's EC Competition Law*, 11 (5th ed., Oxford University Press 2009).
78. Laura Perret, *The Multiple Personalities of EU Competition Law: Time for a Comprehensive Debate on Its Objectives, in* The Goals of Competition Law (Daniel Zimmer ed., Edward Elgar Publishing 2012).
79. Treaty on the Functioning of the European Union, Art. 102 (2008).
80. Laura Perret, *The Multiple Personalities of EU Competition Law: Time for a Comprehensive Debate on Its Objectives, in* The Goals of Competition Law (Daniel Zimmer ed., Edward Elgar Publishing 2012).
81. Simon Bishop & Mike Walker, *The Economics of EC Competition Law: Concepts, Application and Measurement*, 7 (3rd ed.,Sweet & Maxwell 2010).
82. Neelie Kroes, *European Competition Policy – Delivering Better Markets and Better Choices, European Consumer and Competition Day* (2005).
83. John Vickers, *Competition Law and Economics: A Mid-Atlantic Viewpoint*, ECJ 1 (2007).
84. Haley, *Competition Law for the Asia-Pacific Economic Cooperation Community: Designing Shoes for Many Sizes*, 1 Wash. U. Global Stud. L. Rev. (2002).
85. ICN, *ICN Statement of Achievements 2001–2012* (the 11th Annual Conference of the ICN 2012).
86. Paul E. Godek, *One U.S. Export Eastern Europe Does Not Need*, 15 Regulation (1992) (advocating for potential harms from misguided competition policy in emerging economies).

club.[87] Continuing the metaphor, countries tend to too quickly put on these dresses without careful consideration beforehand regarding whether the dresses are suitable for their style, size or stature. The states' eagerness to conform to what they perceive as the global standard has contributed to the proliferation of national competition laws and policies. This is reflected in competition law literature where few question the necessity of competition law. The question is often ignored, taken for granted or simply left unasked.[88] There is much debate on whether countries with smaller markets and in an early stage of development should pursue different goals from countries with larger economies.[89] However, there is no single correct or best goal of competition law that could be applied to any jurisdiction regardless of the local economic and socio-political climates.

In contrast to the smooth development of competition laws in western countries, the emergence of competition laws in developing economies have been more abrupt.[90] They are not a result of internal development but often a top-down legislative approach whereby the competition legislations are taken from western countries' models. The danger resides in introducing a predefined set of goals which came with the imported legislations. Another explanation for the abrupt emergence of competition laws in developing economies is the interventions from international institutions such as the UNCTAD, the OECD, the World Bank and in particular, the Bretton Woods Institutions: the IMF and the WTO[91] who forced developing economies to adopt liberalisation, privatisation, and competition laws. While fighting anticompetitive practices seems desirable for developing economies, the transposition of these competition laws need to be carefully considered. The predefined goals of the above-mentioned organisations for developing economies are to open their markets and force their integration into the global market economy.[92] It means that developing economies' markets are made available to global competition, in particular, international undertakings. Enacting competition law as an accompaniment to liberalisation was considered as merely a façade for the actual objective of protecting competition that gives international undertakings enhanced access to developing economies' markets.[93] This suspicion of western countries' motives for encouraging competition laws in developing economies

87. Haley, *Competition Law for the Asia-Pacific Economic Cooperation Community: Designing Shoes for Many Sizes*, 1 Wash. U. Global Stud. L. Rev. (2002).
88. *Ibid.*
89. *See*, for example, Michal S. Gal, *Competition Policy for Small Market Economies* (Harvard University Press 2003); Round & Zuo, *The Welfare Goal of Antitrust Laws in Asia: For Whom Should the Law Toil?*, 22 Asian-Pacific Economic Literature 2 (2008).
90. Mor Bakhoum, *Reflections on the Concepts of 'Economic Freedom', 'Free Competition' and 'Efficiency' from the Perspective of Developing Countries*, *in* The Goals of Competition Law (Daniel Zimmer ed., Edward Elgar Publishing 2012).
91. Francisco Marcos, *Do Developing Countries Need Competition Laws and Policy?* (EALE Conference, Madrid 2006).
92. Mor Bakhoum, *Reflections on the Concepts of 'Economic Freedom', 'Free Competition' and 'Efficiency' from the Perspective of Developing Countries*, *in* The Goals of Competition Law (Daniel Zimmer ed., Edward Elgar Publishing 2012).
93. *Ibid.*

was shared by Fox[94] who believed that western countries hide behind liberalisation and efficiency to advocate for their version of a universal norm for competition law.

Finally, competition law was seen as an essential part of the efforts by developing economies and countries with economies in transition to restructure their domestic economies and integrate them fully into the global economy.[95] This was to exploit new opportunities to compete and, in particular, to facilitate the move from monopolisation to demonopolisation, and from state control and planning to liberalisation and privatisation.[96] In this regard, the introduction of competition law into national legal systems is a matter of internal choice and a part of the aim to become competitive in a globalised economy.

On the surface, it appears that the goals of competition law in developed and developing economies converge and, as the ICN reported, so do the goals of unilateral conduct laws. These tend to coincide with the goals of ensuring an effective competitive process, economic freedom, economic efficiency, and consumer welfare.[97] However, the convergence is in appearance only and does not translate into enforcement. The same concept does not always carry the same significance in a different jurisdiction. In fact, most of the respondents to the ICN report either do not define the terms or have a different understanding of the terms.[98]

It would appear that developing economies are not content with blindly importing the western models and make an effort to adapt the laws to their specific national needs. Contrary to developed economies, reforming and developing economies tend to have broader goals of competition law in order to assist them with creating a stable economic environment. Their concern seems wider than that of developed economies and they cannot focus solely on economic efficiency to bring about free and fair competition. They tend to make poverty eradication and wealth redistribution their top priorities.[99] Some of the goals stated in developing economies' competition laws are: to expand opportunities for domestic enterprises to participate in world markets;[100] to promote employment; to advance social and economic welfare; to provide the small and medium enterprises (SMEs) with an equitable opportunity to participate in the economy; to increase the economic opportunities of historically disadvantage persons;[101] and to protect access to basic needs.[102] It is to be noted that unlike the US and

94. Eleanor M. Fox, *Economic Development, Poverty and Antitrust: The Other Path*, 13 Sw. J. L. & Trade Am. (2007).
95. *Ibid.* (The desire to integrate more in the world economy is universally shared by many developing countries.)
96. Maher M. Dabbah, *International and Comparative Competition Law*, 36 (Cambridge University Press 2010).
97. ICN, *Unilateral Conduct Working Group* (the 11th Annual ICN Conference, Brazil 2012).
98. ICN, *Report on the Objectives of Unilateral Conduct Laws, Assessment of Dominance/Substantial Market Power, and State-Created Monopolies*, *supra* n. 20.
99. Cassey Lee & Yoshifumi Fukunaga, *Competition Policy Challenges of Single Market and Production Base* (ERIA 2013).
100. ECOWAS, Supplementary Act A/SA.1/06/08 Adopting Community Competition Rules and the Modalities of Their Application within ECOWAS Art. 3 (2008).
101. Republic of South Africa Competition Act, Act No. 89 of 1998 as amended Ch. 1(2) (1998).
102. Taimoon Stewart, et al., *Competition Law in Action: Experiences from Developing Countries*, V (IDRC 2007) (mentioning Mexico and Costa Rica).

the EU, developing economies do not share the ongoing dilemma about whether single or multiple goals are most suitable for them. They seem to have readily adopted the idea of multiple goals.

Some authors maintain that the reasoning behind the multiplicity of social and political goals was the politicians' desire to create jobs and attract foreign investment.[103] Both serve to minimise the social unrest associated with the hardships that typically follow economic reforms. In other words, the policymakers are buying social peace. Even when social peace is not a pressing concern, policymakers are aware that it is crucial to increase both domestic and foreign investment to fully benefit from market reforms and to ensure their re-election.[104]

These multitudes of goals 'constitute not only an administrative nightmare but a source of immense confusion'.[105] Moreover, industrial and trade policies to protect local industries through high import duties also come into conflict with the economic goal of competition policy.[106] In this regard, it is unavoidable that competition policy takes a back seat to industrial and trade policies. It seems accepted that multiple goals contradict the primary competition policy goal that of economic efficiency. The order of importance is said to be resolved politically. Thus, the various goals are implemented in order to ensure that there will always be a legitimate political vehicle available to give expression to latent societal goals.[107] In return, the lack of clarity and a penchant for political resolution contribute to fears in the private sector and cools its activities, thus deliberately creating a false positive. Unlike the developed economies' models, there has been no attempt to balance the goal of economic efficiency with social and political goals. The former is always circumvented for the benefit of the latter since developing economies put more emphasis on issues not pertaining to economic efficiency or the competition process.

§3.03 THE ASEAN'S GOALS OF COMPETITION LAW

The ASEAN did not shy away from the global trend of adhering to the elite club's dress code but dived straight into the question of how best to establish a competition law regime without sufficient prior consideration of the necessity for/or the suitability of a competition law. The reasons behind instituting competition law might not seem important at this stage, especially as the ASEAN has explicitly announced its intention to introduce competition law and policy in all the AMSs before the creation of the region's economic community[108] and as most AMSs have already enacted national

103. A. E. Rodriguez & Ashok Menon, *The Limits of Competition Policy: The Shortcomings of Antitrust in Developing and Reforming Economies*, 100 (Kluwer Law International 2010).
104. *Ibid.*
105. *Ibid.*, at 98.
106. Cassey Lee & Yoshifumi Fukunaga, *Competition Policy Challenges of Single Market and Production Base* (ERIA 2013).
107. A. E. Rodriguez & Ashok Menon, *The Limits of Competition Policy: The Shortcomings of Antitrust in Developing and Reforming Economies*, 98 (Kluwer Law International 2010).
108. ASEAN Secretariat, *ASEAN Economic Community Blueprint*, para. 41 (2007).

competition laws. Indonesia[109] and Thailand[110] were the first AMSs to introduce competition law statutes in 1999 followed by Vietnam[111] and Singapore[112] in 2004. Following the ASEAN's announcement of regional economic integration with competition policy as its pillar, Malaysia,[113] Myanmar,[114] Brunei Darussalam,[115] and the Philippines[116] all passed their competition law bills. Lao PDR was the sole AMSs implementing the country's first comprehensive competition law[117] after the establishment of the AEC. However, the same argument can be made to support examining this important question. The AMSs' established competition law is not without flaws. Defining the rationale behind the existence of each nation's competition law could help reformulate and direct them towards compatibility with the ASEAN regional policy. Furthermore, it could help tailor the remaining AMS competition law that of Cambodia in a way that would keep them aligned with existing members' competition law regimes as well as the ASEAN approach.

The question about the reasons for competition law has never been easy to answer, particularly in the context of the ASEAN where its ten members could not give identical answers. While adapting the law to local conditions is encouraged, too much divergence has the potential to harm the ASEAN's aim for harmonisation at regional level. Conscious of the discordance among the AMSs, the ASEAN organised two conferences, inviting competition authorities and government officials from member countries, to discuss competition law and policy, in particular the necessity of competition law and policy at both regional and national level.[118] The ASEAN Conference on Fair Trade Competition Law and Policy in the AFTA took place in 2003 and the 2nd ASEAN Conference on Competition Policy and Law was held in 2006. However, few officials actually engaged in the discussion of the necessity of the ASEAN regional competition law and instead took the opportunity to introduce their own competition law and policy to other AMSs.[119] Regardless of the actual outcome, in reuniting different opinions on various principles regarding competition law, the conferences were still considered a 'bold first step towards an ASEAN [competition policy]'.[120] Conferences such as these would undeniably promote awareness and sound a 'wake-up call'[121] to all AMSs.

109. Law of the Republic of Indonesia Number 5 Year 1999 Concerning Prohibition of Monopolistic Practices and Unfair Business Competition (1999).
110. Thailand Trade Competition Act (1999).
111. Vietnam Law on Competition, No.27/2004/QH11 (2004).
112. Singapore Competition Act (Ch. 50B) revised on 30 Jan. 2006 (2004).
113. Malaysia Competition Act, Act 712 (2010).
114. The Pyidaungsu Hluttaw Law No. 9 (2015).
115. *Ibid.*
116. Philippines Competition Act, Republic Act No. 10667 (2015).
117. Law on Business Competition (No. 60/NA) (2015) published in the Lao PDR Official Gazette in January 2016.
118. The ASEAN Conference on Fair Competition Law and Policy (5–7 Mar. 2003) and the 2nd ASEAN Conference on Fair Competition Law and Policy: Accelerate Growth and Competitiveness through Competition Policy and Law (14–16 Jun. 2006).
119. Udin Silalahi, The Necessity of ASEAN Competition Law: An Idea (2007).
120. Thant, *Competition Policy and Economic Growth in ASEAN Countries: A Myanmar's Perspective* (The ASEAN Conference on Fair Competition Law and Policy 2003).
121. *Ibid.*

The first conference concluded that there was no binding conclusion to the reasons for competition law. Despite the lack of consensus on what could be considered necessary, there was general acknowledgement that competition law was necessary despite a few different attitudes among AMSs.[122] The economic goal of protection and promotion of the market economy[123] were heavily favoured while some officials were concerned about social goals: consumer welfare,[124] promotion of innovation,[125] and protection of SMEs.[126] Only one representative took his country's economic structure into account through the inclusion of the protection of SMEs and the promotion of innovation. The protection of SMEs is significant in the context of Southeast Asia since SMEs are the dominant basis for growth in this region. Although the globalisation of competition policy is undeniable, competition policy must also resonate at a local level to justify its existence to local taxpayers.[127] The best way to achieve this is to take into consideration the local economic and socio-political climate. Competition policy must combine globalism and localism to combat international cartels which are facilitated by globalisation itself. An example of taking the local context into consideration is responding to citizens' concerns about preserving and securing the benefits of smaller and local firms.[128] A European survey has shown that about 80% of the EU citizens thought that small firms needed to be protected from large firms' competition.[129] While this survey was conducted on the EU citizens, in our globalised world, the EU policies can have an impact on other countries and especially other regional organisation's competition policies.

In spite of the general acknowledgement, not every AMS shared the same optimism regarding the necessity of competition law. The Singaporean representative argued that competition policy was only necessary if economic efficiency could not be achieved through deregulation policies of trade.[130] This implies that competition policy is only a substitute for trade deregulation policy since 'trade policy eliminates governmental barriers to international trade and deregulatory reform eliminates domestic regulation that restricts entry and exit'.[131] In contrast, 'competition policy targets business conduct that limits market access and reduces actual and potential

---

122. Noboyuki Yasuda, *The Evolution of Competition Law in Southeast Asian Countries* (2003).
123. Le Danh Vinh, *Building Competition Law in Vietnam to meet the Need of Regulating Market Economy and in the Light of Trade Liberalisation and International Economic Integration* (2003); Udin Silalahi, The Necessity of ASEAN Competition Law: An Idea (2007); Siripol Yodmuangchareon, *The Urgency of Competition Law* (2003).
124. Thant, *Competition Policy and Economic Growth in ASEAN Countries: a Myanmar's Perspective* (The ASEAN Conference on Fair Competition Law and Policy 2003); Yodmuangchareon, *The Urgency of Competition Law* (2003).
125. Thant, *Competition Policy and Economic Growth in ASEAN Countries: a Myanmar's Perspective* (The ASEAN Conference on Fair Competition Law and Policy 2003).
126. *Ibid.*
127. Maurice E. Stucke, *Antitrust 2025*, CPI Antitrust Journal (2010).
128. *Ibid.*
129. D. G. GoyderCompetition European Commission, *Flash Eurobarometer EU citizens' Perceptions About Competition Policy (No 254)* (2010) (at 7.51% 'totally agreed' and 30% 'somewhat agreed' that small companies needed to be protected from large companies).
130. Chadwick Teo, Competition Policy and Economic Growth (2003).
131. *Ibid.*

competition'.[132] Even if it was decided that competition policy was to be implemented, the Singaporean representative advocated that governmental intervention should only occur in a cost-effective way in order to improve economic outcomes. Nevertheless, Singapore's adoption of its Competition Act in 2004[133] suggests that economic efficiency could not be achieved through trade deregulation policies alone.

It was not until the second conference that the AMSs expressed the needs for a regional competition law within the ASEAN.[134] Since only a few representatives engaged in this debate, it would seem that the AMSs are less enthusiastic about regional competition law compared to national ones. At regional level, competition law could provide an effective protection against unfair competition and strengthen economic integration in the ASEAN.[135] With the impending regional economic integration, competition law became necessary in order to ensure that former statutory obstacles to contestability are not replaced by anticompetitive practices of firms, thus ensuring true trade liberalisation in the process. With an effective regional competition regime in place, the region would project an image of economic and legal certainty to economic participants thus attracting interest in the ASEAN and more FDI. In this regard, regional competition law can reinforce the ASEAN investment regime.[136] Consequently, the ASEAN competition law could play a multifunctional role in regional economies: encourage the free flow of trade and investment, monitor the behaviour of firms, and evaluate the economic role or potential dominance of extra-ASEAN transnational corporations in the region.[137] Moreover, in the case of the ASEAN where most AMSs have adopted competition law statutes, having effective and enforceable unified competition legislation could help fill the void left by national competition laws.[138] The establishment of a competition regime at a regional level may also reduce the costs of applying national competition policies. This would be particularly beneficial for micro-states without national competition laws. These states could follow the example of the EU which only has jurisdiction over cases with significant effect at regional level or trade between Member States, leaving the rest under the jurisdiction of their respective nations.[139]

It was suggested that the AMSs have sufficient knowledge and experience to establish both the ASEAN competition law and a central competition authority.[140] Since the AMSs have already acknowledged the necessity of regional competition law,

132. *Ibid.*
133. Singapore Competition Act (Ch. 50B) revised on 30 Jan. 2006 (2004).
134. Udin Silalahi, The Necessity of ASEAN Competition Law: An Idea (2007).
135. Lawan Thanadsillapakul, *The Harmonization of ASEAN: Competition Laws and Policy from an Economic Integration Perspective, in* Competition Policy and Regional Integration in Developing Countries (Drexl, et al. eds., Edward Elgar 2012); UNCTAD, *Competition Policy and Legislation: Information Note 21* (TD/B/RBP/INF.37 1996).
136. Lawan Thanadsillapakul, *The Harmonization of ASEAN: Competition Laws and Policy from an Economic Integration Perspective, in* Competition Policy and Regional Integration in Developing Countries (Drexl, et al. eds., Edward Elgar 2012).
137. *Ibid.*
138. Lawan Thanadsillapakul, A New Direction for ASEAN Regionalisation in the Changing Global Legal and Economic Environment (2000) (PhD Thesis, Lancaster University).
139. Michal S. Gal, *Competition Policy for Small Market Economies* (Harvard University Press 2003).
140. Udin Silalahi, The Necessity of ASEAN Competition Law: An Idea (2007).

all that remains is the political will to follow through on the project.[141] An AMS should take the initiative together with the ASEAN Secretariat to draft the ASEAN regional competition law. Indonesia volunteered for this role due to its successful experience in the field.[142]

What was missing from the discussion table was whether regional competition law was suitable for the market structure of the ASEAN. The market size and structure, whether regional or national, were never discussed by the officials or the academics.

The *Blueprint*[143] was adopted in 2007 to serve as a master plan to facilitate and ensure the coherence of the AEC. According to the *Blueprint*, each AMS was committed to implementing the competition policy by 2015. The *Blueprint* states that its main competition policy objective is to 'foster a culture of fair competition'.[144] The emphasis on advocacy is reflected in its first action plan regarding competition policy which is to introduce competition policy in all the AMSs by the implementation of the AEC in 2015 with the aid of capacity building programmes and regional guidelines. Unfortunately, the role of competition law in the regional economic integration has not been emphasised in the *Blueprint*.

In 2008, the *Best Practices in the Introduction and Implementation of Competition Policy and Law in East Asia Summit Countries (Best Practices)*,[145] commissioned by the ASEAN Secretariat with financial aid from the Australian government, was published in order to 'undertake a study of best practices in the introduction and implementation of competition policy and law in East Asia Summit Countries'.[146] The East Asia Summit is a regional leaders' forum that was held for the first time in 2005 as 'a forum for dialogue on broad strategic, political and economic issues of common interest and concern with the aim of promoting peace, stability and economic prosperity in East Asia'.[147] The East Asia Summit countries now comprise the ten AMSs, Australia, the People's Republic of China, the Republic of India, Japan, the Republic of Korea, New Zealand, the US and Russia. Despite the title: *Best Practices in the Introduction and Implementation of Competition Policy and Law in East Asia Summit Countries*, this document was only intended to aid the AMSs in developing their own domestic competition laws. The document is part of the Regional Economic Policy Support Facility (REPSF) intended to help the ASEAN Secretariat, its working groups, and offices promote the ASEAN economic integration through economic policy research.[148]

---

141. Lawan Thanadsillapakul, A New Direction for ASEAN Regionalisation in the Changing Global Legal and Economic Environment (2000).
142. Udin Silalahi, The Necessity of ASEAN Competition Law: An Idea (2007).
143. ASEAN Secretariat, *ASEAN Economic Community Blueprint* (2007).
144. *Ibid.*, at 41.
145. Best Practices in the Introduction and Implementation of Competition Policy and Law in East Asia Summit Countries (2008) (Best Practices).
146. *Ibid.*, at 1.
147. *Kuala Lumpur Declaration on the East Asia Summit*, http://www.asean.org/news/item/kuala-lumpur-declaration-on-the-east-asia-summit-kuala-lumpur-14-december-2005 (accessed 12 Dec. 2017).
148. *Regional Economic Policy Support Facility (REPSF) Phase I & II*, http://www.grminternational.com/projects/regional_economic_policy_support_facility_repsf_phases_i_ii (accessed 12 Dec. 2017).

The Best Practices suggest that the common objective of national competition law and policy in the AMSs, citing the World Bank and the OECD,[149] should be 'the maintenance of the competitive process, free competition, or effective competition'.[150] The language used in this document implies that the three objectives could not coexist. Furthermore, the *Best Practices* distinguish between 'the first order objectives'[151] of competition law and policy and the 'second order objectives'.[152] According to the *Best Practices*, the first order objectives are economic efficiency, growth and development, and consumer welfare. These objectives could be achieved through the promotion of competition. However, in certain exceptional cases the promotion of competition may be detrimental to national welfare or other first order objectives such as natural monopoly. The *Best Practices* recognise as second order objectives the promotion and protection of SMEs, the facilitation of FDI, the promotion of technological advancement, the promotion of product and process innovation, the promotion of industrial diversification, job creation, gender equity or the promotion of welfare of particular consumer groups. These second order objectives cover both economic and social objectives and reflect the concerns raised by state officials during the ASEAN Conferences on Competition Policy and Law.

The *Best Practices* encourage the AMSs to freely decide on its national competition policy goals. While it is possible to have multiple, diverse goals, the *Best Practices* strongly advise against this stating that this would generate unnecessary complexities in establishing and implementing national competition policy. In addition, conflicting multiple goals could damage the first order objectives. Therefore, in order to preserve the effectiveness of competition policy goals, the *Best Practices* recommends that the AMSs pursue the second order objectives, particularly social goals, by means of alternative policy instruments without restricting competition or sacrificing the first order objectives. The *Best Practices* recommend prioritising the promotion of economic efficiency as the exclusive goal of competition law and policy, assuring the AMSs that other economic and social goals could be reached even with economic efficiency as the exclusive competition policy goal. Alternatively, it proposes adopting the New Zealand model which allows the government to require the competition authority to give priority to other competition policy over economic efficiency.[153] While this provision brings about certain flexibility in the enforcement of competition policy, it may also disrupt the homogeneity of competition policy. Homogeneity is important in this instance since the ASEAN aims to have a harmonised competition law within the region. It is possible that, even with a single competition goal focusing on economic efficiency, the promotion of competition may conflict with economic efficiency. This conflict is generally resolved by applying the net benefit test where the restriction of

149. World Bank & OECD, *A Framework for the Design and Implementation of Competition Law and Policy*, Ch. 1 (1999).
150. Orr, et al., Best Practices in the Introduction and Implementation of Competition Policy and Law in East Asia Summit Countries. 2008.
151. *Ibid.*, at 2.
152. *Ibid.*
153. New Zealand Commerce Act of 1986, Art. 26 (1986).

competition may be permitted if it confers net efficiency benefits to society and if the restriction of competition is necessary to realise such benefits.[154]

In 2010, the *Guidelines I* were developed, based on the AMSs' experiences and international best practices, to represent a common reference guide for the AMSs. They contain the goals of competition, substantive provisions of competition law, a brief mention of institutional building, competition advocacy, as well as national competition authority's enforcement powers. They reaffirm the common objectives of competition policy as 'the promotion and protection of competitive process'[155] through the introduction of a level playing field to all market players. The *Guidelines I* consider that the pursuit of such objectives will lead to fair or effective competition. The language used in this case follows the example set by the *Best Practices* which do not believe in the coexistence of fair and effective competition. However, fair or effective competition can benefit countries in terms of economic efficiency, economic growth and development, and consumer welfare.

In addition, the *Guidelines I* persuade the AMSs that competition policy is beneficial to developing economies due to the process of globalisation. '[D]eveloping countries need a competition policy, in order to monitor and control the growing role of the private sector in the economy so as to ensure that public monopolies are not simply replaced by private monopolies'.[156] It should be noted that the *Guidelines I* have excluded social goals from the objectives of competition law and include them instead in 'other policy objectives'.[157] Moreover, the integration goal is absent from the document. Despite its purpose of guiding the AMSs towards a common goal, the *Guidelines I* conclude that each AMS may individually decide which objectives to pursue.[158] This final part confirms the ASEAN's lack of persuasive power over the AMSs. The document urges the AMSs to take into account their own national needs when determining the goal or goals of competition law. In retrospect, it is highly possible that the *Guidelines I* have contributed to further diversification of national competition policies to the extent that the AMSs may end up with varying objectives, making any attempt at regional harmonisation more challenging. The *Guidelines II* were published in 2012 but did not feature any discussion on the goals of competition policy instead they focus on the institutional design of competition authority as well as an in-depth discussion of competition advocacy. It is evident that the *Guidelines II*'s purpose is merely to complement the *Guidelines I.*

§3.04 RESOLVING CHALLENGES TO ACHIEVE THE GOALS OF COMPETITION LAW

The introductory chapter has identified the vast differences, notably in economic development and structure, politics and degrees of development, between the AMSs

154. Maurice E. Stucke, *Reconsidering Antitrust's Goals*, 53 B.C. L. Rev. (2012).
155. ASEAN Secretariat, *ASEAN Regional Guidelines on Competition Policy*, Art. 2.2.1 (2010).
156. *Ibid.*, at Art. 2.2.2.
157. *Ibid.*, at Art. 2.2.3.
158. *Ibid.*, at Art. 2.2.5.

and the ASEAN Way as the main challenges faced by the ASEAN in its pursuit of regional economic integration with competition law and policy as one of the principal mechanisms. This section aims to examine the recognition of these challenges by the ASEAN as well as its proposals to overcome them. Throughout the document, The *Guidelines I* recognise a number of challenges such as the different stages of competition policy development among the AMSs,[159] and the problematic access to necessary resources, notably financial and human resources.[160] The *Guidelines II* recognise the challenges faced by the ASEAN in a dedicated section:

- Perceived conflicts with other policy objectives (e.g., employment, promotion of 'national champions') and resistance from 'vested interests'.
- Lack of good governance, in particular due to the strong links between the worlds of politics and business. Such actual or perceived contact gives the public and the business community little faith that the law will be applied free of corruption and in accordance with the rule of law.
- Tension with sector-specific regulators.
- Resources and capacity constraints and limited indigenous expertise in CPL. The (competition authority's) staff and the judiciary have very limited training in competition law and economics (in particular, few staff and fewer judges have any competition-specific university training). Also the (competition authority's) staff and the judiciary have a rigid, literal approach to interpreting and applying the law, divorced from the law's goals. Investigators, managers, commissioners with no legal training or inexperienced lawyers lack a sense of the dynamic nature of the law. Judges avoid the substantive issues and stick to the procedural issues only.
- Lack of political will and independence.
- An underdeveloped judicial system.[161]

While the ASEAN Way is never explicitly mentioned in any documents formulated by the ASEAN, its presence is unavoidable especially in light of the reluctance to properly guide or dictate the path to the AMSs. Indeed both the *Guidelines I* and the *Guidelines II* have repeatedly reminded the AMSs of their non-binding character. [162] In contrast, the concern over the SMEs which have previously been identified as an important part of the AMSs' economy is curiously missing from these texts.

This section will focus on the three primary challenges: the difficulties in designing a competition law and policy framework for the AMSs with deeply rooted varying characteristics; resource restrictions; and foreign influences.

159. *Ibid.*, at Art. 1.3.1.
160. *Ibid.*, at Art. 4.2.2.
161. ASEAN Secretariat, *Guidelines on Developing Core Competencies in Competition Policy and Law for ASEAN*, 43 (2012).
162. ASEAN Secretariat, *ASEAN Regional Guidelines on Competition Policy*, Preface (2010); ASEAN Secretariat, *Guidelines on Developing Core Competencies in Competition Policy and Law for ASEAN*, Introduction (2012).

[A] Accommodating the Differences Within the ASEAN

In Chapter 3, details were given about the considerable diversity among AMSs in terms of their respective economic and political heritage, governance systems, legal institutions, stages of economic development, and exposure to or reliance on foreign trade and investments. As it has been recognised that political and economic regimes have a crucial impact on the implementation of competition law, it is understandable that both *Guidelines* have taken them into account. The *Guidelines II*, in particular, have exhibited a remarkable understanding of the economic, social and political situation within the region. For instance, they acknowledge the existence of an informal economy and an oligarchy and emphasise that the AMSs should take these factors into consideration when drafting a realistic national competition law.[163] They also refer to the small economies of many AMSs. The *Guidelines II* question whether this issue has an effect on competition law in general before concluding that the size of the economy does not affect the economic analysis of competition law.[164] However, this analysis does not take into account other characteristics of small economies, such as the concentration of business actors and the difficulty in accessing the market, which would have an impact on the economic analysis of competition law. Most importantly, however, the different stages of competition policy development in the region are included in the *Guidelines I*.[165]

In this respect, the ASEAN has exhibited an unequivocal awareness of the imbalance in the development of different areas and respect the differing capabilities of each member. Indeed, the ASEAN affirms that the AMSs 'should consider and choose what best suits their particular characteristics and needs'.[166] It denies the one-size-fits-all approach and favours a tailor-made competition law in accordance with specific situations. There is a legitimate concern about whether the ASEAN's approach to competition law and policy would, rather than harmonising existing and in-development competition regimes, actually increase the differences among the AMSs. Nevertheless, when considering the differences among the AMSs and their ability to adopt competition law, it is almost impossible to formulate a central model appropriate for all the AMSs. By encouraging the AMSs' liberty in adopting their own vision of competition law, the ASEAN has opted for the most prudent and realistic approach. In this context, the broad and often ambiguous terminology in both *Guidelines* is necessary to accommodate the differences. Accordingly, the only expectation is the adherence to international standards of competition law. It is worth reiterating that the expectation is not absolute because all AMSs have the freedom to adopt their own vision of competition law and policy.

163. ASEAN Secretariat, *Guidelines on Developing Core Competencies in Competition Policy and Law for ASEAN*, 13–14 (2012).
164. *Ibid.*, at 29.
165. ASEAN Secretariat, *ASEAN Regional Guidelines on Competition Policy*, Art. 1.3.1 (2010).
166. ASEAN Secretariat, *Guidelines on Developing Core Competencies in Competition Policy and Law for ASEAN*, 5 (2012).

[B] Overcoming Resource Restriction

There is no shortage of issues related to resource restrictions in this region. The issues, recorded in both *Guidelines,* include financial restrictions and qualified human resources.[167] The financial issue, being the most pressing, requires resolution as soon as the competition authority is established.[168] The budget for the authority usually derives from the state's government which can lead to doubts about the competition authority's independence. However, reliance on the ministerial budget could significantly alleviate financial concerns[169] and can be a justifiable temporary compromise. In addition, the ASEAN proposes that:

> The [competition authority] also draws from an independent source of financing. It can be done, for example, by introducing procedural fees, such as filing fees for notifications (e.g. for merger clearance or exemptions). Fees should be set at a level corresponding to the average costs of the authority handling a particular category of matter, in order to minimise the risks of distorting effects on the [competition authority's] priorities. Additionally, the [competition authority] could be granted a share of the fines imposed.[170]

The *Guidelines II* publish an extensive list of recommendations to the AMSs to overcome the challenge of the shortage of qualified human resources.[171] The *Guidelines I* also stress the importance of optimising available resources. For this purpose, the competition authority should be allowed to:

> Introduce 'prioritisation criteria' to determine in an objective and consistent manner which investigations are to be pursued with priority. The priorities may remain confidential to the competition regulatory body or made public through annual plans or the annual report of the competition regulatory body, specifying industries or sectors, as well as types of conduct that are of particular interest.[172]

These criteria should reflect the time and resources at the national competition authority disposal.[173] Therefore, the work requirement must be proportionate to these resources. For instance, per se infringement cases with serious impact on relevant market should be made a priority. While complex cases that require cross-border investigation and international cooperation might present too big a hurdle. Similarly, a case that can be brought through private enforcement might not be worth pursuing by national competition authority with resource restriction issue. Most importantly,

---

167. *See*, in particular, ASEAN Secretariat, *ASEAN Regional Guidelines on Competition Policy*, Art. 4.2.2 (2010); ASEAN Secretariat, *Guidelines on Developing Core Competencies in Competition Policy and Law for ASEAN*, 38–40 (2012).
168. ASEAN Secretariat, *Guidelines on Developing Core Competencies in Competition Policy and Law for ASEAN*, 38 (2012).
169. Marco Botta, *Fostering Competition Culture in the Emerging Economies: The Brazilian Experience*, 32 World Competition (2009).
170. ASEAN Secretariat, *Guidelines on Developing Core Competencies in Competition Policy and Law for ASEAN*, 38 (2012).
171. *Ibid.*, at 39.
172. ASEAN Secretariat, *ASEAN Regional Guidelines on Competition Policy*, Art. 4.2.1 (2010).
173. *Ibid.*, at Art. 4.2.2.

prioritisation criteria should not lead to de facto exemptions which would unnecessarily restrict the scope of enforcement of the authority.

[C] Optimising Foreign Influences

It is noteworthy that the ASEAN readily embraced the concept of foreign help when drafting national competition law.[174] Moreover, it has admitted to borrowing from the AMSs' experiences and international best practices.[175] Although both *Guidelines* liberally reference the experiences of its AMSs by name, the *Guidelines I* are more reluctant to cite their international sources. Foreign origins have never been explicitly identified, perhaps in an attempt to further establish an authentic ASEAN vision of competition law and policy. In contrast, the *Guidelines II* acknowledge foreign influences and their role in introducing competition law and advising decision makers in matters regarding competition law. They give ample examples of foreign practices in the field of competition law, ranging from mature regimes such as the EU and the US to newer regimes like India, Jamaica, and Armenia.

The ASEAN's action of importing foreign rules is not unique. Competition law is often based on the experience of other countries.[176] However, this situation has not always been the case since most mature competition law regimes have had a chance to enact and adapt their own competition rules before adapting these in light of international agreements.[177] The same pattern cannot be applied to new competition law jurisdictions. Fox and Padilla aptly named this trend 'the follower phenomenon'.[178] This phenomenon includes transplanting a foreign rule to imitating a foreign law's interpretation. The transplantation may be partial or complete. The follower phenomenon is not a recent phenomenon since transplant has always been a major form of legal development.[179]

The motivation behind the adoption of competition law based on foreign experiences varies and there is no shortage of incentives for introducing foreign ideas. Generally, the motivation is the desire to save costs, both financial and institutional. Developing new competition law jurisdiction entirely internally will be a lengthy and costly process. In a resource-restricted jurisdiction, this would be simply impossible. Further, importing a successful concept could help ease the acceptance of the law in the

174. ASEAN Secretariat, *Guidelines on Developing Core Competencies in Competition Policy and Law for ASEAN*, 17 (2012).
175. ASEAN Secretariat, *ASEAN Regional Guidelines on Competition Policy*, Foreword (2010).
176. Michal S. Gal, *The 'Cut and Paste' of Art. 82 of the EC Treaty in Israel: Conditions for a Successful Transplant*, 9 European Journal of Law Reform (2007).
177. Maher M. Dabbah, *Competition Law and Policy in Developing Countries: A Critical Assessment of the Challenges to Establishing an Effective Competition Law Regime*, 33 World Competition (2010).
178. Eleanor M. Fox & A. Jorge Padilla, *The Follower Phenomenon: Implications for the Design of Monopolization Rules in a Global Economy*, 76 Antitrust L.J. (2010).
179. Michal S. Gal, *The 'Cut and Paste' of Art. 82 of the EC Treaty in Israel: Conditions for a Successful Transplant*, 9 European Journal of Law Reform (2007).

host country,[180] thus alleviating the burden on the competition advocacy programme. Nonetheless, the successful implementation of competition law abroad does not guarantee it would also be beneficial to the follower jurisdiction. Commentators warn that the latter needs to proceed with caution in order to obtain successful transplantation.[181] In this context, success is presumed when the recently transplanted competition law receives optimal implementation locally. The newly enacted law may not be applicable unless the special characteristics of the host state, such as the socioeconomic conditions, are effectively addressed. Furthermore, even if all the conditions for the successful transplant of the law are met, there is still the possibility that the law may be misapplied or applied differently from its foreign version. While this scenario is not desirable, especially in light of the process of the harmonisation of competition law, it can be justified when considering the special characteristics of the state in question.

Pitfalls when foreign laws are transplanted are more likely to occur if there has been excessive foreign pressure to adopt the laws. There is no evidence to indicate that this scenario applies to the ASEAN. It is likely that the choice to adopt foreign experiences is made voluntarily, thus implying that the ASEAN is aware of the potential benefits and pitfalls that could transpire. This awareness would explain why the ASEAN limits itself to simply following the universal consensus-based competition law and repeatedly suggests that AMSs take their special characteristics into consideration when designing national competition laws, even when its ultimate goal is to support regional economic integration.

Notwithstanding the study of foreign experiences, the ASEAN accepts two forms of foreign help: intellectual and financial resources.

[1] Technical Assistance

Developed economies have a duty of cooperation to aid developing economies in their efforts to combat international anticompetitive practices since developing economies lack the necessary resources and enforcement reach to treat them.[182] This duty of cooperation is due to the anticompetitive conduct being concocted in developed economies but taking place in developing economies since developing economies' tools to combat international anticompetitive conduct are often inadequate. The proposed solution is to extend developed economies' jurisdiction so as to make hard-core export cartels illegal. This suggestion of extraterritoriality of established competition jurisdiction is not necessarily the best alternative. Another proposed alternative is in the form of the concept of duty of cooperation on the part of developed

180. Eleanor M. Fox & A. Jorge Padilla, *The Follower Phenomenon: Implications for the Design of Monopolization Rules in a Global Economy*, 76 Antitrust L.J. (2010).
181. *See*, in particular, Michal S. Gal, *The 'Cut and Paste' of Art. 82 of the EC Treaty in Israel: Conditions for a Successful Transplant*, 9 European Journal of Law Reform (2007); Eleanor M. Fox & A. Jorge Padilla, *The Follower Phenomenon: Implications for the Design of Monopolization Rules in a Global Economy*, 76 Antitrust L.J. (2010).
182. Eleanor M. Fox, *Economic Development, Poverty and Antitrust: The Other Path*, 13 Sw. J. L. & Trade Am. (2007).

economies.[183] While duty of cooperation appears less hostile to foreign jurisdiction, the success of competition law enforcement in new jurisdiction is entirely dependence on the support from international organisations. In the case of the ASEAN, such support does not appear to be lacking.

Technical assistance provided to countries can be divided into two categories: the OECD model and the UNCTAD model.[184] The difference between the OECD and the UNCTAD lies, first, in their membership. The UNCTAD has broad and universal membership and includes most of the Member States of the UN, while the OECD is usually considered the 'club of rich nations'[185] because of its inclusion of thirty-four of the most industrialised economies of the world. Despite its best efforts in adding more diversity to its composition, the OECD is still heavily criticised limiting its membership to developed economies only.[186] Despite this difference, both organisations pursue the same activity - the convergence of competition law standards.

In the area of competition law and policy, the OECD is best known for its *Recommendations and Best Practices*.[187] Many competition authorities, even from non-OECD members, use these works as highly authoritative sources in the field of competition law. Among the different OECD publications in the field of competition law, the most influential is the *Recommendation Concerning Effective Action against Hard Core Cartels*, published in 1998.[188] Using this *Recommendation*, the OECD is working on obtaining substantive soft harmonisation in the field of hard-core cartels. The OECD's emphasis on fighting hard-core cartels is because the conduct of cartels is unambiguously harmful and countries unanimously condemn them. The OECD activities are not limited to hard-core cartels. It also deals with a variety of issues of competition law and policy including mergers, cooperation between competition authorities and Member States and fighting bid-rigging.[189] Equally important to the *Recommendations and Best Practices* is the OECD work on cooperation between the competition authorities of its Member States. The OECD has created an important competition forum as part of its Competition Committee called the Global Forum on Competition. This forum allows the OECD to further widen its policy dialogue to include non-OECD members. Today the Global Forum on Competition unites more

183. Maher M. Dabbah, *Competition Law and Policy in Developing Countries: A Critical Assessment of the Challenges to Establishing an Effective Competition Law Regime*, 33 World Competition (2010).
184. Cassey Lee, *Model Competition Laws*, *in* Competitive Advantage and Competition Policy in Developing Countries (Paul Cook, et al. eds., Edward Elgar 2007). (In his analysis, he used the OECD 1999 and UNCTAD 2003 model.)
185. Marco Botta, *Competition Policy: The EU and Global Networks*, *in* EU Policies in a Global Perspective: Shaping or Taking International Regimes? (Gerda Falkner & Patrick Müller eds., Routledge, Taylor & Francis Group 2014).
186. David J. Gerber, *The Extraterritorial Application of German Antitrust Law*, 77 American Journal of International Law (1983).
187. Eleanor M. Fox & Daniel A. Crane, *Global Issues in Antitrust and Competition Law*, 535 (West 2010).
188. Recommendation of the Council concerning Effective Action Against Hard Core Cartels (25 Mar. 1998).
189. *See*, in particular, OECD, *Recommendation of the Council concerning Co-operation between Member Countries on Anticompetitive Practices affecting International Trade* (1995); OECD, *Recommendation on Fighting Bid Rigging in Public Procurement* (2012).

than 100 competition authorities around the world.[190] It is intended to be a forum where the OECD members' convergence experience can be shared with non-members and at the same time, non-members' concerns can be heard. Another key function of the OECD in the field of competition law is to conduct peer reviews of national competition laws and policies. Through the peer reviews, the OECD can evaluate competition law regimes around the world and recommend how best to increase each one's effectiveness. In practice, this means that countries are free to submit their competition law regimes to OECD scrutiny but are under no obligation to implement the recommendations made in the review. Nonetheless, countries are encouraged to make legitimate domestic changes. The reviews are a useful convergence mechanism; newly established authorities can use them to lobby the government of its country to amend the competition law.[191] In other words, what the peer review lacks in binding obligation is compensated for by peer pressure.

The UNCTAD entered the field of competition law and policy in 1973 when it began its negotiation on the control of restrictive business practices. Since the nature of the UNCTAD's work already centred on trade policy, its expansion to the field of competition law should not be regarded as surprising but rather a natural progression as the Conference develops. It aims to facilitate a more efficient and equitable globalised economy through enhancing competitiveness and economic growth in developing economies by spreading a competition-based culture and elevating consumer welfare. The UNCTAD has produced some notable contributions to the field of global competition law over the years. Perhaps its best-known work is *The United Nations Set of Principles and Rules on Competition*,[192] more commonly known as the *UNCTAD Code* or the *UNCTAD Set*. Notwithstanding its nature as a multilateral agreement, the *UNCTAD Code* is generally regarded as a code of conduct on competition policy that aims to provide developing countries with equitable rules to protect them from anticompetitive harm.[193] It also recognizes the development dimension of competition law and policy and provides a framework for international operation and exchange of best practices.[194] When examining the text, it is evident that the *UNCTAD Code* is a compromise of different interests. The *UNCTAD Code*'s substantive provisions contain basic competition law principles generally consistent with the western concept of anticompetitive conduct. The *UNCTAD Code* has a two-tiered structure of rules and principles addressed both to countries and firms and contains classic competition law provisions. Nevertheless, the effects of the *UNCTAD Code* are extremely limited for two main reasons. First, in the eyes of developed economies, in particular the US, the *UNCTAD Code* represents a populist conception of competition

190. OECD, *Global Forum on Competition*, http://www.oecd.org/competition/globalforum/ (accessed 12 Dec. 2017).
191. Marco Botta, *Competition Policy: The EU and Global Networks*, *in* EU Policies in a Global Perspective: Shaping or Taking International Regimes? (Falkner & Müller eds., Routledge, Taylor & Francis Group 2014).
192. UNCTAD, *The United Nations Set of Principles and Rules on Competition* (2000) (the UNCTAD Code).
193. *Ibid.*, at s. A(5).
194. *Ibid.*, at s. D.

law which contrasts with the prevailing economic efficiency rationale.[195] As a consequence, developed economies tend to disregard the *UNCTAD Code* although the part of the *UNCTAD Code* that overlaps with their conception of efficient competition law continues to be cited approvingly. Second, the absence of a clear and legally binding effect reduces the political importance of the *UNCTAD Code*. Beside the *UNCTAD Code*, the UNCTAD has contributed to the globalisation of competition law through other measures such as the *Model Law on Competition*[196] which is based on the *UNCTAD Code*. This was adopted to give Member States a source of reference when drafting or amending domestic competition laws.

The UNCTAD also provides capacity building and technical assistance to developing economies and economies in transition which seek to implement competition law and policy in their jurisdictions. In this, the UNCTAD works closely with national competition authorities, competition experts, and development partners such as the OECD and the ICN.

Finally, the UNCTAD also has a peer review system similar to that of the OECD. The peer reviews are voluntary which means that countries are free to submit their competition law regimes for review; the recommendations made are not mandatory. The peer reviews are conducted by different competition experts to provide an objective assessment of the competition law regime for the purpose of identifying its shortcomings and proposing suggestions as well as technical assistance when needed. The UNCTAD peer review exercise is unique in terms of its development perspective and rich experience in working with developing economies.

Although there is no supporting evidence attesting to direct involvement of the OECD and the UNCTAD in capacity building and technical assistance within ASEAN, the *Best Practices* cite the OECD recommendations and the *Guidelines II* mention both the OECD and the UNCTAD body of work, in particular the *UNCTAD Model Law*, as their sources of competition law recommendations and best practices. Moreover, the ASEAN has received direct aid from some foreign nations; for instance, the *Guidelines I* was produced by InWent Capacity Building International while the *Guidelines II* was produced with the support of the Deutsche Gesellschaft für Internationale Zusammenarbeit (GIZ) for its capacity building for the ASEAN Secretariat project. Both projects were funded by the Foreign Office of the Federal Republic of Germany. In addition to the direct help, the ASEAN also receives technical assistance from the ASEAN-Australia Development Cooperation Programme Phase II and the ASEAN-Australia-New Zealand Free Trade Agreement (AANZFTA). Both programmes have offered ample technical assistance as evidenced by the frequent organisation of capacity-building workshops and conferences in the region.[197]

195. Ioannis Lianos, *The Contribution of the United Nations to the Emergence of Global Antitrust Law*, 15 Tul. J. Int'l & Comp. L. (2007).
196. UNCTAD, *The Model Law on Competition* (2010) (the Model Law).
197. ASEAN, *ASEAN Annual Report 2013–2014*, 4 (July 2014).

[2] *Financial Assistance*

The financial assistance provided to the ASEAN is essential for its initiative in developing its competition law and policy framework since the AMSs' contribution is minimal. In 2013, the Member States' contribution only accounted for USD 16.2 million.[198] This covered little more than the ASEAN Secretariat's operational costs. Consequently, the ASEAN is currently not financially self-reliant and foreign financial contributions are more-or-less imperative. For example, the ASEAN-Australia Development Cooperation Programme Phase II, which was launched in 2009 and is expected to last until 2019, has offered a budget of AUD 57 million (roughly USD 44.7 million).[199] Given the lack of public transparency regarding financial expenditure within the ASEAN structure, it is impossible to determine how much has been distributed to the development of the ASEAN competition law and policy projects.

§3.05 CONCLUSION

The ASEAN ambition of creating a highly competitive region that is fully integrated with the global economy is laudable, but the task ahead seems colossal. Its first task is to set the goals of competition law that is acceptable to all the AMSs. Through the *Guidelines I*, the ASEAN confirms the common objectives of competition policy as 'the promotion and protection of competitive process'[200] through the introduction of a level playing field to all market players. It strongly believes that the pursuit of such objectives will lead to fair or effective competition in the single market. In addition, the *Guidelines I* persuade the AMSs that competition policy is beneficial to developing economies due to the process of globalisation. '[D]eveloping countries need a competition policy, in order to monitor and control the growing role of the private sector in the economy so as to ensure that public monopolies are not simply replaced by private monopolies.'[201] It should be noted that the *Guidelines I* have relegated social goals from the objectives of competition law to 'other policy objectives'.[202] Most importantly, the integration goal is absent. The absence of integration goal from the goals advocated by the ASEAN signify a humbler adjustment in the execution of the ASEAN regional competition law.

In addition, the *Guidelines I* conclude that each AMS may individually decide which objectives to pursue.[203] This confirms the ASEAN's lack of persuasion power over the AMSs. While it is true that encouraging the AMSs to take into consideration their own national needs when determining the goal or goals of competition law will ensure effective actual enforcement of competition law, in retrospect, it is highly

198. Jörn Dosch, *The ASEAN Economic Community: The Status of Implementation, Challenges and Bottlenecks*, 13 (CARI 2013). (The calculation is based on the principle of equal annual contributions under The ASEAN Charter, Art. 30.2 (2007).)
199. ASEAN, *ASEAN Annual Report 2013–2014*, 4 (July 2014).
200. ASEAN Secretariat, *ASEAN Regional Guidelines on Competition Policy*, Art. 2.2.1 (2010).
201. *Ibid.*, at Art. 2.2.2.
202. *Ibid.*, at Art. 2.2.3.
203. *Ibid.*, at Art. 2.2.5.

possible that the *Guidelines I* have contributed to further diversification of national competition policies to the extent that the AMSs may end up varying objectives, making any attempt at regional harmonisation more challenging. Markedly different national competition laws could adversely affect the overall progress of ASEAN competition law development.

This chapter identifies the discrepancies in the political systems and the economic development, along with the deeply rooted ASEAN Way as the principal challenges to establishing the ASEAN regional competition policy. The ASEAN simply proposed overcoming these obstacles by acting in accordance with the nature of each AMSs without any suggestion at regional level. Yet, it is evident that the issues analysed in this chapter need to be addressed in the development of the ASEAN competition law for the benefit of the continual pursuit of regional economic integration. If they are not overcome or minimised, they possess the ability to hinder the establishment of the ASEAN single market since competition law occupies a central place at the foundation of the AEC.

CHAPTER 4

The ASEAN Regional Competition Law

Establishing a new competition law regime is never an easy task, especially for developing economies. Generally, there are three accepted models.[1] The first model is the formulation of competition law based on its own vision distinct from that of the developed economies.[2] This model is strongly advocated since developing economies sustain a different market reality from that of developed ones because of the smallness of their market which are often plagued with high level of concentrations.[3] It follows that competition law rules that flourish in big economies would struggle to find enforcement in small market economies. Yet, the proposal of such a model usually begins with the examination of current existing competition law regimes, especially those belonging to developed economies. This practice suggests that in reality, the formulation of developing economies' competition law model is at best, merely an adaptation of competition law from more matured regimes. The restriction in resources, both financial and technical, within developing economies further exacerbates developing economies' chance of developing an originally expressed law tailored to the specificities of those economies. In this regard, no competition law is entirely tailor-made for a developing economy.

However, it is not impossible to properly adjust existing laws to correspond to the special considerations of small market economies.[4] The challenge to adopting this

1. Heba Shahein, *Designing Competition Laws in New Jurisdictions: Three Models to Follow, in* New Competition Jurisdiction: Shaping Policies and Building Institutions (Richard Whish & Christopher Townley eds., Edward Elgar Publishing 2012). Employs the same distinctions using a different language to describe the three models: cut and paste model, contextualised approach, and tailor-made model.
2. Ajit Singh, *Competition and Competition Policy in Emerging Markets: International and Developmental Dimensions*, 15 (2002).
3. *See*, in particular, Michal S. Gal, *Size Does Matter: the Effects of Market Size on Optimal Competition Policy*, 74 S. Cal. L. Rev. (2001); Michal S. Gal, *Competition Policy for Small Market Economies* (Harvard University Press 2003).
4. *See*, in particular, William E. Kovacic, *Designing and Implementing Competition and Consumer Protection Reforms in Transitional Economies: Perspectives from Mongolia, Nepal, Ukraine, and Zimbabwe*, 44 DePaul L. Rev. (1995).

second model lies in understanding when foreign law is appropriate for the host country. This condition is crucial in light of the law's acceptance of legitimacy by the people. At the other end of the difficulty spectrum is the adoption of a universal consensus-based competition law.[5] Admittedly, this movement has weakened considerably since the abandonment of the *Draft International Antitrust Code*[6] and does not seem to have recovered its momentum since.[7] The main argument in support of this model is the convenience of travelling on a path well-paved and well-travelled especially since reinventing a new path can prove difficult and costly.[8] This is especially true in light of developing economies' lack of resources and experience to adequately manage the complex issues of developing a new competition law regime.

This chapter will concentrate on the ASEAN's efforts to establish a regional framework for competition law. The ASEAN initiative in establishing its own competition law framework was once underestimated in 2010.[9] Since then the ASEAN has produced a number of documents and both organised and participated in various activities in the hope of creating its own competition law framework. Outwardly, the ASEAN gives the impression of adhering to all the accepted provisions of competition law.

There are currently five documents produced by the ASEAN. The *Best Practices*[10] are the first to be introduced in 2008. As the name implies, the aim of the *Best Practices* is to study best international practices for introducing and implementing competition policy. The document generally uses affirmative words such as *recommend* to ensure that the document is suggesting a certain position or direction. The *Handbook on Competition Policy and Law for Business*[11] illustrates competition law and policy and related legislations in each of the AMS and is addressed primarily to interested foreign business. There are two *Guidelines*[12] written under the auspices of the ASEAN Secretariat. Lastly, *An ASEAN Competition Action Plan (2016-2015)*[13] charts the strategic goals, initiatives, and outcomes on competition law and policy in the ASEAN over the next ten years after the arrival of the AEC.

5. *See*, for example, Andrew T. Guzman, *The Case for International Antitrust*, 22 Berkeley J. Int'l Law (2004); Makan Delrahim, *The Long and Winding Road: Convergence in the Application of Antitrust to Intellectual Property*, 13 Geo. Mason L. Rev. (2005); Richard M. Steuer, *The Simplicity of Antitrust Law*, 14 U. Pa. J. Bus. L. (2012).
6. *Draft International Antitrust Code as a GATT-MTO-Plurilateral Trade Agreement (reprint)*, 64 Antitrust & Trade Reg. Rep. (1993).
7. *Interview with Anne K. Bingaman*, 8 Antitrust (1993). As seen in Gerber, *Global Competition: Law, Markets and Globalisation*, 103 (Oxford University Press 2010).
8. Eleanor M. Fox, *Economic Development, Poverty and Antitrust: The Other Path*, 13 Sw. J. L. & Trade Am. (2007).
9. Maher M. Dabbah, *International and Comparative Competition Law*, 394 (Cambridge University Press 2010).
10. Jennifer Orr, et al., *Best Practices in the Introduction and Implementation of Competition Policy and Law in East Asia Summit Countries* (REPSF II Project No. 07/008 2008).
11. ASEAN Secretariat, *Handbook on Competition Policy and Law for Business* (2010); ASEAN Secretariat, *Handbook on Competition Policy and Law for Business 2013* (2013).
12. ASEAN Secretariat, *ASEAN Regional Guidelines on Competition Policy* (2010); ASEAN Secretariat, *Guidelines on Developing Core Competencies in Competition Policy and Law for ASEAN* (2012).
13. An ASEAN Competition Action Plan (2016–2015).

These efforts have been warmly welcomed because they are expected to assist in the development of the region's competition law and policy framework.[14] On the other hand, they have been criticised for the absence of well-established specifications and the lack of clarity.[15] Both *Guidelines* contain a double message to the AMSs: on the one hand, they are encouraged to introduce or reform an efficient competition law based on essential competition law principles and on the other hand, to establish clear competition rules. The clarity of the competition law is crucial in the case of developing economies which do not have sufficient resources to handle a heavy work load in their competition agencies. The *Guidelines I* are identified as a common reference guide without any binding power over the AMSs. The language used in the *Guidelines I* is less persuasive than in the *Best Practices* and does not demand any form of commitment from the AMSs regarding competition law and policy with the exception of the sole commitment to introduce national competition law before the unveiling of the AEC in 2015. The words often employed are; *may*, *could*, and *can* while *should* is rarely used. Despite its name, the *Guidelines I* simply collate the already available knowledge on general competition law practices and institutional building. In this endeavour, at least, the *Guidelines I* are extremely successful since the final product is highly educative. The *Guidelines II* were introduced two years after the introduction of the *Guidelines I* in a complementary role. The arrangement of both documents is starkly different. While the *Guidelines I* use chapters and articles, these traits are absent from the *Guidelines II*, hinting that they were developed by different participating authors.[16] The purpose of the *Guidelines II* is to guide the AMSs in building core competencies in the field of competition policy with a focus on how best to develop a competition law enforcement mechanism. The focal point is on competition authority attributes and competencies. Indubitably, both *Guidelines* are well-researched drawing from both the AMSs' and existing competition regimes' experiences. However, building an ASEAN-specific legal framework does not appear to be their focal subject matter. *An ASEAN Competition Action Plan* was introduced after the creation of the AEC with an aim to recommit to the harmonisation of competition law in the ASEAN. Most importantly, the document extends the deadline for a complete legal framework on competition law in all the AMSs to the end of 2016.

This chapter examines the approach taken by the ASEAN in order to achieve regional economic integration with competition law and policy as one of the principal mechanisms. It is mainly concerned with the substantive rules; discussion on the institutional aspect will be presented in Chapter 5. Many of the substantive rules are

14. Luu Huong Ly, *Regional Harmonization of Competition Law and Policy: An ASEAN Approach*, 2 Asian J. Int. Law (2012).
15. Stéphanie Yon-Courtin, *ASEAN: L'ASEAN Publie des Lignes Directrices en Matière de Concurrence*, 4 Revue Concurrences (2010).
16. The *Guidelines I* were produced by InWent Capacity Building International whose project was funded by the Foreign Office of the Federal Republic of Germany. France's l'Autorité de la Concurrence is also documented as having participated. The *Guidelines II* were produced with the support of the Deutsche Gesellschaft fur Internationale Zusammenarbeit (GIZ) for its capacity building for the ASEAN Secretariat project. The project was also funded by the Foreign Office of the Federal Republic of Germany. In addition, the *Guidelines II* subcontractor is FratiniVergano – European Lawyers.

covered by *Guidelines I* since *Guidelines II* do not delve much into this area, preferring instead to focus on institutional development. This chapter is organised to reflect the organisation of the *Guidelines I*. It covers the application of competition law, prohibitions on anticompetitive agreements, abuse of dominant position, and anticompetitive mergers.

§4.01 THE SCOPE OF COMPETITION LAW

To understand the reach of the competition law application, defining *undertaking* is crucial. At first glance, it might appear that the *Guidelines I* opt for a broad and general definition of an *undertaking* claiming that competition law applies to 'all businesses engaged in commercial economic activities in all economic sectors, including State-owned enterprises having effect within the members' territory, unless exempted by law'.[17] The *Guidelines I* further explain that the term includes:

> [A]ny person, being an individual, a body corporate, an unincorporated body of persons or any other entity, capable of carrying on commercial or economic activities relating to goods or services. It includes individuals operating as sole proprietorships, companies, firms, businesses, partnerships, cooperatives, societies, business chambers, trade associations and non-profit making organisations, whatever their legal and ownership status (foreign or local, government or nongovernment), and the way in which they are financed.[18]

This formulation shifts the focus from the organisation of an entity to its activity. The ASEAN seems to be more concerned with the functional approach than the institutional approach. It is reminiscent of the EU's competition law where the term is defined by case laws as 'every entity engaged in an economic activity, regardless of the legal status of the entity and the way in which it is financed'.[19]

The functional approach relies heavily on the concept of economic activity which the *Guidelines I* refer to as 'any activity that could be performed in return for payment and normally, but not necessarily, with the objective of making a profit'.[20] In contrast, non-economic activity or public interest activity, that is, is any activity that could not be performed for payment and without the objective of making a profit, would escape the application of competition law. This definition is precariously narrow since it reduces economic activity to pecuniary interest and thus widens the public/private divide.[21] Notwithstanding the language used to demonstrate the ASEAN's fixation on the pecuniary aspect of economic activity, the interpretation of the term is borrowed from EU law. In comparison, EU law's definition of economic trade applies regardless

17. ASEAN Secretariat, *ASEAN Regional Guidelines on Competition Policy*, Art. 3.1.2. (2010).
18. *Ibid.*, at Art. 3.2.1.4.
19. *Höfner and Elser v. Macroton GmbH*, Case 41/90, para. 21 (ECR I-1979 1991); *Poucet and Pistre v. Assurances Générales de France*, Cases 159 & 160/91, para. 17 (ECR I-637 1993); *Fédération Française des Sociétés d'Assurance v. Ministry of Agriculture and Fisheries*, Case 244/94, para. 14 (ECR I-4013 1995).
20. ASEAN Secretariat, *ASEAN Regional Guidelines on Competition Policy*, Art. 3.1.2. (2010).
21. For more information on the public and private divide, *see*, Okeoghene Odudu, *The Boundaries of EC Competition Law: The Scope of Art. 81*, 47 (Oxford University Press 2006).

of whether or not the activity is profit making.[22] Supplementary indicators include the offering of goods or services on the market,[23] the bearing of the financial risks attached to the performance of the economic activities[24] and where that activity could, at least in principle, be carried on by a private undertaking in order to make profits.[25]

In addition, the *Guidelines I* later introduce an even broader and non-exhaustive list of exemptions and exclusions from the application of competition law. The long list includes:

- The Government, statutory bodies or any person acting on their behalf. For example, Government officials and statutory bodies exercising prerogatives arising from their public powers or acting for the fulfilment of public service objectives, or any persons acting on their behalf, may be excluded from the prohibitions. These exemptions apply insofar as the Government activities are connected with the exercise of sovereign power;[26]
- Certain agreements and conduct which have significant countervailing benefits, such as contributing to or improving the production or distribution of goods and services, or promoting technical or economic progress, while allowing consumers a fair share of the resulting benefit. The exemptions may be allowed only to the extent that is appropriate and indispensable to reach their intended aims, and should not afford the undertakings concerned the possibility of eliminating competition in respect of a substantial part of the goods or services in question;[27]
- Specific industries or activities includes strategic and national interest, security, public, economic and/or social considerations;[28]
- Block exemptions granted to research and development cooperation and intellectual property rights contracts;[29] and
- Small and medium-sized enterprises (SMEs).[30]

While most items on the list exemplify the idea of entities performing public interest functions, the inclusion of the SMEs is quite peculiar. It is possible that the ASEAN is simply trying to protect the SMEs since, as discussed in Chapter 3, this was one of the principal concerns expressed by the AMSs.

22. *Commission Decision of 20 Jul. 1999 relating to a proceeding under Art. 82 of the EC Treaty and Art. 54 of the EEA Agreement (1998 Football World Cup Finals)*, OJ L5/55, para. 65 (2000).
23. *Commission v. Italy*, Case 118/85, para. 7 (ECR 2599 1987).
24. *Wouters, Savelbergh and Price Waterhouse Belastingadviseurs BV v. Algemene Raad van de Nederlandse Orde van Advocaten*, Case 309/99, para. 48 (ECR I-1577 2002).
25. *Albany International BV v. Stichting Bedrijfspensioenfonds Textielindustrie*, Case 67/96, para. 311 (ECR I-5751 1999).
26. ASEAN Secretariat, *ASEAN Regional Guidelines on Competition Policy*, Art. 3.5.4 (2010).
27. *Ibid.*, at Art. 3.5.3.
28. *Ibid.*, at Art. 3.5.1.
29. *Ibid.*, at Art. 3.5.6.
30. *Ibid.*, at Art. 3.5.5.

Eventually, the *Guidelines II* directly contradict the *Guidelines I* and extend the list of limitations to state-owned enterprises, while admitting that the inclusion of state-owned enterprises in the general application of competition law would be better.[31] The reason for this reversal lies in the historical context of Southeast Asian countries. It is possible that the ASEAN changed its tone on this matter in order to address the AMSs' concern. Historically, the AMSs' government has played a leading role in economic activity through the construction of necessary infrastructures because of its public nature and economies of scale and scope.[32] The exclusion of the state as an economic actor to which competition law applies is detrimental to the success of the enforcement rate of the law. Not only does it greatly diminish the domain of competition law, but it also invites cronyism and exploitation in the market. Excluding the state from the domain of competition law will inevitably lead to interest groups shifting their anticompetitive conduct through government protection. Instead of eliminating it, the anticompetitive behaviour will simply change form. Consequently, competition law may cause inefficiencies that are worse than the allocative losses that it was designed to counteract.[33] This will render the adoption of competition law obsolete.

It remains unclear which vision prevails since both documents are mere guidelines with no binding power. The lack of a cohesive understanding of the scope of competition law indicates that the ASEAN approach to substantive competition law is heading towards an uncertain start.

§4.02 THE PROHIBITION OF ANTICOMPETITIVE AGREEMENTS

This prohibition is of particular importance in light of developing economies' natural market conditions which tend to facilitate collusive agreements.[34] The ASEAN is consciously aware of this necessity. The *Guidelines I* assert that the 'AMSs should consider prohibiting horizontal and vertical agreements between undertakings that prevent, distort or restrict competition in the AMSs' territory, unless otherwise exempted'.[35] In analysing the anticompetitive agreements, it is imperative to first consider the definition of the term before progressing to an assessment of the agreement.

This section will discuss the meaning of the term *agreement* as intended by the *Guidelines I.* Agreements must contain two elements: the willingness to agree and the restriction of competition in the market.

31. ASEAN Secretariat, *Guidelines on Developing Core Competencies in Competition Policy and Law for ASEAN*, 27 (2012).
32. Chadwick Teo, *Competition Policy and Economic Growth* (2003).
33. A. E. Rodriguez & Mark D. Williams, *The Effectiveness of Proposed Antitrust Programs for Developing Countries*, 19 NCJ. Int'l L. & Com. Reg. 209 (1994).
34. Michal S. Gal, *Competition Policy for Small Market Economies*, 168 (Harvard University Press 2003).
35. ASEAN Secretariat, *ASEAN Regional Guidelines on Competition Policy*, Art. 3.2.1. (2010).

[A] The Willingness to Agree

The term *agreement* has a broad definition. It is described as:

> Both legally enforceable and non-enforceable agreements, whether written or oral; it also includes so-called gentlemen's agreements. An agreement may be reached via a physical meeting of the parties or through an exchange of letters or telephone calls, or by any other means. All that is required is that parties arrive at a consensus on the actions each party will, or will not, take.[36]

The only prerequisite of the term *agreement* is an occurrence of wills between undertakings regardless of their form or content. This is a close adaptation of settled EU case law.[37]

The concept of agreement is further expanded to encompass concerted practices. In this context, concerted practice covers 'any form of coordination or implicit understanding or arrangement between undertakings, but which do not reach the stage where an agreement properly so-called has been reached or concluded'.[38] Similarly to the EU case law,[39] this liberal concept is seemingly designed to include all forms of coordination between undertakings that might escape the literal interpretation of the term *agreements*. In the case of the ASEAN, whose AMSs largely comprise developing economies with relatively small market economies, the necessity of a broad definition is even more significant. Not only does it need to conform to the hybrid and flexible nature of both global and local business, but it needs to compensate for the difficulty in obtaining the evidence of actual and tacit collusive agreements.

[B] The Restriction to the Competition Test

The mere existence of an agreement is not always indicative of an anticompetitive characteristic. Agreements need to be put under the restriction to competition test. The *Guidelines I* explain that:

> The terms 'prevent,' 'distort' or 'restrict' refer, respectively, to the elimination of existing or potential competitive activities, the artificial alteration of competitive conditions in favour of the parties of the agreement, and the reduction of competitive activities. They are meant to include all situations where competitive conditions are adversely affected by the existence of the anticompetitive agreement.[40]

Regarding the evaluation of the agreements, the *Guidelines I* suggest that:

> [The] AMSs should evaluate the agreement by reference to its object and/or its effects where possible. [The] AMSs may decide that an agreement infringes the law only if it has as its object or effect the appreciable prevention, distortion or

36. *Ibid.*, at Art. 3.2.1.3.
37. *Bayer AG v. Commission*, Case T-41/96, para. 69 (ECR II-3383 2000).
38. ASEAN Secretariat, *ASEAN Regional Guidelines on Competition Policy*, Art. 3.2.5. (2010).
39. *ICI v. Commission*, Case 48/69, para. 64 (ECR 619 1972).
40. ASEAN Secretariat, *ASEAN Regional Guidelines on Competition Policy*, Art. 3.2.1.5. (2010).

> restriction of competition. [The] AMSs may consider identifying specific 'hardcore restrictions,' which will always be considered as having an appreciable adverse effect on competition (e.g., price fixing, bid-rigging, market sharing, limiting or controlling production or investment), which need to be treated as *per se* illegal[41]

By indicating that the evaluation made to the agreements should be done with reference to their object and/or their effect the appreciable prevention, distortion, or restriction of competition, the *Guidelines I* bear a close resemblance to Article 101(1) of the *TFEU*. Generally, the evaluation can be distinguished by two different classifications: the per se rule and the rule of reason.

First, there is global agreement that cartels are bad.[42] All competition laws prohibit horizontal collaboration outright without allowing any reasonable defences[43] since it is assumed that this type of agreement outweighs the few possible procompetitive justifications.[44] The ASEAN is no stranger to this attitude and hard-core restrictions are prohibited as well under the per se rule. The *Guidelines I* identify price-fixing, bid-rigging, market sharing, limiting, or controlling production or investment as examples in this category. They further clarify that:

- 'Price-fixing' involves fixing either the price itself or the components of a price such as a discount, establishing the amount or percentage by which prices are to be increased, or establishing a range outside of which prices are not to move.
- 'Bid-rigging' includes cover bidding to assist an undertaking in winning the tender. An essential feature of the tender system is that tenderers prepare and submit bids independently.
- 'Market sharing' involves agreements to share markets, whether by territory, type or size of customer, or in some other ways.
- 'Limiting or controlling production or investment' involves agreements which limit output or control production, by fixing production levels or setting quotas, or agreements which deal with structural overcapacity or coordinate future investment plans.[45]

It is believed that the clear and strict prohibition of hard-core cartels is especially important for small economies in which cartelistic behaviour is widespread owing to underlying market conditions that are relatively more conducive to collusion.[46] This belief was not shared by the ASEAN who excludes vertical agreements from this category while remaining silent on the matter of the burden of proof. Vertical

41. *Ibid.*, at Art. 3.2.2.
42. Eleanor M. Fox & Daniel A. Crane, *Global Issues in Antitrust and Competition Law*, 5 (West 2010).
43. A. E. Rodriguez & Ashok Menon, *The Limits of Competition Policy: The Shortcomings of Antitrust in Developing and Reforming Economies*, 87 (Kluwer Law International 2010).
44. Manisha M. Sheth, *Formulating Antitrust Policy in Emerging Economies*, 86 Geo. L. J. (1997).
45. ASEAN Secretariat, *ASEAN Regional Guidelines on Competition Policy*, Art. 3.2.2 (2010).
46. Michal S. Gal, *Competition Policy for Small Market Economies*, 170 (Harvard University Press 2003).

agreements commonly contain price (minimum or maximum resale price maintenance) and non-price restraints (exclusive territorial or customer arrangements, exclusive dealings, tie-ins, selective distribution, and quantity forcing).[47] They are generally efficient and thus procompetitive.[48] Therefore, there is some justification for excluding vertical agreements from hard-core restrictions. The *Best Practices*, which form the basis of the *Guidelines I*, seem to concur with this position and warn that refusal to do so would create a cumbersome provision and result in welfare reduction.[49] In addition, it was established that setting the burden-of-proof thresholds too high could result in difficulties with prosecuting hard-core cartels.[50] Limiting the competition authority's power to prosecuting hard-core cartels only in the presence of hard evidence such as written agreements between undertakings would render hard-core cartels hard to detect and subsequently prosecute. This is due to the fact that tacit collusion in developing economies is easier to establish because of the oligopolistic structure of their market.[51] Moreover, communication between undertakings is easier and typically not in written form. For this reason, the *Best Practices* recommend that the standard of proof for collusion in the case of per se prohibition should be especially high.[52] Yet, this specific consideration is not included in the *Guidelines I*.

Secondly, the rule of reason is often considered the exception to the per se rule. However, the rule of reason analysis remains necessary in order to limit too literal an interpretation of the broad language used in the law. Such a method of interpretation could cause harm to the process of competition by eliminating efficiency. The rule of reason analysis is also included in the *Guidelines I*. They provide that: [53]

> With the exclusion of the hardcore restrictions which are treated as *per se* illegal, AMSs may decide to analyse the agreements by 'rule of reason' (e.g., via market share thresholds and efficiency considerations) and safe harbour provisions (e.g., appreciability test). For example, the AMSs may decide that an agreement by undertakings, which exceeds a certain percentage of any relevant market affected by the agreement, will have an appreciable effect on competition.

The inclusion of the market share threshold within the rule of reason test is done without any further recommendation on how to determine the aforementioned threshold. The efficiency consideration could be included under the rule of reason test as well, especially given the constant pressure to allow some exceptions to the general prohibitions for agreements with procompetitive effect, such as achieving minimum efficient scale and lowering costs to a level that an undertaking acting alone can never

47. OECD, *Trade and Competition Policies for Tomorrow*, 43 (OECD Publishing 1999).
48. Paul E. Godek, *A Chicago-School Approach to Antitrust for Developing Countries*, 43 The Antitrust Bulletin (1998).
49. Jennifer Orr, et al., *Best Practices in the Introduction and Implementation of Competition Policy and Law in East Asia Summit Countries*, 3 (REPSF II Project No. 07/008 2008).
50. A. E. Rodriguez & Ashok Menon, *The Limits of Competition Policy: The Shortcomings of Antitrust in Developing and Reforming Economies*, 88 (Kluwer Law International 2010).
51. Manisha M. Sheth, *Formulating Antitrust Policy in Emerging Economies*, 86 Geo. L. J. (1997).
52. Jennifer Orr, et al., *Best Practices in the Introduction and Implementation of Competition Policy and Law in East Asia Summit Countries*, 3 (REPSF II Project No. 07/008 2008).
53. ASEAN Secretariat, *ASEAN Regional Guidelines on Competition Policy*, Art. 3.2.3. (2010).

achieve. This exception is crucial for small market economies,[54] therefore the *Guidelines I* provide that:

> AMSs may also set up a procedure to consider granting exemptions or exclusions to certain agreements and conduct which have significant countervailing benefits, such as contributing to or improving the production or distribution of goods and services, or promoting technical or economic progress, while allowing consumers a fair share of the resulting benefit. The exemptions may be allowed only to the extent that is appropriate and indispensable to reach their intended aims and should not afford the undertakings concerned the possibility of eliminating competition in respect of a substantial part of the goods or services in question.[55]

Essentially, the *Guidelines I* illustrate agreements with countervailing benefits, such as contributing to or improving the production or distribution of goods and services, or promoting technical or economic progress, while allowing consumers a fair share of the resulting benefit. Nonetheless, there is a limit to this exception. The *Guidelines I* warn that the exemptions should only be allowed to the extent that is appropriate and indispensable to reach their intended aims and should not eliminate competition in respect of a substantial part of the goods or services in question.

§4.03 THE PROHIBITION OF ABUSE OF DOMINANT POSITION

Competition law also prohibits behaviours by a single undertaking. These behaviours are sometimes described as unilateral conducts. If competition laws are in agreement regarding the prohibition of anticompetitive agreements, the same could not be said with regard to abuse of dominant position. There are disparities, well documented by the ICN, in how abuse of dominance is treated in different jurisdictions.[56] The report speculated that the divergence in competition law practices, in particular between the US and the EU, was due to different theoretical economic frameworks. This report is further corroborated that the size of the market does not contribute to a divergence in how prohibition of abuse of dominant position is practiced.[57] Both small and large economies suffer from abuse of dominance in a similar way but to a more intense degree in countries with small economies. The intensity is possibly due to the natural condition of a small market economy where the levels of concentration tends to be high in both upstream and downstream markets. This naturally erects barriers to market entry. It is precisely this natural condition of small market economies that makes erasing the abuse of dominant position more challenging for developing economies. If the suffering is identical, developing economies find it more difficult to alleviate the pain.

---

54. Michal S. Gal, *Competition Policy for Small Market Economies*, 162 (Harvard University Press 2003).
55. ASEAN Secretariat, *ASEAN Regional Guidelines on Competition Policy*, Art. 3.5.3 (2010).
56. *See*, in particular, ICN, *Report on the Objectives of Unilateral Conduct Laws, Assessment of Dominance/Substantial Market Power, and State-Created Monopolies* (2007).
57. Michal S. Gal, *Size Does Matter: the Effects of Market Size on Optimal Competition Policy*, 74 S. Cal. L. Rev. (2001).

The *Guidelines I* confirm that the AMSs should consider prohibiting the abuse of a dominant position.[58] Whether an undertaking holds a dominant position is a crucial prerequisite to categorising the abuse.

[A] The Definition of Dominant Position

The *Guidelines I* clarify that:

> 'Dominant position' refers to a situation of market power, where an undertaking, either individually or together with other undertakings, is in a position to unilaterally affect the competition parameters in the relevant market for a good(s) or service(s), e.g., able to profitably sustain prices above competitive levels or to restrict output or quality below competitive levels.[59]

The language chosen by the ASEAN signify that dominant position is not exclusively held by a single undertaking but can be shared between several undertakings.

The first step in determining whether an undertaking holds a dominant position is to identify the relevant market. Failure to do so could result in the non-enforcement of competition law.[60] Curiously, information about relevant markets do not appear in the *Guidelines I* under the provision of abuse of dominant position, forcing observers and interested parties to refer back to the definition of relevant market as it appears under the prohibition of anticompetitive agreements. The relevant market is described there as 'the product range and the geographic area where competition takes place between undertakings'.[61] This formulation covers both the product and the geographical market. Relevant market is commonly determined through means of the test of substitutability in both large and small economies.

The second step is to analyse the market power held by the undertaking. In the case of a monopoly, it can be challenging to analyse the market power of an undertaking. The ASEAN does not suggest ways to assess market dominance assessment; it leaves the decision-making power entirely in the hands of its AMSs. The *Guidelines I*[62] makes slight reference to market share and then only as a mere possibility. The ASEAN's silence is understandable as there is no single formulation to assess market dominance.[63] Nonetheless, most jurisdictions rely on market share as the main indicator of market power.[64] While this method has often been criticised for

58. ASEAN Secretariat, *ASEAN Regional Guidelines on Competition Policy*, Art. 3.3.1 (2010).
59. *Ibid.*, at Art. 3.3.1.1.
60. This occurred in the EU case law, *see*, *Europemballage Corporation and Continental Can Company Inc. v Commission of the European Communities*, Case 6/72 (ECR 215 1973).
61. ASEAN Secretariat, *ASEAN Regional Guidelines on Competition Policy*, Art. 3.2.3.2 (2010).
62. *Ibid.*, at Art. 3.3.1.1.
63. Michal S. Gal, *Competition Policy for Small Market Economies*, 68 (Harvard University Press 2003).
64. *See*, for example, George A. Hay, *Market Power in Antitrust*, 60 Antitrust L.J (1991); *Hoffmann-La Roche & Co. AG v. Commission*, Case 85/76 (ECR 461 1979).

its high inaccuracy,[65] the pragmatic benefits gained from it are considerable. The loss of technical accuracy is more than compensated for by the gain in administrative convenience and the reduction of litigation costs,[66] thus reinforcing the appeal of the market share criterion. Incidentally, developing economies prefer using the criterion of market share as proof of dominance; assessing evidence from a set of complex economic factors requires high capability and experience on the part of the national competition authority.[67] However, because of the questionable accuracy of the market share criterion, other indicators should be used in conjunction with market share, for example, the ease of access to the market.

Unsurprisingly, the ASEAN does not provide any guidance relative to the market share threshold. Emerging economies were advised to use a lower market share threshold than that of developed economies because small economies have higher barriers to entry to the market but fewer constraints placed upon undertakings which have gained entry to potentially be abusive.[68] Therefore, the market share necessary to infer dominance in a relevant market is lower. Regrettably, the *Guidelines I* have missed the opportunity to encourage a lower threshold of market share to the AMSs.

[B] Classification of Abuse

The possession of dominant position in the relevant market in itself is not a violation of competition law unless it is accompanied by abuse. On the definition of *abuse*, the *Guidelines I* describe it as follow:

> 'Abuse' of a dominant position occurs where the dominant enterprise, either individually or together with other undertakings, exploits its dominant position in the relevant market or excludes competitors and harms the competition process. It is prudent to consider the actual or potential impact of the conduct on competition, instead of treating certain conducts by dominant enterprises as automatically abusive.[69]

According to this description, there are two types of abuse of dominant position: exploitative and exclusionary abuses. Exploitative behaviours of an undertaking may cause harm to consumer directly while exclusionary conducts affect market structure. In this regard, the ASEAN elects the same distinction as that of the CJEU.[70]

65. Jonathan B. Baker & Timothy F. Bresnahan, *Estimating the Residual Demand Curve Facing a Single Firm*, 6 International Journal of Industrial Organization (1988); John Vickers, *Market Power in Competition Case*, 2 European Law Journal (2006).
66. Michal S. Gal, *Competition Policy for Small Market Economies*, 61 (Harvard University Press 2003).
67. Eleanor M. Fox, *Linked-In: Antitrust and the Virtues of a Virtual Network*, 43 Int'l Law (2009).
68. Manisha M. Sheth, *Formulating Antitrust Policy in Emerging Economies*, 86 Geo. L. J. (1997).
69. ASEAN Secretariat, *ASEAN Regional Guidelines on Competition Policy*, Art. 3.3.1.2 (2010).
70. *Europemballage Corporation and Continental Can Company Inc. v. Commission of the European Communities*.

To illustrate the abuse of dominant position, the *Guidelines I* present a non-exhaustive list of abusive conduct encompassing:

- Exploitative behaviour towards consumers, customers and/or competitors (e.g., excessive or unfair purchase or sales prices or other unfair trading conditions, tying);
- Exploitative behaviour towards consumers, customers and/or competitors (e.g., excessive or unfair purchase or sales prices or other unfair trading conditions, tying);
- Exclusionary behaviour towards competitors (e.g., predatory pricing by an undertaking which deliberately incurs losses in the short run by setting prices so low that it forces one or more undertakings out of the market, so as to be able to charge higher prices in the longer run; margin squeeze);
- Discriminatory behaviour (e.g., applying dissimilar pricing or conditions to equivalent transactions and vice-versa);
- Limiting production, markets or technical development to the prejudice of consumers (e.g., restricting output or illegitimate refusal to supply, restricting access to/use of/ development of a new technology).[71]

The *Guidelines II* later reduce this list to only exploitative behaviour and exclusionary behaviour.[72] There is no explanation for this reduction.

The *Guidelines I* further inform that 'it is prudent to consider the actual or potential impact of the conduct on competition, instead of treating certain conducts by dominant enterprises as automatically abusive'.[73] Evidently, the ASEAN is embracing both the form- and the effect-based analysis to ensure the effectiveness of competition law. It is not enough to confine enforcement of abuse of dominant position only to the actual impacts. The competition authority should be able to prevent potential anticompetitive conduct before it presents.

§4.04 MERGER CONTROL

Merger control is one of the most important competition rules, as reflected in the *Guidelines I*. A merger occurs when independent undertakings combine into one. There are two categories of merger. A horizontal merger involves undertakings that are actual or potential competitors, while a vertical merger involves undertakings at different levels of the production chain. There are generally two main concerns with mergers.[74] The first concern is that a horizontal merger may result in substantial market power, creating unilateral anticompetitive effects. The second is that mergers can reduce the number of competitors, resulting in the formation of a cooperative oligopoly. Merger control can then be seen as a natural extension of the prohibition of

71. ASEAN Secretariat, *ASEAN Regional Guidelines on Competition Policy*, Art. 3.3.2 (2010).
72. ASEAN Secretariat, *Guidelines on Developing Core Competencies in Competition Policy and Law for ASEAN*, 19 (2012).
73. ASEAN Secretariat, *ASEAN Regional Guidelines on Competition Policy*, Art. 3.3.1.2 (2010).
74. Mark Furse, *Antitrust Law in China, Korea and Vietnam*, 53 (Oxford University Press 2009).

abuse of dominant position and anticompetitive agreements. Merger control operates under the assumption that a pre-emptive review of a merger is both less costly and less complicated than attempting to deconcentrate an anticompetitive merger that has already been realised.

[A] The Definition of Merger

The ASEAN chooses the term *merger* to encompass the full extent of the concentrations of undertakings including: mergers, acquisitions, takeovers, and joint ventures. The *Guidelines I* explain that:

> 'Mergers' refers to situations where two or more undertakings, previously independent of one another, join together. This definition includes transactions whereby two companies legally merge into one ('mergers'), one firm takes sole control of the whole or part of another ('acquisitions' or 'takeovers'), two or more firms acquire joint control over another firm ('joint ventures') and other transactions, whereby one or more undertakings acquire control over one or more undertakings, such as interlocking directorates.[75]

In essence, a merger occurs when previously independent undertakings are transformed into a single new entity irrespective of the precise nature and language of the concentration. In this regard, the *Guidelines I* broadly paraphrased Article 3 of the *EUMR*.[76] For the purpose of this book and to avoid confusion, the term *merger* will be used to describe all types of concentrations of undertakings.

[B] The Organisation of Control of Concentration

The merger control is especially important for developing economies which typically have small market economies. As mergers reduce the number of competitors and increase the market share of the merged entities resulting in an increase in any concentration already present in the market.[77] Nevertheless, the increased concentration could also help achieve efficiencies that were unattainable pre-merger.

[1] The Appraisal of Merger

The *Guidelines I* indicate that mergers should be appraised on their economic effect. The 'AMSs may consider prohibiting mergers that lead to a substantial lessening of competition or would significantly impede effective competition in the relevant market or in a substantial part of it, unless otherwise exempted'.[78] Accordingly, the analysis of the impact of mergers must be examined from three different perspectives: an analysis

75. ASEAN Secretariat, *ASEAN Regional Guidelines on Competition Policy*, Art. 3.4.1.1 (2010).
76. Council Regulation (EC) No. 139/2004 on the Control of Concentrations between Undertakings (2004).
77. Jurgita Malinauskaite, *Efficiency Tests in the Merger Control Regimes of the Baltic Countries: Myth or Reality*, 18 International Company and Commercial Law Review (2007).
78. ASEAN Secretariat, *ASEAN Regional Guidelines on Competition Policy*, Art. 3.4.1 (2010).

of the structure of the market before the merger, an analysis of the potential effect of the merger on the structure of the market, and an analysis of the impact of the structural changes on the functioning of the market.

Interestingly, the *Guidelines I* have abandoned the *Best Practices*' recommendation of a dominance test.[79] The opinion expressed in *Best Practices* is that the substantial reduction of the competition test is unsuitable for new competition law authorities who might not be able to handle the informational and analytical demands crucial to the use of this test. The *Guidelines I* opt instead for a combining of both the US antitrust law which uses the term 'substantially to lessen competition'[80] (the SLC test) and the EU competition law which prefers the term 'significantly impede effective competition'[81] (the SIEC test). The inclusion of the US term is undoubtedly because the US introduced the first merger control in the world.[82] Under section 7 of the *Clayton Act*,[83] the appraisal criterion is whether a merger will result in a substantial lessening of competition. *The Horizontal Merger Guidelines of 1992*[84] later reiterate the SLC test and emphasise that the SLC test takes into consideration the competitive effect of merger and the resulting changes in the competitive equilibrium. The other party is the EU law which has shifted the focus of its merger control to the SIEC *test*. In this respect, the scope of application of the test is no longer limited to a consideration of dominant position. The focal point is now on the potential effect of the merger. In this respect, the merger control could be extended to oligopolistic markets. While observers agreed that the SIEC and the SLC tests have some striking similarities,[85] this is unsurprising. The adoption of the new EU test was considered to be a mere reorganisation of the original test of market dominance[86] partly to more resemble the SLC test.[87] It would appear that the change in the wording of the test does not completely alter the appraisal criteria in the merger control law[88] and the similarities between the SIEC and the SLC test remain, rendering the ASEAN's repetition of both tests redundant.

---

79. Jennifer Orr, et al., *Best Practices in the Introduction and Implementation of Competition Policy and Law in East Asia Summit Countries*, 3 (REPSF II Project No. 07/008 2008).
80. The Clayton Act, 15 USC. §§ 12-27, 29 USC. §§52-53 (2006).
81. Council Regulation (EC) No. 139/2004 on the Control of Concentrations between Undertakings Art. 2(2) (2004). The previous criterion of dominant position has been reduced to a mere example of significant impedance of effective competition. However, dominant position has not completely been erased from the *EUMR*. It still appears on the regulation as a prime indication of concentration between undertakings incompatible with the common market. *See* Art. 2(3) of the *EUMR*.
82. Anna-Louise Hinds, *The New EC Merger Regulation – The More Things Change the More They Stay the Same?*, 17 European Business Law Review (2006).
83. The Clayton Act, 15 USC. §§ 12-27, 29 USC. §§52-53 (2006).
84. US Department of Justice & Federal Trade Commission, *Horizontal Merger Guidelines* (1992 revised 1997).
85. Michael G. Egge, *The New EC Merger Regulation: Recipe for Profound Change or More of the Same?* (2004); Vijay S.V. Selvam, *The EC Merger Control Impasse: Is there a Solution to this Predicament*, 25 E.C.L.R. (2004).
86. Council Regulation (EC) No. 4064/89 on the Control of Concentrations between Undertakings (1989).
87. Alison Jones & Brenda Sufrin, *EU Competition Law: Text, Cases, and Materials*, 1182 (5th ed.,Oxford University Press 2014).
88. Sven B. Volcker, *Mind the Gap: Unilateral Effects Analysis Arrives in EC Merger Control*, 25 E.C.L.R. (2004).

It is impossible for the appraisal of mergers not to include an efficiency defence since mergers may improve efficiency or other socio-political goals. Such a defence would exempt mergers that substantially reduce the competition or significantly impede effective competition in the relevant market as this could result in economies of scale. Put another way, competition authorities need to do a trade-off between strict regulations and efficiency. The latter is of more importance since it offers greater social gains in term of economic growth and eventual consumer welfare. In practice, however, this balancing approach is harder to execute. The difficulties have to do with the analysis of the potential efficiency that mergers could bring. Moreover, the balancing approach of the efficiency defence is not without flaws. It is inherently vague, giving competition authorities a large margin of flexibility and discretion in their analysis of mergers.[89] This flexibility would inevitably threaten legal certainty. The efficiency test can also be burdensome for the competition authorities of newly developed competition law regimes who often lack the necessary experience and resources to prove efficiency.[90]

The balancing approach figured in the *Guidelines I* which disclose that:

> AMSs may also set up a procedure to consider granting exemptions or exclusions to certain agreements and conduct which have significant countervailing benefits, such as contributing to or improving the production or distribution of goods and services, or promoting technical or economic progress, while allowing consumers a fair share of the resulting benefit. The exemptions may be allowed only to the extent that is appropriate and indispensable to reach their intended aims and should not afford the undertakings concerned the possibility of eliminating competition in respect of a substantial part of the goods or services in question.[91]

It is unclear whether the ASEAN has taken into consideration the difficulties of analysing efficiency gains with the crippling lack of resources within the AMSs when including the efficiency defence. Excluding the efficiency test from the merger control provisions is not unheard off. In fact, the Baltic countries, recognising the insurmountable difficulty this task would pose for their inexperienced authorities, decided to exclude the balancing approach from their competition laws.[92]

[2] The Control Exercised by the National Competition Authority

The ASEAN cannot support the existence of a central mechanism in charge of handling mergers with a regional dimension. Therefore, the task is exclusively under the discretion of each AMS's national competition authority. The merger control relies largely on structural metrics to establish a presumption of anticompetitive pricing

89. Philip Lowe, *The Substantive Standard for Merger Control, and the Treatment of Efficiencies in Merger Analysis: An EU Perspective* (2002).
90. Jurgita Malinauskaite, *Efficiency Tests in the Merger Control Regimes of the Baltic Countries: Myth or Reality*, 18 International Company and Commercial Law Review (2007).
91. ASEAN Secretariat, *ASEAN Regional Guidelines on Competition Policy*, Art. 3.5.3 (2010).
92. Jurgita Malinauskaite, *Efficiency Tests in the Merger Control Regimes of the Baltic Countries: Myth or Reality*, 18 International Company and Commercial Law Review (2007).

emerging.[93] The control can be either structural or behavioural. Structural control is a one-time measure that seeks to restore or maintain the competitive structure of the market.[94] Since by nature, mergers affect the structure of the relevant market, it has been widely acknowledged that the control should also be structural, such as divestiture of a stand-alone business.[95] It is no coincidence that the most common form of structural remedy is divestiture.[96] On the other hand, behavioural control is an ongoing measure that seeks to regulate or contain the behaviours of the concerned undertaking.[97] It may include promises by the parties to abstain from certain commercial behaviour.[98] It has been suggested that structural control might be of limited effectiveness in small market economies and behavioural commitments should be used instead as a more viable alternative.[99] Nonetheless, behavioural control must be exercised cautiously by new competition authorities, since their unpreparedness or lack of expertise in the implementation of a behavioural remedy could jeopardise the effectiveness of the chosen remedy.[100]

The *Guidelines I* advise the AMSs to equip their national competition authorities with the power to decide, notwithstanding the power to authorise the merger, 'to stop the merger or, as part of the clearance, impose conditions on or require commitments from the merging enterprises to address any competition concerns arising from the merger'.[101] In this way, the national competition authorities exercise three distinctive powers: the power of pure and simple authorisation; the power of conditional authorisation; and the power of refusal. These contain both structural and behavioural remedies. The three powers are a straightforward reiteration of Articles 8 (1), (2) and (3) of the *EUMR*. It would seem that the ASEAN readily applies the pre-merger control regimes, following the examples of most competition law jurisdictions in the world.[102] There is no mention of the possibility of post-merger control whereby the competition authority controls a merger transaction after its conclusion in the *Guidelines I*. Only a few regimes use this method because of significant legal uncertainty for the undertakings concerned and the high cost of untangling merged undertaking should the transaction reveals to be anticompetitive.[103]

93. A. E. Rodriguez & Ashok Menon, *The Limits of Competition Policy: The Shortcomings of Antitrust in Developing and Reforming Economies*, 90 (Kluwer Law International 2010).
94. Competition Commission, *Merger Remedies: Competition Commission Guidelines* (2008).
95. Alexandr Svetlicinii & Külliki Lugenberg, *Merger Remedies in a Small Market Economy: The Estonian Experience*, E.C.L.R. (2012).
96. Commission Notice on Remedies Acceptable under Council Regulation (EEC) No. 4064/89 and under Commission Regulation (EC) No. 447/98, para. 13 (2001).
97. Competition Commission, *Merger Remedies: Competition Commission Guidelines* (2008).
98. *Commission Decision of 13 October 1999 Declaring a Concentration to be Compatible with the Common Market and the EEA Agreement (Telia/Telenor)*, COMP/M.1439 (1999).
99. Michal S. Gal, *Size Does Matter: The Effects of Market Size on Optimal Competition Policy*, 74 S. Cal. L. Rev. (2001).
100. Alexandr Svetlicinii & Külliki Lugenberg, *Merger Remedies in a Small Market Economy: the Estonian Experience*, E.C.L.R. (2012).
101. ASEAN Secretariat, *ASEAN Regional Guidelines on Competition Policy*, Art. 3.4.4 (2010).
102. Katri Paas-Mohando, *Choice of Merger Notification System for Small Economies*, 34 E.C.L.R. (2013).
103. *Ibid.* (identified Russia and Korea as the regimes which use post-merger notification system for certain merger transactions).

The pre-merger notification process has been identified as a crucial component of the pre-merger control exercised by the national competition authorities.[104] It is important to include a pre-merger notification system into a jurisdiction, not least because the majority of merger control regimes have it[105] but also because obtaining the competition authority clearance to proceed with the merger before its realisation could lessen the business cost. The pre-merger notification system can be divided into two categories: mandatory and voluntary notifications. The mandatory notification system is the most commonly used. In this instance, undertakings concerned must notify the competition authority prior to the completion of the merger in question when certain criteria are met. The criteria often constitute worldwide or national turnover threshold. In a voluntary notification system, undertakings are not obliged to notify the competition authority of their merger plan. However, they face the risk of *post-merger* investigation by the competition authority. This method can be difficult and costly to implement since it involves undoing the already merged undertaking.

With regard to the ASEAN approach, the *Guidelines I* do not decide between voluntary or mandatory notification, leaving the choice instead to respective AMSs:

- A specific procedure may be established by which the competition regulatory body is tasked to assess mergers, following a (voluntary or mandatory) notification by the merging undertakings, or otherwise following a complaint or by their own motion. [For this purpose],
- 'Mandatory notification' prevents the undertakings from implementing the transaction until they have received merger clearance from the competition regulatory body. This helps to avoid a situation where anti-competitive mergers have to subsequently be subject to difficult and costly de-concentration measures imposed by the competition regulatory body.
- 'Voluntary notification' allows businesses to do their own merger self-assessment, to decide if they should notify the competition regulatory body to clear the merger. It helps to reduce business costs while not impeding competition regulatory body's authority to investigate any merger which raises competition concerns.[106]

Before deciding on this important matter, the AMSs should first take into consideration the high cost of imposing mandatory notification as well as their competition authority's ability to process notified merger plans within the legal time limit. Nonetheless, the Australian experience has proven that the outcomes of both mandatory and voluntary notifications do not substantially differ since most notified merger cases do not raise competition concerns.[107] On the other hand, voluntary notification leads to substantial lessening of the cost for both the competition authority

---

104. A. E. Rodriguez & Ashok Menon, *The Limits of Competition Policy: The Shortcomings of Antitrust in Developing and Reforming Economies*, 90 (Kluwer Law International 2010).
105. Paas-Mohando, *Choice of Merger Notification System for Small Economies*, 34 E.C.L.R. (2013).
106. ASEAN Secretariat, *ASEAN Regional Guidelines on Competition Policy*, Art. 3.4.2 (2010).
107. Chongwoo Choe & Chander Shekhar, *Compulsory or Voluntary Pre-merger Notification?: A Theoretical and Empirical Analysis*, http://www.iss.u-tokyo.ac.jp/~matsumur/CCNote68.pdf (accessed 26 Sept. 2014).

and the undertakings concerned.[108] It was further suggested that since most mergers do not raise any competition concerns, it would be more cost effective, especially for small market economies, to favour the voluntary notification system provided that it is accompanied by the proper design of the deterrent mechanisms and enforcement measures.[109]

The mandatory merger notification is usually triggered by the size of the sale or assets of the firms involved in transaction, the size of the combined market shares of the merger participants, or the size of the pre-acquisition market share of any on party.[110] Authorities do not need to be notified of any mergers that fall below the level of the threshold. Generally, because the calculation of an undertaking's market share is subject to more manipulation than that of the transaction size and thus prone to more mistakes, most competition regimes resort to the transaction size threshold.[111] When adopting a merger threshold, new competition law regimes need to be aware of the resources available to their competition authorities. If the threshold is set too low, there is the chance that the agency would be inundated with reviewable cases, including those with no conceivable competition significance, without the means to properly enforce the merger assessment. In contrast, establishing an excessively high threshold is deemed to be the only appropriate measure for newly installed competition agencies on which to focus their limited resources.[112]

In the case of the ASEAN:

> [The] AMSs may establish that only mergers above a given threshold shall (or may) be notified to - and approved by - the competition regulatory body. Thresholds may refer, for instance, to the (national and/or worldwide) turnover of the merging parties in the last completed financial year, market shares of the parties or a combination of both criteria. Thresholds may be adjusted when necessary to take account, for example, of increases in the GDP deflator index. AMSs may also consider introducing a standstill provision by which mergers, which are subject to the competition regulatory body evaluation, cannot be implemented before they are approved.[113]

Accordingly, the thresholds may be fixed according to national and/or worldwide turnover of the merging parties in the last completed financial year, and the market shares of the parties or a combination of both criteria. Inexplicably, the more reliable criterion of transaction size is not included in this case. However, the *Guidelines I* admit that the threshold may also be adjusted when necessary, for example, in order to take into account, but not limited to, the increase in the GDP deflator index.

108. *Ibid.*
109. Paas-Mohando, *Choice of Merger Notification System for Small Economies*, 34 E.C.L.R. (2013).
110. William E. Kovacic, *Merger Enforcement in Transition: Antitrust Controls on Acquisitions in Emerging Economies*, 66 U. Cin. L. Rev. (1998).
111. A. E. Rodriguez & Ashok Menon, *The Limits of Competition Policy: The Shortcomings of Antitrust in Developing and Reforming Economies*, 90 (Kluwer Law International 2010).
112. William E. Kovacic, *Merger Enforcement in Transition: Antitrust Controls on Acquisitions in Emerging Economies*, 66 U. Cin. L. Rev. (1998).
113. ASEAN Secretariat, *ASEAN Regional Guidelines on Competition Policy*, Art. 3.4.3 (2010).

§4.05 CONCLUSION

This chapter has examined the ASEAN's approach to substantive competition law. It has revealed that most of the work has concentrated on supporting the installation of national competition laws. To this effect, the ASEAN's contribution is in the form of various conferences and publications aimed at connecting the AMSs with global attitudes to competition law. It has always been mindful of both its own limitations, in particular the absence of a centralised organ with allocated power necessary to impose a model, as well as differing AMSs' specificities. This was translated into an offering of collections of traditional and globally accepted competition rules that could be adapted according to each AMS's needs. The ASEAN seems more preoccupied with gaining acceptance and inviting more participation from its own AMSs. It is now an opportune time to question whether the approach taken will lead the ASEAN to its ambitious goal of harmonising competition law to complement its regional economic integration.

In this respect, the process of soft harmonisation as a non-binding multilateralism which relies on the power of persuasion, as described in Chapter 2, most resembles the ASEAN's effort in competition law and policy thus far. This process responds well to the ASEAN's inherent limitations and ambition. The ASEAN has never proposed a framework unique to its vision; it is instead content with gathering accepted up-to-date best practices in the field of competition law and policy accompanied by a large margin of discretion that the AMSs' competition authorities could enjoy. At the same time, it also inherits all the shortcomings of soft harmonisation. The AMSs are free, and to a certain degree encouraged, to neglect the ASEAN's approach as assembled in the *Guidelines* in favour of their own particular necessities or situations. In the end, one is left to wonder whether the path of soft harmonisation chosen by the ASEAN does not further widen the divergence between members instead of bridging it.

By electing the soft harmonisation approach with respect to the competition regulatory design to pursue its economic integration goal, the ASEAN has retained its uniqueness in comparison with other regional experiences. It is the only regional organisation with an integration goal not to undertake a unified and centralised approach to substantive design. Conversely, its approach more resembles the NAFTA's free trade approach.

CHAPTER 5
The ASEAN Institutional System

'Jurisdictions need sound and thoughtful institutional design that will best help advance their competition law and policy.'[1] Yet, the subject of institutional design is often relegated to 'a relatively obscure corner'[2] with more attention paid to substantive policy development. It was argued that 'if theory is not grounded in the engineering of effective institutions, it will not work in practice'.[3] Put differently, if the construction of an institutional structure for competition is not appropriate to house substantive interiors, the entire policy could collapse.

Accompanying the previous chapter on the ASEAN's approach to substantive competition law through the process of soft harmonisation, this chapter turns to the institutional design of competition law which housed the process of regional harmonisation. The ASEAN's guidance in the field of institutional design appears more developed than that of the substantive law. Indeed, the *Guidelines I* introduce the concept of institutional building that is impressively expanded in the *Guidelines II*, including suggestions on institutional design, attributes and competencies, core values and organisational structure. If the ASEAN refrains from entering into details about substantive law, such restraint is not present in its institutional building recommendations. It is evident that the issue of substantive law and institutional design do not receive equal treatment. Such a cautious approach regarding substantive law is inexplicable since both the areas of substantive law and institutional construction involve a high degree of national choice placed under the discretion of the AMSs.

Five factors influencing the design of regional competition structures have been unearthed: 'the number of states and the level of integration of the regional market; the fluidity of trade between member states; the respective institutional capacities of the member states and the Union; the existence or lack of a competition culture in the

1. Eleanor M. Fox, *Antitrust and Institutions: Design and Change*, 41 Loy. U. Chi. L. J. (2010).
2. Peter H. Schuck, *Is a Competent Federal Government Becoming Oxymoronic?*, 77 George Washington L. Rev. (2009).
3. William E. Kovacic, *The Institutions of Antitrust Law: How Structure Shapes Substance*, 110 Mich. L. Rev. (2012).

member states; and the time dimension'.[4] The ASEAN is a regional organisation composed of ten neighbouring states in Southeast Asia with the ambitious goal of economic integration. The current level of trade between the AMSs is not high but it is believed that market integration could help its fluidity. The competition culture of the AMSs is not firmly established and the AMSs have varying degrees of success in the enforcement of competition law. Furthermore, the institutional capacities attached to the ASEAN are fragile due to the principle of non-interference between the AMSs, which lies at the heart of the organisation, and the lack of a centralised mechanism. Since the ASEAN cannot support the existence of a central mechanism in charge of handling regional competition law issues, the task is therefore exclusively under the discretion of each AMS's competition authority. Facing its limitations, the ASEAN endeavours instead to support each AMS in its establishment and modernisation of a national competition institution. The only regional competition structure available to the ASEAN is the AEGC which, as the name would suggest, is merely a network of national competition authorities. Despite having an ambitious goal of introducing a single market that fully integrates all the AMSs, the ASEAN is deprived of a centralised decision-making ability. Consequently, in its current state it is legally impossible for the ASEAN to gain a regional authority in charge of competition law. In relation to the inevitable regional issues of competition law that are bound to emerge during the regional economic integration, the ASEAN resorts instead to extraterritoriality and regional cooperation.

§5.01 THE ASEAN'S MODEL FOR NATIONAL COMPETITION AUTHORITY

The design of a competition law institution is compared to the design of a house:

> Good institutional design is a critical component of good competition policy and competition law enforcement. The design of the institutions is like the design of a house: it must facilitate life within the house. Good institutional design takes account of the family's values and empowers life within its walls. Designs cannot be conjured in the abstract; they must fit the family that lives in the house, its aspirations, possibilities, and practical limits. Therefore, the good architect lives with the family before conceptualizing the design.[5]

It follows that the design of a competition structure must not be undertaken in the abstract and must take into consideration the specificities, the goals, the capacities and the restrictions of the country or the region. In other words, it is the context that shapes the design of the institution. Consequently, the perfect internationally agreed template for competition institutional design does not exist. The ASEAN demonstrates its awareness of this aspect when it declares that 'there is no one-size-fits-all answer and

4. Bakhoum & Molestina, *Institutional Coherence and Effectiveness of a Regional Competition Policy: the Case of the West African Economic and Monetary Union (WAEMU)*, *in* Competition Policy and Regional Integration in Developing Countries (Josef Drexl, et al. eds., Edward Elgar Publishing 2012).
5. Eleanor M. Fox, *Antitrust and Institutions: Design and Change*, 41 Loy. U. Chi. L. J. (2010).

the optimal solution must be coherent with the country's general legal framework and regulatory history. The solution can vary from country to country and even across industries within the same country.'[6] Furthermore, many new competition jurisdictions faced daunting challenges in building the institutional foundations for successful implementation.[7] The challenges are fuelled principally by resource restrictions, namely the financial investment by the state, limited knowledge, lack of personnel, and lack of experience. In this regard, the ASEAN faces similar challenges to many developing economies in their construction of a regional framework of substantive competition law.

[A] Considerations for an Effective Framework

It is important to first recognise the qualities and attributes that a competition authority should possess before proceeding to the appropriate design of institution as envisioned by the ASEAN. Generally, the values include independence, accountability, expertise, transparency, due regard for confidentiality, efficiency, due process, and predictability.[8] The *Guidelines I* state that the responsibilities of the competition agency are: to implement and enforce national competition law; to interpret and elaborate; to advocate; to provide advice; and to act as the representative of the country in international competition matters.[9] The *Guidelines II* further expand that in order to carry out these responsibilities, it is fundamental for a competition agency to possess the following attributes and competencies: independence, accountability, fairness, transparency, confidentiality, effective powers, influence, resources, and cooperation skills.[10] Among these attributes and competencies, independence is given an apparent priority. What is noteworthy in this institutional building section is the ASEAN's adoption of a firmer language. The term *should* is used deliberately when discussing the attributes of national competition authorities.

[1] The Prevalence of Independence

It is accepted knowledge that the principle of independence is at the core of competition authorities.[11] Regardless, jurisdictions often differ in their formulation of independence. Ideally, competition agencies should be insulated from 'political and budgetary

6. ASEAN Secretariat, *Guidelines on Developing Core Competencies in Competition Policy and Law for ASEAN*, 31 (2012).
7. William E. Kovacic, *Extraterritoriality, Institutions, and Convergence in International Competition Policy*, 97 Am. Soc'y Int'lL. Proc. (2003).
8. Michael J. Trebilcock & Edward M. Iacobucci, *Designing Competition Law Institutions*, 25 World Competition (2002).
9. ASEAN Secretariat, *ASEAN Regional Guidelines on Competition Policy*, Art. 4.1.1 (2010).
10. ASEAN Secretariat, *Guidelines on Developing Core Competencies in Competition Policy and Law for ASEAN*, 36 (2012).
11. UNCTAD, *The Role of Competition Policy in Promoting Economic Development: The Appropriate Design and Effectiveness of Competition Law and Policy* (TD/RBP/CONF.7/3 2010).

interference'.[12] A competition authority is independent when it can exercise its decision-making power free from the influences of elected and non-elected officials or other subjects under the scope of competition law. It is believed that there is a direct correlation between an agency's independence and its improvement in enforcement.[13] It follows that independence merely serves to ensure objective functionality and effectiveness of a competition authority. Objectivity in this context could lead in turn to legal certainty in the competition enforcement of the agency.

The principle of independence in a competition agency is highly regarded by the ASEAN as evidenced by the fact that it is the most developed consideration in both *Guidelines*. The ASEAN categorises independence in two interlinked forms: financial and administrative independence. The *Guidelines I* suggest that the AMSs' competition regulatory body should be equipped with the necessary resources and legal powers to carry out their responsibilities.[14] In addition, the determination of the budget of the competition regulatory body should be free from political interference. The proposed method in achieving financial independence is to separate the competition authority's budget from other governmental functions, and then make the budget transparent to the public.[15] In practice, however, financial independence is but an illusion. Even with the suggested separation, the competition agency's budget is still generally controlled by the legislature which possesses the power to alter it if it is dissatisfied with the performance of the agency. The competition agency could resort to self-generated income, for example through the fees for merger notification, but it is susceptible to economic growth ('[a]mid a recession, the filings and the funding diminish dramatically').[16] Hence, this method of assuring income might not be sufficiently reliable to sustain the agency. The other form of independence is administrative. The *Guidelines I* suggest that the AMSs accord the competition authority as much administrative independence as necessary and as possible in order to avoid the political influence.[17] In order to achieve this aim, the *Guidelines I* recommend the appointment of independent commission members in charge of the competition regulatory body with a fixed term of reasonable duration without the possibility of being dismissed. The process of nomination and appointment is left to the discretion of the AMSs. In contrast, the World Bank has a more restrictive view of autonomy since it delimits the notion to independence with regards to the government.[18] This means that members of the competition agency should be appointed by a committee or the parliament instead of the head of

12. R. Shyam Khemani & Mark A. Dutz, *The Instruments of Competition Policy and Their Relevance for Economic Development, in* Regularities Policies and Reform: A Comparative Perspective (Claudio R. Frischtak ed., World Bank 1995).
13. Tay-Cheng Ma, *Competition Authority Independence, Antitrust Effectiveness, and Institutions,* 30 Int'l Rev. L. & Econ. (2010).
14. ASEAN Secretariat, *ASEAN Regional Guidelines on Competition Policy*, Art. 4.1.3 (2010).
15. *Ibid.*, at Art. 4.3.3.
16. William E. Kovacic & David A. Hyman, *Competition Agency Design: What's on the Menu?*, 8 European Competition Journal (2012).
17. ASEAN Secretariat, *ASEAN Regional Guidelines on Competition Policy*, Art. 4.3.3 (2010).
18. World Bank, *World Development Report 2002: Building Institutions for Markets*, 142 (Oxford University Press 2002).

state. Until then, it seemed that the ASEAN broadly followed agreement by consensus on the principle of independence.

Two years later, the *Guidelines II* adopt a sterner position than the *Guidelines I*. The *Guidelines II* boldly announce that '[t]o be effective, a [competition authority] should be independent. Especially it should be free from both political and business influence'.[19] In this regard, a checklist is developed as follows:

- The [competition authority] should be a distinct statutory authority, free from day-to-day ministerial control;
- There should be an appointment according to well-defined professional criteria and with the involvement of both the executive and the legislative branches of the government;
- Any Head (or equivalent) and members of the adjudicating body should be appointed for a fixed-term, with a prohibition on their removal except for clearly pre-defined due cause with the appropriate judicial review;
- The term periods of the members of the (collegiate) adjudicating body should be staggered (i.e. arranged in alternating or overlapping time periods);
- The [competition authority] should have an adequate and reliable source of funding;
- There should be adequate salary levels (e.g. through an exemption from civil service salary limits);
- The executive should be prevented from overturning the [competition agency's] decisions, or limiting the [competition authority's] power, unless as set out in clearly pre-defined exceptional instances.[20]

Nonetheless, the case for independence is not so straightforward for developing economies with a newly adopted competition law culture. In a country where competition law has been transplanted into an environment where the concept of competition was previously unknown, a competition authority without any link to other ministerial bodies is in danger of becoming an isolated institution, incapable of enforcing the competition statutes.[21] Being part of an influential Ministry can help boost the agency authority and aid in its actual enforcement against both private entities and other governmental bodies. The temporary inclusion of a competition authority within an influential Ministry is therefore a more attractive option for most of the AMSs during the early stages of competition enforcement.

Ideally, the competition authority should be independent of both political and financial pressure but remain accountable for the exercise of its powers and expenditure of public resources.[22] Accountability can be achieved in various ways. It can be exhibited through judicial review, the public control of financial resources, direct

19. ASEAN Secretariat, *Guidelines on Developing Core Competencies in Competition Policy and Law for ASEAN*, 36 (2012).
20. *Ibid.*
21. Marco Botta, *Fostering Competition Culture in the Emerging Economies: The Brazilian Experience*, 32 World Competition (2009).
22. William E. Kovacic & David A. Hyman, *Competition Agency Design: What's on the Menu?*, 8 European Competition Journal (2012).

nomination to the agency by executive branch or legislature or through the transparency of the agency. The choices made regarding accountability will inevitably affect the degree of independence of the authority.

According to the ASEAN, a competition authority should be accountable to the government and/or the legislator, the public, and the business community.[23] In this regard, an agency is held accountable for its decisions by every stakeholder. The *Guidelines II* give a comprehensive list describing measures that a competition authority could undertake in order to ensure its accountability:

> The competition law and [competition agency's] statutes should be published, clearly specifying the [agency's] duties, responsibilities, rights and obligations;
>
> Judicial review of the [competition authority's] decisions should be ensured ...;
>
> The [competition authority] should be requested to publish annual reports on its activities and establish a formal review of its performance by independent auditors, and/or an oversight committee of the legislature;
>
> Rules should be established for the removal of board members if they show evidence of misconduct or incompetence;
>
> All interested parties should be allowed to make submissions to the [competition authority] on matters under review;
>
> The [competition authority] should be mandated to publish its reasoned decisions.[24]

The viability of a judicial review as a means to increase a competition authority's accountability merits closer analysis. 'It is widely held that independent judicial review of the decisions of competition authorities, whether through the regular courts or through administrative tribunals, is desirable for the sake of the fairness and integrity of the decision-making process.'[25] Its importance is reflected in the inclusion of the right to appeal the competition agency's actions to the nation's judiciary by every competition law,[26] at least as prescribed within its procedures.

The *Guidelines I* recognise the role of the judiciary in the enforcement of competition law. The document proposes that the AMSs include both direct access to the judicial authority and the judicial review of administrative decisions in the enforcement process.[27] Regarding the judicial review, the *Guidelines I* give the AMSs two possible models: either an administrative appeal independent of the competition regulatory body or a common judicial authority.[28] The AMSs could choose to put the entire set of the competition authority's decisions under judicial review, or reserve it for substantive law or procedural law.[29] The *Guidelines II* later contradicted this suggestion and insist that it is crucial to introduce some limits to the judicial review to

23. ASEAN Secretariat, *Guidelines on Developing Core Competencies in Competition Policy and Law for ASEAN*, 36 (2012).
24. *Ibid.*, at 37.
25. UNCTAD, *Independence and Accountability of Competition Authorities* (TD/B/COM.2/CLP/67 2008).
26. A. E. Rodriguez & Ashok Menon, *The Limits of Competition Policy: The Shortcomings of Antitrust in Developing and Reforming Economies*, 113 (Kluwer Law International 2010).
27. ASEAN Secretariat, *ASEAN Regional Guidelines on Competition Policy*, Art. 7.1.4 (2010).
28. *Ibid.*, at Art. 4.3.2.
29. *Ibid.*, at Art. 7.1.4.2.

allow some degree of deference to the competition authority's decisions.[30] It is suggested that the appeal be confined to a consideration of the law, including a review of the procedures. The judicial review is intended to prevent the court from substituting the competition authority's decisions or undermining them. The role of the judiciary is simply to ascertain whether the competition authority has abused its discretionary power. In this context, the judge must accept the facts as found by the authority.

There are some lingering doubts about whether the judiciary in developing economies is capable of employing proper economic analyses of the underlying competition principles or an understanding of the business practices that may have arisen in the case.[31] The complexity of business practices challenged by the competition authority in the practice of competition law demands considerable experience as well as some sophistication in- and knowledge of economics. Moreover, in newly developed competition regimes with few enforcement decisions, it is impossible for the judiciary to refer to past case law and therefore a challenge for the judiciary to pass a precise and accurate competition law-related judgment. Rodriguez and Menon proposed overcoming the lack of expertise by relying on the adversarial court procedure where independent competition law experts are invited to give testimony.[32] The testimony is especially useful when experts disagree, thus providing the judiciary with well-rounded information.

[2] Other Considerations

The *Guidelines I* also recognise fairness, equality, transparency, consistency, non-discriminatory treatment under the law,[33] confidentiality of commercially sensitive information and details of an individual's private affairs,[34] and due process[35] among the second-tiered values. With the exception of equality, the *Guidelines II* repeat all considerations given in the previous list.[36] Among the secondary considerations, transparency is prominent. The importance of maintenance and public disclosure of a comprehensive and informative database on competition law enforcement cannot be underestimated.[37] Transparency encompasses enforcement standards and procedures

30. ASEAN Secretariat, *Guidelines on Developing Core Competencies in Competition Policy and Law for ASEAN*, 42 (2012).
31. Sheth, *Formulating Antitrust Policy in Emerging Economies*, 86 Geo. L. J. (1997).
32. A. E. Rodriguez & Ashok Menon, *The Limits of Competition Policy: The Shortcomings of Antitrust in Developing and Reforming Economies*, 113 (Kluwer Law International 2010).
33. ASEAN Secretariat, *ASEAN Regional Guidelines on Competition Policy*, Art. 3.1.3 (2010).
34. *Ibid.*, at Art. 6.4.
35. *Ibid.*, at Ch. 7.
36. ASEAN Secretariat, *Guidelines on Developing Core Competencies in Competition Policy and Law for ASEAN*, 36 (2012).
37. William E. Kovacic, *Achieving Better Practices in the Design of Competition Policy Institutions*, 50 The Antitrust Bulletin (2005).

and the broader issue of the decision-making framework of the agency on various substantive antitrust issues.[38] This type of transparency could help inform the public of ongoing investigation, leading to better participation by the public and interested parties in the enforcement. By communicating detailed and useful information about the enforcement system, the competition authority could ensure better legal certainty. Nonetheless, limiting administrative discretion might be more feasible in a culture that has rules promoting transparency, fairness and suppression of corruption in public administration.[39] Many new and developing jurisdictions might not have such rules. Furthermore, an attempt at increased transparency could negatively impact on already scarce financial resources of the agency. However, the potential benefits of increased transparency, including greater predictability and accountability, for the agency should outweigh its cost.[40]

Transparency in the administration of competition law enforcement will always be in tension with confidentiality. Transparency includes the release of confidential information used by the competition agency in its case analysis, even if the analysis does not result in a decision.[41] Much of the information provided by involved parties, competitors, suppliers, and customers to the competition authority is of the sensitive nature. Making this type of information publicly available might damage their legitimate commercial interest affect the parties' cooperation in future cases.

It appears that each consideration interacts and sometimes contradicts the other. The trade-off of values is unavoidable. The balance of values is 'a quintessential polycentric and highly contestable exercise'[42] in which there is no singular model combination. Jurisdictions can simply make their choices dependent on the context surrounding their competition policy at the time. In this regard, the AMSs must proceed cautiously with their balancing of considerations relevant to the adoption of a national competition institution by taking into consideration the local political and economic context upon which the competition institution is to be constructed. Only then will the likelihood of achieving an effective institutional framework for the AMSs be possible.

[B] Institutional Models

The perfect model of competition law institution does not exist. Although there is a striking diversity in the design of competition institutions,[43] there are three accepted referential models: the bifurcated judicial model, the bifurcated agency model, and the

38. John M. Nannes, *Transparency in Federal Antitrust Enforcement Decisions: A Reaction to Professor Grimes*, 51 Buff. L. Rev. (2003).
39. William E. Kovacic, *Getting Started: Creating New Competition Policy Institutions in Transition Economies*, 23 Brook. J. Int'l L. (1997).
40. D. Daniel Sokol, *Designing Antitrust Agencies for More Effective Outcomes: What Antitrust Can Learn from Restaurant Guides*, 41 Loyola University Chicago Law Journal (2010).
41. Malcolm B. Coate, *Theory Meets Practice: Barriers to Entry in Merger Analysis* (2008).
42. Michael J. Trebilcock & Edward M. Iacobucci, *Designing Competition Law Institutions: Values, Structure, and Mandate*, 41 Loy. U. Chi. L.J. (2010).
43. The OECD thoroughly chronicles the different models adopted by countries in the OECD, *Countries Review of Competition Law*, http://www.oecd.org/regreform/sectors/countryreviewsofcompetitionpolicyframeworks.htm (accessed 11 Nov. 2017).

integrated agency model.[44] These models are based on how the three principal functions of competition enforcement (investigation, enforcement, and adjudication) are arranged. Nevertheless, the differences in experience do not necessarily imply significant differences in practical outcomes. The ASEAN readily adopts the three-model categorisation[45] but exhibits its preference for the integrated agency model.

[1] The Bifurcated Judicial Model

Under the bifurcated judicial model, the investigative and enforcement authorities are separated.[46] In addition, they must bring formal complaints before the court for remedial relief. The recourse to the judiciary helps elevate the accountability of this model while at the same time draws attention to its lack of expertise in the field of competition law. The model relies heavily on an effective judicial system. Thus, it would not be suitable for countries whose court is perceived to be 'corrupt and undependable'. [47] The bifurcated judicial model is particularly suitable for criminal offences since it ensures adequate standards of due process.While this model could strike a reasonable balance between transparency and respect of confidentiality, it will result in a higher cost of administrative process which might ultimately affect its efficiency. This model existed in Canada until the competition law reform in 1976 but continued with criminal matters under the Canada Competition Act[48] as the Bureau of Competition Policy.[49] It is currently the model followed by the US Department of Justice's Antitrust Division (DOJ). When initiating enforcement proceedings, the DOJ relies on federal courts to substantiate its views of the US antitrust policy.[50] While the Antitrust division can bring both criminal and civil cases before the court, only civil cases can be subjected to judicial appeal. It is noteworthy that in the US the bifurcated judicial model is accompanied by an integrated agency model in the form of the US Federal Trade Commission (FTC) and is complemented by an established system of private enforcement.[51]

Intriguingly, the ASEAN refers to the bifurcated judicial model as the adversarial judicial model. It is possible that the notion *adversarial* conveys the separation of organs and powers. According to the ASEAN, '[t]he adversarial judicial model requires

44. This is based on the three accepted referential models: the bifurcated judicial model, the bifurcated agency model, and the integrated agency model seen in Michael J. Trebilcock & Edward M. Iacobucci, *Designing Competition Law Institutions*, 25 World Competition (2002).
45. ASEAN Secretariat, *Guidelines on Developing Core Competencies in Competition Policy and Law for ASEAN*, 31 (2012).
46. Michael J. Trebilcock & Edward M. Iacobucci, *Designing Competition Law Institutions*, 25 World Competition (2002).
47. A. E. Rodriguez & Ashok Menon, *The Limits of Competition Policy: The Shortcomings of Antitrust in Developing and Reforming Economies*, 113 (Kluwer Law International 2010).
48. Canada Competition Act (RSC., 1985, c. C-34.) (1985).
49. Doern & Wilks, *Comparative Competition Policy: National Institutions in a Global Market*, 75 (Oxford University Press 1996).
50. *Ibid.*, at 47.
51. *Ibid.*, at 48.

the separation of the investigative and enforcement functions (entrusted to a specialised agency) and the adjudicating powers (entrusted to the law courts)'.[52] The *Guidelines II* subsequently discarded this model attesting that it was not suitable for the AMSs whose limited resources are better allocated to a united institution.[53]

[2] The Bifurcated Agency Model

The bifurcated agency model separates investigative and enforcement functions from the adjudicating function.[54] Separated specialised investigative and enforcement agencies bring competition complaint before specialised adjudicative agencies. This model relies on the division of agencies. On the surface, this model is designed to achieve a reasonable balance of the numerous values identified earlier in this chapter.[55] It ensures a high level of independence in the performance of the adjudicative function while ensuring some degree of accountability through the judicial appeal process. The proceedings are transparent with a reasonable degree of respect of confidentiality. However, as seen from the Canadian experience, the bifurcated agency model has failed to meet expectations.[56] First, a disappointing number of cases have been brought to the Competition Tribunal partly because of the preference for compliance over the enforcement approach by both the firms and the competition agencies.[57] It is possible this is to avoid high enforcement costs, both temporal and monetary, and the legal uncertainty compared with the compliance approach. Second, the Competition Tribunal is dominated by judicial members, thus undermining its own motive of a specialised adjudicative agency.[58]

As in the case of the bifurcated judicial model, the ASEAN elects to use the term *adversarial agency model*. However, the *Guidelines II* do not recommend the adversarial agency model.[59] The bifurcated models are not the preferred alternatives by competition law experts since 'wise designers would not design such a two-headed system from scratch'.[60]

52. ASEAN Secretariat, *Guidelines on Developing Core Competencies in Competition Policy and Law for ASEAN*, 31 (2012).
53. *Ibid.*, at 32.
54. Michael J. Trebilcock & Edward M. Iacobucci, *Designing Competition Law Institutions*, 25 World Competition (2002).
55. Michael J. Trebilcock & Edward M. Iacobucci, *Designing Competition Law Institutions: Values, Structure, and Mandate*, 41 Loy. U. Chi. L.J. (2010).
56. Doern & Wilks, *Comparative Competition Policy: National Institutions in a Global Market*, 77 (Oxford University Press 1996).
57. Michael J. Trebilcock & Edward M. Iacobucci, *Designing Competition Law Institutions: Values, Structure, and Mandate*, 41 Loy. U. Chi. L.J. (2010).
58. Doern & Wilks, *Comparative Competition Policy: National Institutions in a Global Market*, 77 (Oxford University Press 1996).
59. ASEAN Secretariat, *Guidelines on Developing Core Competencies in Competition Policy and Law for ASEAN*, 32 (2012).
60. Eleanor M. Fox, *Antitrust and Institutions: Design and Change*, 41 Loy. U. Chi. L. J. (2010).

[3] *The Integrated Agency Model*

With the integrated agency model, a single agency incorporates all the functions of investigation, enforcement, and adjudication.[61] This model offers a higher level of expertise since agency officials and commissioners are involved in all aspects of competition law on a daily basis. Naturally, this leads to more consistency throughout the process of competition proceedings. The agency undertakes the policy-making function through the adoption of guidelines and referential notices. The integrated agency model also yields a high level of accountability through its multi-member composition. Nonetheless, the integrated agency model has the potential to show partiality since all the competition law-related functions are concentrated in a single agency. This concern can easily be mitigated through the judicial review. The renowned examples of this model are the US FTC[62] and the EU Competition Commission.[63]

The *Guidelines II* evidently favour this model, referring to it as the 'inquisitorial model'.[64] The document draws attention to the fact that for competition law to be effective within a reasonable time, the AMSs need to efficiently allocate their limited resources to a single integrated organ.[65] Furthermore, since this is the model selected by more experienced competition regimes, the ASEAN felt reassured in travelling this path.[66]

§5.02 THE ASEAN COMPETITION LAW INSTITUTION

Conscious of its own institutional limitation, the ASEAN leaders readily endorsed the concept of a platform for competition law authorities. This platform was intended to be a network of authorities or agencies to serve on a forum to discuss and coordinate competition policies[67] as at the time there was no official ASEAN body for cooperative work on competition law and policy. Thus, the AEGC was established and serves as a network for authorities to exchange experience and institutional norms on relevant competition subjects. With the establishment of the AEGC, the ASEAN gained its first and only regional competition institution.

61. Michael J. Trebilcock & Edward M. Iacobucci, *Designing Competition Law Institutions*, 25 World Competition (2002).
62. Harry First, et al., *The United States: The Competition Law System and the Country's Norm, in* The Design of Competition Law Institutions: Global Norms, Local Choices (Eleanor M. Fox & Michael J. Trebilcock eds., Oxford University Press 2012).
63. Ioannis Lianos & Arianna Andreangeli, *The European Union: The Competition Law System and the Country's Norm, in* The Design of Competition Law Institutions: Global Norms, Local Choices (Eleanor M. Fox & Michael J. Trebilcock eds., Oxford University Press 2012).
64. ASEAN Secretariat, *Guidelines on Developing Core Competencies in Competition Policy and Law for ASEAN*, 32 (2012).
65. *Ibid.*, at 15.
66. *Ibid.*, at 32.
67. ASEAN Secretariat, *ASEAN Economic Community Blueprint*, 18 (2007).

The AEGC is regarded as a cooperation channel similar to the ICN and the OECD.[68] The similarity with competition networks like the ICN is easily observed since the AEGC shares the same composition consisting of competition authorities and the same mission of harmonisation of competition laws with the network forum. What is striking in this case is the omission of other forms of regional organisation, especially those with an economic integration structure, suggesting that the structure and role of the AEGC is not regarded as part of regional cooperation. Furthermore, the OECD has been strongly criticised for its restrictive membership; membership is reserved for developed economies[69] and its design does not include the intention to cooperate in the field of international competition law.[70] A comparison of the AEGC with the OECD is thus inappropriate. This section will instead draw a comparison with other regional cooperation organisations and the network dynamic.

The AEGC membership encompasses the AMSs' national competition authorities or agencies associated with competition policy enforcement. The use of 'expert' is a false denomination since it exclusively includes national competition authorities or related governmental officials. In this regard, private entities with knowledge and experience in the area are deliberately excluded. The AEGC is organised into five working groups that concentrate on pressing issues of competition law within the region: the establishment of the ASEAN regional guidelines; the handbook of competition policy; capacity building; and regional competition advocacy. Each working group is supported by different AMSs on a rotating basis. The rotating chairmanship of each working group reflects the chairmanship of the ASEAN Secretariat. It is possible that this is to factor in the ASEAN's operational financing challenge and to encourage better participation from the host members.

In its own words, the AEGC is a network of competition authorities concentrating on competition advocacy, aiding the AMSs with their construction of national competition law, and providing a networking forum among the AMSs as well as with external entities. The use of the word *socialisation* is certainly cogent in this instance since it demonstrates a deviation from the purpose of coordination as appeared in the *Blueprint*.[71] It is essentially a networking organ concentrating on assisting the AMSs in their development of competition laws. This is echoed in the activities which strongly recommend conferences and workshops with foreign partners in a bid to provide foreign technical assistance.

Most noteworthy in the functioning of the AEGC is the absence of the peer review system. In the voluntary peer review process, countries are free to submit their competition law regimes to the scrutiny of their peers without any obligation to

68. The chairman of Australia's Competition and Consumer Commission's, Rod Sim, speech at the inaugural GCR Asia Law Leaders conference can be found at Global Competition Review, *ACCC's Sims Pushes for More Regional Cooperation*, http://www.globalcompetitionreview.com/news/article/31471/acccs-sims-pushes-regional-cooperation (accessed 13 Nov. 2017).
69. David Gerber, *Global Competition: Law, Markets and Globalisation*, 88 (Oxford University Press 2010).
70. Nathalie Jalabert-Doury, Les Instruments de Coopération Plurilatéraux et Multilatéraux de Soft Law Élaborés par l'OCDE (2007).
71. ASEAN Secretariat, *ASEAN Economic Community Blueprint*, Art. 41 (2007).

implement the recommendations given during the review process. Scrutiny of any nation's competition enforcement regime should be undertaken regularly. 'Every jurisdiction at regular intervals should undertake a basic evaluation of the effectiveness of its competition policy institutions.'[72] Conducting peer reviews of national competition laws and policies is regarded as the key function for both the OECD and the UNCTAD. Through the peer reviews, multilateral organisations evaluate competition law regimes and recommend how best to increase their effectiveness. The reviews are usually thorough and deal with both regulatory and structural issues. In the OECD, the review prepared by its internal staff is presented to the OECD members or the Global Forum on Competition. During the presentation, participating countries are encouraged to comment, and the target country is welcome to answer questions and explain its policy. While there is no legal obligation to implement the recommendations, there is encouragement for countries to make legitimate domestic change. The reviews are taken seriously and are the object of national public debates. A negative peer review from the OECD members would imply a need for domestic change or risk losing face.[73] It follows that peer reviews can be used to broker domestic changes to the law. While the peer review lacks binding obligations, peer pressure compensates for this and acts as a strong motivation to change. The UNCTAD has a peer review system similar to that of the OECD. In this case, peer reviews are conducted by different competition experts who provide an objective assessment of a competition law regime to identify its shortcomings. They propose suggestions and offer technical assistance when needed. The UNCTAD peer review exercise is unique in its development perspective and its rich experience in working with developing economies. The AEGC's omission of such a beneficial function would eventually reduce its importance to a mere 'talking-shop'[74] focusing more on discussion than productive work. However, the absence of the peer review exercise is not the only difference separating the AEGC from the UNCTAD and the OECD. Notwithstanding the composition which focuses on geographic proximity in Southeast Asia, the AEGC is distinctively dissimilar to the OECD and the UNCTAD due to its integration mission whereas both the OECD and the UNCTAD aim to promote policies that will improve social and economic well-being.

As a communication forum exclusively related to competition policy within the regional integration structure, it is difficult to compare the AEGC with other institutions. In contrast to other regional organisations, the AEGC as the ASEAN's sole regional organ relating to competition policy is not equipped with the power to enforce or monitor the AMSs' enforcement of the law. Yet, the AEGC is expected to act as the harbinger of the harmonisation of the AMSs' competition laws. It is possible that the AEGC shares similarities with the network forum, in particular, the ICN. Both are networks comprising competition authorities, although in the case of the ICN not

72. William E. Kovacic, *Achieving Better Practices in the Design of Competition Policy Institutions*, 50 The Antitrust Bulletin (2005).
73. Maher M. Dabbah, *International and Comparative Competition Law* (Cambridge University Press 2010).
74. Philip Marsden, *Acta Non Verba: 'Talking Shop', Don't Become Another Talking Shop, in* The International Competition Network at Ten: Origins, Accomplishments and Aspirations (Paul Lugard ed., Hart Publishing 2011).

exclusively so, who are not representatives of their states. They share the same objective of better harmonisation of competition laws between members through discussion. It is within the membership requirement where they diverge since the AEGC is exclusively reserved for the AMSs and therefore has to serve the regional integration aim of the ASEAN. There have been concerns that the function of the AEGC and the ICN may overlap. However, the AEGC could act as a complementary institution by providing a more comfortable socialisation platform for the AMSs with reference to the fact that there is under participation from developing economies in the ICN. Regardless of its potential, the AEGC does not officially count the ICN among its external partners, although some AMSs do.[75] The AEGC is also different from the ECN, another networking group within the regional integration structure. The only similarity shared with the ECN is that it is a network platform for competition authorities in the construction of regional economic integration. Both organisations differ greatly in their objectives. The AEGC is not constructed to aid better relations with the central competition enforcement organ since the ASEAN simply does not have one.

In conclusion, the AEGC is a distinctive regional competition institution in its organisation and role. It is the sole competition policy organ for regional economic integration without the ability to either enforce or monitor law enforcement by the Member States. In this regard, it is unlike other regional competition-related organs and more resembles a competition law network at international level. Nonetheless, it is not without its virtue. One of the main factors explaining the failure cooperation between competition law authorities is their mistrust of each other.[76] Thus, a forum reuniting different national competition authorities may be the only occasion when they can meet each other to facilitate future day-to-day cooperation.[77] Though the effect of such a forum is not immediate, general benefits derived from it should not be easily discarded. While the AEGC may lack the common attributes of other regional competition organs and have questionable measures to realise regional harmonisation, its communication forum service is unquestionably useful for the AMSs in their first endeavour to regional integration.

§5.03 SOLUTIONS FOR REGIONAL COMPETITION ISSUES

As a single market, regional and transnational issues of competition law are certain to arise, the ASEAN is quick to recommend a national authority model for its Member States potentially to compensate for its own lack of a centralised institution. Indeed, the ASEAN only has the AEGC as its competition-related internal organ. The obvious

75. ASEAN Competition Policy and Law, *Regional ASEAN-Level Cooperation with External Partners*, http://www.aseancompetition.org/cooperation/regional-asean-level-cooperation-external-partners (accessed 19 Feb. 2015). The list includes Australia, New Zealand, and Germany.
76. Marco Botta, *The Cooperation between the Competition Authorities of the Developing Countries: Why Does It Not Work? Case Study on Argentina and Brazil*, 5 Comp. L. Rev. (2009). (The other factor is the lack of resources to realise the cooperation.)
77. Russell W. Damtoft & Ronan Flanagan, *The Development of International Networks in Antitrust*, 43 The International Lawyer (2009).

discrepancy between substantive and institutional designs warrants a deeper study into how the ASEAN resolves regional competition law issues.

The internationalisation of markets gave rise to global competition problems such as the disconnection between anti-dumping laws and predatory pricing, jurisdictional gaps allowing export cartels, parochial use of measures that immunise private action, and the lack of a coherent view of world competition and trade and competition problems.[78] Having an effective competition law regime is important to address the issue of cross-border competition dispute, in particular, since international cartels are more likely to have significant economic effect to trade in developing economies.[79] Yet, developing economies rarely apply their laws to such conduct.[80] The importance is intensified in the context of a regional integrated market where cross-border disputes are unavoidable. In its pursuit of a regional economic integration, the ASEAN needs a mechanism to address foreign or national conduct with anticompetitive consequences for the region.

If the ASEAN had set its sight on the creation of regional economic integration, it failed, however, to foresee the necessity for a mechanism to deal with the inevitable competition issues at regional level as became evident in 2013, when it was noted that the ASEAN did not have an appropriate mechanism to deal with competition-related cross-border disputes.[81] That assessment is still applicable today. The *Guidelines I* suggest resolving regional competition infringements through the extraterritorial application of national competition law[82] or through regional cooperation,[83] while the *Guidelines II* remain silent on this matter, preferring instead to concentrate solely on national institutional building. The ASEAN's choice to make extraterritoriality and regional cooperation equal alternatives to compensate for its lack of a central mechanism is peculiar considering that cooperation is usually regarded as the measure to curb the effects of the unilateral assertion of national law presented in the principle of extraterritoriality.[84] Nonetheless, on the scale of global competition law, the use of extraterritoriality in combination with cooperation are regarded as the most visible and effective answer to international anticompetitive practice.[85]

78. Eleanor M. Fox & Janusz A. Ordover, *Internationalising Competition Law to Limit Parochial State and Private Action: Moving towards the Vision of World Welfare,* 24 Int'l Bus. Law. (1996).
79. Margaret Levenstein & Valerie Y. Suslow, *Contemporary International Cartels and Developing Countries: Economic Effects and Implications for Competition Policy,* 71 Antitrust L.J. (2004).
80. Michal S. Gal, *Antitrust in a Globalized Economy: The Unique Enforcement Challenges Faced by Small and Developing Jurisdictions,* 33 Fordham Int'l L.J. (2009).
81. McEwin's testimony appeared in Faaez Samadi, *Convergence Issues Loom Large for ASEAN,* Global Competition Review (2013).
82. ASEAN Secretariat, *ASEAN Regional Guidelines on Competition Policy,* Art. 5.1.3.2 (2010).
83. *Ibid.*, at Art. 10.2.1.4.
84. Damien Geradin, et al., *Extraterritoriality, Comity and Cooperation in EU Competition Law, in* Cooperation, Comity, and Competition Policy (Andrew T. Guzman ed., Oxford University Press 2010).
85. Bruno Zanettin, *Cooperation between Antitrust Agencies at the International Level,* 2 (Hart Publishing 2002).

[A] Extraterritoriality

Historically, the foremost solution to solving the problem of global anticompetitive practice has been to extend the scope of national law by applying it extraterritorially. The ASEAN advised the AMSs to include a provision on the extraterritorial application of national competition law in the *Guidelines I*.[86] This particular recommendation subsequently disappeared from the *Guidelines II*, ostensibly because of the focus on competition institutional building. There are implications of this simple suggestion, although appearing only once, for the regional economic integration ambitions of the ASEAN. By definition, there is a discernible conflict between extraterritoriality as an expression of the unilateral approach of competition law and the regional approach of the ASEAN. It is difficult to understand how promoting this unilateral approach could help the ASEAN achieve its regional integration goal.

[1] Understanding Extraterritoriality of Competition Law

As a result of globalisation, physical conduct in one country could have harmful economic effects in another. Certain countries believe that it is imperative to address all forms of harmful economic conduct whether it originates from within or outside their territories.[87] For this reason, they extend the reach of competition law beyond their territories. The term *extraterritoriality* generally refers to 'the power to secure the enforcement of the law outside the jurisdiction in which the law was made'.[88] This idea expands the traditional jurisdiction principle that authorises a state to regulate conduct in its territory, by authorising a state to regulate conduct that occurs outside its territory when that conduct has particular effects within its territory.[89]

On the basis of the traditional territorial principle, a country is able to enact law and enforce it only within its national borders. As ensconced in the *Lotus* case: 'all that can be required of a State is that it should not overstep the limits which international law places upon its jurisdiction; within these limits, its title to exercise jurisdiction rests in its sovereignty'.[90] In this regard, 'jurisdiction is an aspect of sovereignty'[91] and is thus limited to the latter. However, when globalisation began reducing the importance of national borders, the principle of territoriality began to be incompatible with world progress.[92] The traditional approach, applying the principle of territoriality, would prevent countries from protecting their legitimate interests from conduct or behaviour occurring outside their national borders. This disparity presents companies with an

86. ASEAN Secretariat, *ASEAN Regional Guidelines on Competition Policy*, Art. 5.1.3.2 (2010).
87. David Gerber, *The Extraterritorial Application of German Antitrust Law*, 77 American Journal of International Law 756 (1983).
88. Alastair Sutton, *'Extraterritoriality' in Competition Law from a European Perspective*, 16 AUT Int'l L. Practicum (2003).
89. David Gerber, *The Extraterritorial Application of German Antitrust Law*, 77 American Journal of International Law 756 (1983).
90. *France v. Turkey*, Series A, No. 10, para. 47 (PCIJ. 1927).
91. Frederick A. Mann, *The Doctrine of Jurisdiction in International Law* (Académie de Droit International, Receuil des Cours 1964).
92. Gary B. Born, *A Reappraisal of Extraterritorial Reach of U.S. Law*, 24 Law & Pol'y Int'l Bus (1992).

opportunity to engage in harmful conduct abroad without facing punishment back in their home state. Moreover, certain countries could transform into competition law 'havens'[93] by attracting private firms wishing to avoid competition regulations in their home countries. Accordingly, an exception to the principle of territoriality was necessary and inevitable.[94] The *Lotus* case recognised this problem and stated that:

Far from laying down a general prohibition to the effect that States may not extend the application of their laws and the jurisdiction of their courts to persons, property and acts outside their territory, it leaves them in this respect a wide measure of discretion, which is only limited in certain cases by prohibitive rules; as regards other cases, every State remains free to adopt the principles which it regards as best and most suitable ...[95]

Admitting an extension of national law makes it possible for countries to extend their jurisdiction beyond their national boundaries in certain situations. In this age of globalisation, it has become increasingly difficult to disagree with the principle of extraterritoriality.

While the principle of extraterritoriality has been validated, it remains a natural source of conflict. Foreign governments have objected vehemently to the aggressive use of the doctrine. These reactions are not surprising since the question of jurisdiction is related to sovereignty.[96] In this regard, excessive pursuit of extraterritoriality can be interpreted as an act of aggression towards a country's sovereignty. The foreign sovereigns' reactions range from soft diplomatic protests to strong retaliation statutes.

Diplomatic protest by foreign governments against extraterritorial assertion of domestic competition laws is the most common and immediate reaction.[97] Foreign governments usually protest that such assertion adversely affects the legitimate interests of the countries concerned and constitutes an intrusion into their domestic affairs.[98] Nonetheless, it is by far the least efficient reaction since few diplomatic protests have led to fruitful solutions.[99]

The unproductiveness of diplomatic protests has forced countries to take unilateral steps in retaliation to extraterritorial assertion of jurisdiction. Countries started introducing the same effects doctrine in their territory,[100] thus aiding in the generalisation of extraterritoriality. Another retaliatory option is to enact blocking statutes.

93. Maher M. Dabbah, *International and Comparative Competition Law* (Cambridge University Press 2010).
94. Donald F. Turner, *Application of Competition Laws to Foreign Conduct: Appropriate Resolution of Jurisdictional Issues*, 10 World Competition (1986).
95. *France v. Turkey*.
96. Frederick A. Mann, *The Doctrine of Jurisdiction in International Law* (Académie de Droit International, Receuil des Cours 1964).
97. *See*, for example, the response of the UK to the assertion of jurisdiction by the EU in the *Dyestuffs* case, in which a note of diplomatic protest was sent to the Commission.
98. Deepa Rishikesh, *Extraterritoriality Versus Sovereignty in International Antitrust Jurisdiction*, 14 World Competition (1991).
99. *Ibid.*
100. OECD, *Restrictive Business Practices of Multinational Enterprises: Report of the Committee of Experts on Restrictive Business Practices* (1977).

These blocking statutes aim at prohibiting nationals, who are the subject of competition law investigations by foreign authorities, from complying with requests or orders issued by the latter.[101] The scope of these blocking laws can be broad, ranging from impeding discovery outside of the territory of the enacting country[102] to rendering certain types of foreign competition law judgment unenforceable in domestic courts.[103] In light of these blocking laws, an attempt by foreign authorities to apply their competition laws extraterritorially would be difficult. Nonetheless, the proportionality of the blocking statutes in response to extraterritoriality has been called into question. These blocking measures are regarded as too drastic[104] and could trigger more conflicts between countries. However, resorting to such drastic measures shows meaningful desperation on behalf of the blocking country in the face of what it perceives as a highly intrusive extraterritorial assertion of jurisdiction on its sovereignty.

Countries have also enacted legislation seeking to recover damages paid in satisfaction of foreign antitrust judgments. The UK was one of the first countries to enact such a statute. It adopted the *Protection of Trade Interests Act*[105] in response to a perceived increase in aggressiveness in the extraterritorial enforcement of the US antitrust and trade law.[106] This type of legislation is commonly known as the clawback statute.[107] It makes it possible for defendants who have paid multiple damage judgment in a foreign country to recover the multiple portions of that judgment from the successful plaintiff. It is obvious that the language used in the clawback statute, such as multiple damage judgment, is aimed at the treble damages available under the US antitrust law.[108] Nonetheless, this legislation lacks international law support and is based solely on the desire to protect British nationals and businesses from what the UK perceives as the American's excessive assertion of jurisdiction.[109] Similar clawback laws have been enacted in other countries such as Canada[110] and Australia.[111]

101. Joseph E. Neuhas, *Power to Reverse Foreign Judgments: The British Clawback Stature under International Law*, 81 Colum. L. Rev. (1981).
102. (Canada) Ontario Business Records Protection Act, RSO. Ch. 54 (1950). (France) Loi n° 80-538 du 16 juillet 1980 relative à la Communication de Documents ou Renseignements d'Ordre Economique, Commercial ou Technique à des Personnes Physiques ou Morales Etrangeres (1980). (This French law makes it a crime to request certain type of documentation located in France.)
103. (Australia) Foreign Proceedings (Excess of Jurisdiction) Act, 1984, No. 3 (1984).
104. Deepa Rishikesh, *Extraterritoriality Versus Sovereignty in International Antitrust Jurisdiction*, 14 World Competition (1991).
105. Protection of Trading Interests Act (1980). Read in light of Civil Jurisdiction and Judgments Act (1982).
106. Joseph E. Neuhas, *Power to Reverse Foreign Judgments: The British Clawback Stature under International Law*, 81 Colum. L. Rev. (1981).
107. Joseph P. Griffin, *Foreign Governmental Reactions to U.S. Assertions of Extraterritorial Jurisdiction*, 6 Geo. Mason L. Rev. (1997).
108. The Clayton Act, 15 U.S.C. §§ 12-27, 29 U.S.C. §§52-53 (2006).
109. Joseph E. Neuhas, *Power to Reverse Foreign Judgments: The British Clawback Stature under International Law*, 81 Colum. L. Rev. (1981).
110. Foreign Extraterritorial Measures Act, Ch. 49 1984 CAN. STAT. 1867 (1984). An earlier bill was introduced in 1980 Foreign Proceedings and Judgments Act, Bill C-41, 32d Parl., Ist Sess. (1980).
111. 973 Parl. Deb., H.C. (5th ser.) 1544 (1979).

The doctrine of extraterritoriality is essentially unilateral. It is designed to protect nations' legitimate interests outside their territories in the absence of a multilateral framework, bilateral cooperation, or regional convergence. The validity of the doctrine is not contested since it is a natural advancement under globalisation, but extraterritoriality needs to be tamed in order to avoid the limitlessness of the manner in which it is used. Its aggressive application tends to create more foes than friends and harms international relations between countries. Animosity at regional level would injure any attempt at cooperation thus further hamper efforts to establish harmonised competition law within the ASEAN. In recent years, the tension created by extraterritoriality seems to be on the decline. This is principally a result of the proliferation of competition laws around the world[112] and more understanding and acceptance of other countries' extraterritoriality even when it affects their own territoriality.[113] After *Gencor*, the South African government did not call into question the EU's jurisdiction, and merely expressed its preference for intervention in specific cases of collusion when they arose rather than the outright prohibition of the transaction.[114] It is not uncommon for small jurisdictions to 'free ride'[115] on the enforcement efforts of more developed jurisdictions. Other authors have recognised the possibility that the effective extraterritorial application of foreign competition law to conduct committed by an international cartel may protect a developing economy with either a weaker or no competition regime.[116] In addition, the promotion of bilateral and regional cooperation seems to have considerably reduced the friction caused by extraterritoriality.

[2] Leading Jurisdictions' Experiences

[a] The Extraterritorial Application of the US Antitrust Law

The US is one of the first to adopt the principle of extraterritoriality in competition law.[117] The antitrust policy in the US has been shaped largely by a triad of early legislations: the *Sherman Act,*[118] the *Clayton Act*[119] and the *Robinson-Patman Act*[120] each plays a significant role in local and foreign business. The *Sherman Act* imposes

112. Damien Geradin, *The Perils of Antitrust Proliferation: The Globalisation of Antitrust and the Risks of Overregulation of Competitive Behavior,* 10 Chi. J. Int'l L (2009), describing this phenomenon as a decentralised globalisation.
113. Bruno Zanettin, *Cooperation between Antitrust Agencies at the International Level,* 36 (Hart Publishing 2002).
114. *Gencor v. Commission,* Case T-102/96, para. 104 (ECR II-753 1999).
115. Brendan Sweeney, *Combatting Foreign Anti-competitive Conduct: What Role for Extraterritoriality?,* 8(1) Melbourne J. Int'l L. (2007).
116. Eleanor M. Fox & Michal S. Gal, *Drafting Competition Law for Developing Jurisdictions: Learning from Experience, in* The Economic Characteristics of Developing Jurisdictions: Their Implications for Competition Law (Michal S. Gal, et al. eds., Edward Elgar Publishing 2015).
117. Bruno Zanettin, *Cooperation between Antitrust Agencies at the International Level,* 8 (Hart Publishing 2002).
118. The Sherman Act, 26 Stat. 209, 15 U.S.C. (1890).§§ 1-7
119. The Clayton Act, 15 U.S.C. §§ 12-27, 29 U.S.C. §§52-53 (2006).
120. The Robinson-Patman Act, 15 U.S.C. §§ 13-13b 21a (1936).

criminal penalties on antitrust violation by both interstate and foreign commerce.[121] Criminal prosecution under this *Act* is usually confined to traditional violations of the law including price-fixing, bid-rigging and other cartel-like conduct considered unlawful in most countries.[122] The *Clayton Act* supplements the *Sherman Act* by including prohibitions against interlocking directorates, exclusive dealing, tying of deals and acquisitions with the potential to substantially decrease competition or create monopolies. Similar to the *Sherman Act*, the *Clayton Act*'s non-criminal penalties also apply to commerce 'among the several states and to foreign nations'.[123] Finally, the *Robinson-Patman Act* prohibits large retailers from selling goods at discriminatorily low prices that could disadvantage small retailers.[124] Although the *Robinson-Patman Act* only prohibits price discrimination within the US, the *Antidumping Act*[125] applies similar prohibitions to foreign commerce. Extraterritorial concern was one of the factors in each of these Acts. Each provides an important measure to attain the two principal goals of US antitrust law: to preserve competition and economic efficiency in the market.[126]

The US courts' interpretation of the antitrust statutes has been important in developing the doctrine of extraterritoriality over the years. The US effects doctrine dated back to *Sisal*[127] which ruled that jurisdiction under the US antitrust law may be asserted in relation to conduct taking place both within and outside the US national borders. *Sisal* marked an important departure from the traditional territorial approach whereby the court admitted that the US competition law did not apply to activities occurring outside the US's national boundaries[128] and paved the way for the development of the US effects doctrine. Subsequently, *Alcoa*[129] heralded the effects principle in which the US courts have jurisdiction and the *Sherman Act* applies if foreigners acting abroad with the intent to affect the US commerce caused a direct effect as intended. By focusing solely on the US interests, the court failed to take into consideration legitimate foreign interests that created friction between the US and other countries who claimed it was a clear violation of international law.[130] In response to criticisms and threats of retaliation by foreign governments, the US courts[131] made an attempt to apply restrictions to the US extraterritorial doctrine. They decided that they may not require

121. The Sherman Act, 26 Stat. 209, 15 U.S.C. (1890).
122. US Department of Justice & Federal Trade Commission, *Antitrust Enforcement Guidelines for International Operations* (1995).
123. The Clayton Act, 15 U.S.C. §§ 12–27, 29 U.S.C. §§52–53 §§ 12 (2006).
124. The Robinson-Patman Act, 15 U.S.C. §§ 13–13b §§ 13 (1936).
125. Antidumping Act, 15 U.S.C. §§ 71–74 (1916).
126. Eleanor M. Fox, et al., *Cases and Materials on United States Antitrust in Global Context* (2nd ed., West 2004).
127. *United States v. Sisal Sales Corp.*, 274 US 268 (1927).
128. *American Banana Co. v. United Fruits Co.*, 29 S.Ct. 511 (1909).
129. *United States v. Aluminium Company of America*, 148 F.2d 416 (1945) (*hereinafter* Alcoa).
130. *See*, for example, George Winthrop Haight, *International Law and Extraterritorial Application of the Antitrust Laws*, 63 Yale L. J. (1954); Nicholas de BelleVille Katzenbach, *Conflicts on an Unruly Horse: Reciprocal Claims and Tolerances in Interstate and International Law*, 65 Yale L. J. (1956).
131. *See*, *Timberlane Lumber v. Bank of America*, 549 F.2d 597 (9th Cir. 1976); *Mannington Mills Inc. v. Congoleum Corp.*, 595 F.2d 1287 (3rd Cir. 1979) (*hereinafter* Timberlane I).

foreign firms acting in their home territory to do what their home governments forbid or to abstain from doing what the home government requires.[132] Such an order would undoubtedly intrude on other nations' sovereignty. The balancing principle states that the courts either lack jurisdiction or should refrain from exercising jurisdiction if foreign nations' and foreign nationals' interests in the non-application of the US law outweigh US interests.[133] In *Timberlane II,* the Circuit Court held that in asserting national jurisdiction, a court should examine: '(1) the effect or intended effect on the foreign commerce of the United States; (2) the type and magnitude of the alleged illegal behaviour; and (3) the appropriateness of exercising extraterritorial jurisdiction in light of considerations of international comity or fairness'.[134] Nonetheless, the effectiveness of the *Timberlane* factor is called into question in *Laker* when the Court held that it is incommensurable to balance foreign interests with domestic interests.[135]

Hartford Fire[136] announced an important shift from the balancing test in the extraterritoriality doctrine. The Supreme Court held that the *Sherman Act* applies to 'foreign conduct that was meant to produce and did in fact produce some substantial effect in the United States'.[137] Consequently, 'passing the effects test is virtually as easy as showing that a particular transaction or business practice falls within the rubric of interstate commerce [...]. Effects can almost always be found'.[138] After *Hartford Fire,* the District Courts remained divided. Some Courts held that *Hartford Fire* did not overrule *Timberlane*[139] and merely added another principle to the doctrine of extraterritoriality, while others followed *Hartford Fire.*[140]

Empagran[141] would later attempt to refine the decision in *Hartford Fire*. The Court looked into the *Foreign Trade Antitrust Improvement Act*[142] and found that it was designed to limit 'but not to expand in any significant way the Sherman Act's scope as applied to foreign commerce'.[143] It steered the extraterritoriality doctrine back to its original track by ending the *Hartford Fire*'s trend of excessive expansion of the US antitrust law. The Court admitted that interference with foreign sovereignty is admissible in so far that there is domestic injury involved. In order to further clarify the exception of domestic injury, the Court distinguished between dependent and independent effect to US commerce. If the domestic injury is independent from the foreign

132. *United States v. Watchmakers of Switzerland Info. Center,* Trade Cases P 70,600, order modified, Trade Cases P 71,352 (SDNY. 1963, 1965).
133. Eleanor M. Fox & Daniel A. Crane, *Global Issues in Antitrust and Competition Law* (West 2010).
134. *Timberlane Lumber Co. v. Bank of America National Trust and Savings Association,* 749 F.2d 1378 (1984) (*hereinafter* Timberlane II).
135. *Laker Airways Ltd. v. Sabena, Belgian World Airlines,* 731 F.2d 909 (1984).
136. *Hartford Fire Ins. Co. v. California,* 509 U.S. 764 (1993).
137. *Ibid.,* at para. 2909.
138. Dean Brockbank, *The 1995 International Antitrust Guidelines: The Reach of U.S. Antitrust Law Continues to Expand,* 2 J. Int'l Legal Stud. (1996).
139. *See,* e.g., *Metro Indus. Inc. v. Sammi Corp.,* 82 F.3d 839, 846 (1996); *Filetech SARL v. France Telecom,* 978 F. Supp. 464 (SDNY. 1997); *Trugman-Nash Inc. v. New Zealand Dairy Board,* 945 F. Supp. 733, 736 (1997).
140. *See,* for example, *United States v. Nippon Paper Industries Co., Ltd.,* 109 F.3d 1 (1997); *Caribbean Broad Sys. v. Cable and Wireless Plc.,* 148 F.3d 1080 (1998).
141. *Hoffman – La Roche Ltd. v. Empagran* S.A., 124 S. Ct. 2359 (2004).
142. The Foreign Trade Antitrust Improvement Act, 15 U.S.C. § 6a [1982].
143. *Hoffman – La Roche Ltd. v. Empagran.*

harm, foreign plaintiffs could not bring their claim before the US courts. Regrettably, the Court did not give sufficient indication as to what it considered dependent effect to the US commerce and therefore even after *Empagran*, the courts remain divided on the question of extraterritoriality.[144] It appears that *Empagran* has left more judicial uncertainty on the question of extraterritoriality.[145]

The US experience has reflected the unpredictable nature of the doctrine of extraterritoriality. It seems that extraterritoriality will continue being used differently by different courts. Some courts might favour a more restrictive application while others may be in favour of a more expansive application of extraterritoriality. Waller predicts that 'years of additional litigation or statutory change will be necessary to resolve this critical question'.[146]

[b] The Extraterritorial Application of the EU Competition Law

The EU competition law shares some similarities with the US antitrust, yet still differs in many fundamental respects. Even though the European doctrine of extraterritoriality is younger and the pursuit of extraterritorial assertion of jurisdiction is less vigorous than that of the US, it should not be underestimated.[147] Dissimilarly from the US experience, the EU's doctrine of extraterritoriality does not find its foundation within the Treaties; instead the doctrine has been established by the Commission and the judiciary. Articles 101 and 102 of *TFEU* prohibit certain conduct that affects trade between Member States and has an anticompetitive effect within the Common Market. The Commission later clarified that the effect must be *appreciable* which means more than *de minimis* but less than *substantial.*[148] Similarly to the US experience, however, are the historical changes the doctrine has undergone throughout the years. Generally, there are three accepted doctrines in the EU regarding extraterritoriality: the single economic entity; the implementation; and the effects doctrine.

It was in *Grosfillex*[149] that the Commission first considered the effects doctrine. The Commission reasoned that the EU competition law regime was compatible with the effects doctrine since the territorial scope of the EU competition law was determined neither by the domicile of the firm nor by where the agreement was concluded or carried out. The decisive criterion here is whether an agreement affects competition

144. *See*, for instance, *Intel Corp. v. Advanced Micro Devices, Inc.*, 124 S. Ct. 2466 (2004). Rejected the narrow view in *Empagran* in favour of a broader one despite strong objection from the European Competition Commission.
145. Salil K. Mehrar, *More Is Less: A Law-and-Economics Approach to the International Scope of Private Antitrust Enforcement*, 77 Temp. L. Rev. (2004).
146. Spencer Weber Waller, *The Internationalization of Antitrust Enforcement*, 77 B.U. L. Rev. (2002).
147. Barbara C. George, et al., *Increasing Extraterritorial Intrusion of European Union Authority into U.S. Business Mergers and Competition Practices: U.S. Multinational Businesses Underestimate the Strength of the European Commission from GE/Honeywell to Microsoft*, 19 Conn. J. Int'l L. 571 (2004).
148. *Notice on Agreements of Minor Importance [1986] OJ C231/2, as amended, [1994] OJ C368/20 and [1997] OJ C372/13.*
149. *Grosfillex – Fillistorf*, OJ 58/915 (1964).

within the Common Market. *Grosfillex* made it clear that the Commission fully embraced the US extraterritorial doctrine.

The *Dyestuffs*[150] judgment marked the first occasion when the CJEU was invited to express its view on the doctrine of extraterritoriality. However, the CJEU avoided the question of extraterritoriality, preferring instead to rely on the doctrine of economic entity. The Court held that jurisdiction should be asserted on the basis of the principle of territoriality by relying on the existence of a single economic entity. In this case, the CJEU ruled that the parent company, which was non-EU-based, exercised control over the strategic business behaviour of its EU-based subsidiary. Therefore, the participation of the subsidiary in illegal conduct could be attributed to the parent company even though the latter was non-EU-based. On this basis, Article 101 *TFEU* could be applied to the foreign-based company without having to resort to the doctrine of extraterritoriality. The group economic unit doctrine is considered 'the most established basis in EC competition law for asserting jurisdiction over foreign companies'.[151] Historically, the CJEU's position reflected that of the EU's politics which at that time fervently criticised the use of extraterritoriality by the US.[152]

The CJEU would later establish a different doctrine called the implementation doctrine in the *Wood Pulp* case.[153] It held that the EU competition law could only apply extraterritorially when the price-fixing agreement was implemented within the EU. The decisive factor was the location where the conduct occurred. If the conduct was implemented within the EU, then its competition law would apply. In this case, the price-fixing agreement was established within the Internal Market, thus the CJEU was entitled to apply the EU competition law to non-EU-based undertakings. It is irrelevant whether foreign undertakings implemented the conduct through subsidiaries, agents, sub-agents or branches within the EU. Under this doctrine, foreign conduct or behaviour would be in violation of the EU competition law, not on the ground of its effects within the Internal Market but because it had the effect of implementing the infringement.

In 2004, the Commission adopted the *Guidelines on Effects on Trade between Member States*[154] as part of the Commission's modernisation package. The Guidelines demonstrate the Commission's desire to fully embrace the extraterritoriality doctrine by providing that Articles 101 and 102 *TFEU* 'apply to agreements and practices that are capable of affecting trade between Member States even if one or more of the parties are located outside the Community'.[155] Moreover, the EU competition law applies regardless of the location of the undertakings or the location where the agreement has been concluded provided that the agreement or practice is either implemented or produces

150. *ICI v. Commission* (*hereinafter* Dyestuffs).
151. D. G. Goyder, et al., *Goyder's EC Competition Law*, 581 (5th ed., Oxford University Press 2009).
152. James J. Friedberg, *The Convergence of Law in an Era of Political Integration: The Wood Pulp Case and the Alcoa Effects Doctrine*, 52 U. Pitt. L. Rev. (1991).
153. *Ahlström Osakeyhtiö v. Commission*, Case 89/85 (ECR I-1307 1993) (*hereinafter* Wood Pulp).
154. *Guidelines on Effect on Trade between Member States, O.J. C-101/81* (2004).
155. *Ibid.*, at para. 100.

effects inside the Union.[156] In the end, the Commission chose to compromise by combining the CJEU implementation doctrine with the US effects principle.

The principle of extraterritoriality also has significance in the case of mergers, especially with the pre-merger notification requirement that gives competition authorities an opportunity to assert jurisdiction over non-EU companies. The most notable instrument was the *Regulation 139/2004 (EUMR)*.[157] The *EUMR* gives the Commission the power to assert jurisdiction over mergers, takeovers, certain joint ventures and the purchase of minority controlling interests provided that the concentration has a Community dimension.[158] The Commission became the central authority with regard to concentration operations. The *EUMR*'s community dimension is a broad concept implying that it is not indispensable for merger operations to have an effect in the EU provided that the financial threshold is met. Therefore, the Commission could assert control over non-EU-based parties even though the merger operation only produces minimal or no effect within the Community. The Commission's pursuit of the extraterritoriality doctrine, as demonstrated in *Boeing/McDonnell Douglas*[159] when the Commission based its analysis on the possible effect on the market after the merger operation, was categorised as an aggressive form of the effects doctrine.[160]

At this stage, a question has been raised about the possible incompatibility of the Commission's application of the effects doctrine with the CJEU's implementation doctrine. On the surface, the two doctrines seem incompatible since the *EUMR* could only be applied with the effects doctrine. *Gencor*[161] provided that the *EUMR* does not require the company concerned to be incorporated or established in the EU. The GCEU ruled that the *EUMR* is compatible with public international law if the merger operation's effects within the EU are immediate, substantial, and foreseeable.[162] It further concluded that the concept of the Community dimension in the *EUMR* is consistent with the implementation doctrine as established in *Wood Pulp* by the CJEU. Another notable merger case is *GE/Honeywell*.[163] This case marks the first time that US antitrust authorities approved a merger between US-based multinational companies only to be stopped by the European Commission.[164] On appeal, the GCEU confirmed

156. *Ibid.*
157. Council Regulation (EC) No. 139/2004 on the Control of Concentrations between Undertakings (2004). (The original merger regulation was the Council Regulation (EC) No. 4064/89 on the Control of Concentrations between Undertakings (1989) which was later replaced by the Council Regulation (EC) No. 1310/97 Amending Regulation (EEC) No. 4064/89 on the Control of Concentrations between Undertakings (1997).)
158. Council Regulation (EC) No. 139/2004 on the Control of Concentrations between Undertakings, Art. 1 (2004).
159. *Boeing/McDonnell Douglas*, OJ C372, para. 17 (1997).
160. Maher M. Dabbah, *International and Comparative Competition Law*, 479 (Cambridge University Press 2010).
161. *Gencor v. Commission* (*Gencor*).
162. *Ibid.*, at para. 90.
163. *General Electric/Honeywell*, COMP/M.2220 (2001) (*GE/Honeywell*).
164. Barbara C. George, et al., *Increasing Extraterritorial Intrusion of European Union Authority into U.S. Business Mergers and Competition Practices: U.S. Multinational Businesses Underestimate the Strength of the European Commission from GE/Honeywell to Microsoft*, 19 Conn. J. Int'l L. 571 (2004).

the Commission's decision and dismissed GE's action for annulment.[165] This case provoked heavy criticism from the US. In particular, the Commission was accused of protecting competitors and not the competition process.[166]

The seeds of divergence between the positions of the US and the EU rested primarily on the different tests used at the time. The US used the substantial lessening of the competition test[167] in which a merger will be prohibited if it leads to substantial lessening of the competition. On the other hand, the EU employed the dominance test[168] in which a merger will not be approved if it creates or strengthens a dominant position which will significantly or substantially impede competition in the Common Market. This test would later be modified in the *EUMR* by relegating the question of dominance from the sole consideration to the main consideration. Fox claimed the change was provoked by US influence.[169] While the EU clearly asserts extraterritorial jurisdiction, the Commission is more constrained in its use of unilateral application of the EU competition law because of the attitude of the Member States who have expressed an aversion to the doctrine of extraterritoriality.[170]

[3] The Application of Extraterritoriality by the AMSs

There are some lingering doubts about whether the AMSs are capable of extraterritorially and whether they are able to enforce their national laws to regional problems within the region. First, the principle of extraterritoriality as a whole relies heavily on a country's ability to exert its political and economic power.[171] Furthermore, '[e]xtraterritoriality is an efficient tool for large jurisdictions that possess sufficient power over foreign firms to command obedience. Small ones often lack the requisite power to discipline foreign entities that harm them. It is thus not surprising that most do not have developed doctrines of extraterritoriality ...'[172] Countries with strong economic and political persuasive power coupled with a more established system of competition law possess the necessary tools to extend their competition laws to extend their reach. They can also do so in a more aggressive manner than others. This is not surprising since only stronger states are able to extend their jurisdiction to where their interests lie in order to control, what they perceived to be, conduct harmful to their interests. On the other hand, weaker states do not have the capacity to extend their reach of domestic

165. *General Electric v. Commission*, Case T-210/01 (ECR II-5575 2005).
166. *Department of Justice Press Release*, http://www.justice.gov/atr/public/press_releases/2001/8510.htm. (accessed 11 Nov. 2017).
167. The Clayton Act, 15 U.S.C. §§ 12–27, 29 U.S.C. §§52–53, s. 7 (2006).
168. Council Regulation (EC) No. 4064/89 on the Control of Concentrations between Undertakings, Art. 2 (1989).
169. Eleanor M. Fox, *GE/Honeywell the U.S. Merger that Europe Stopped-A Story of the Politics of Convergence*, *in* Antitrust Stories (Eleanor M. Fox & Daniel A. Crane eds., Foundation Press 2007).
170. D. G. Goyder, *EC Competition Law*, 499 (4th ed., Oxford University Press 2003).
171. David Gerber, *The Extraterritorial Application of German Antitrust Law*, 77 American Journal of International Law 756 (1983).
172. Michal S. Gal, *Extra-territorial Application of Antitrust – The Case of a Small Economy (Israel)*, *in* Cooperation, Comity, and Competition Policy (Andrew T. Guzman ed., Oxford University Press 2010).

laws to undertakings originating from stronger states and may fear of economic and political retaliation. Their inability to effectively enforce competition law could lead to a legal vacuum where the behaviour is never enforced under any competition law regime. This is particularly true when the harm is confined only to the national territory or when such conduct produces positive effects elsewhere. Moreover, an attempt to enforce competition law by a perceived weaker jurisdiction could potentially result in negative welfare effect.[173] For instance, external constituencies could exit the national market, leaving the market more vulnerable than before the competition law enforcement. At the same time, the limited resources made available to new and developing competition law authorities prevent them from extending their enforcement reach.[174] The limited resources, both financial and human, can be more severely felt in the field of extraterritoriality since the proof of anticompetitive conduct by foreign firms, especially in the case of international cartels, is costly in both time and money.[175]

Currently, only two AMSs' competition laws contain extraterritoriality provisions. The Malaysia Competition Act applies to behaviours outside Malaysia having an effect on competition in any market in Malaysia.[176] The language used hints at the effect doctrine. In addition, Singapore's competition law is explicitly applicable to conduct and agreements outside Singapore insofar as there is appreciable object or affect competition within Singapore[177] or in the case of abuse of dominant position, in so far as there is a negative effect on competition within Singapore.[178] This reach is more extensive than that of the EU legislation.[179] This wide-ranging measure is claimed necessary for Singapore because of its small and open economy that is highly reliant on imported commerce, although he expressed his concerns over practical enforcement limitations.[180]

There are some examples of AMSs use of extraterritoriality. One such example is the case involving Singapore, in *Ball Bearings*,[181] which involved the violation of section 34 of the *Singapore Competition Act* on the prohibition of anticompetitive agreements by the Japanese parent companies and Singaporean subsidiaries. The Commission decided that the jurisdiction should be asserted on the basis of the principle of the territoriality by relying on the existence of a single economic entity. In this case, the Japanese parent companies exerted a decisive influence over the behaviour of the Singaporean subsidiaries and were therefore jointly and severally liable for the infringement committed by the subsidiaries.[182] On this basis, the

173. *Ibid.*
174. *Ibid.*
175. Brendan Sweeney, *Combatting Foreign Anti-competitive Conduct: What Role for Extraterritoriality?*, 8(1) Melbourne J. Int'l L. (2007).
176. Malaysia Competition Act, Act 712, Art. 3 (2010).
177. Singapore Competition Act (Ch. 50B) revised on 30 Jan. 2006, Art. 33(1) (2004).
178. *Ibid.*, at Art. 47(3).
179. Mark Williams, *The Lion City and the Fragrant Harbor: The Political Economy of Competition Policy in Singapore and Hong Kong Compared*, 54 Antitrust Bulletin (2009).
180. Burton Ong, *The Origins, Objectives and Structure of Competition Law in Singapore*, 29 World Competition (2006).
181. *CCS Imposes Penalties on Ball Bearings Manufacturers involved in International Cartel*, CCS 700/002/11 (2014) (*Ball Bearings*).
182. *Ibid.*, at para. 369.

Singapore Competition Act could be applied to the foreign-based company without having to resort to the doctrine of extraterritoriality enshrined in section 33(1). This decision is reminiscent of the CJEU *Dyestuffs* doctrine of economic entity which was also cited in *Ball Bearings*. The same analysis continued in *Freight Forwarders*[183] but with the addition of the application of section 33(1) read in light of section 34 of the *Singapore Competition Act*. The Commission found that the subsidiaries' violation could be attributable to foreign parent companies in accordance with the doctrine of single economic unity. It ruled that section 34 was applicable to the parent companies' anticompetitive agreements carried out outside Singapore's territory in accordance with the doctrine of extraterritoriality in section 33(1).[184] In the case of Indonesia, it was reported[185] that the Supreme Court applied the CJEU *Dyestuffs* doctrine of economic entity and attributed the subsidiary anticompetitive agreement to the foreign parent firm.[186] More recently, the Indonesian Competition Commission (Komisi Pengawas Persaingan Usaha or the KPPU) also employed the doctrine of economic entity.[187] This is an interesting case since Indonesia's competition law does not have an explicit extraterritorial provision. The Commission creatively used this doctrine to expand the interpretation of the definition of *undertaking* in the *Law of the Republic of Indonesia Number 5 Year 1999* which provides that '[e]ntrepreneur is an individual person or a company, in the form of a legal or non-legal entity established and domiciled or engaged in activities within the legal territory of the Republic of Indonesia, conducting various kinds of business activities in the economic sector through contracts, both individually or collectively'[188] to cover foreign parent firms. In this regard, the Commission managed to overcome the territorial limitation by interpreting the criterion of engagement in activities within the territory in a broad manner. The KPPU decision was upheld by the Supreme Court.[189]

These examples demonstrate that the AMSs possess the capability and willingness to extend their national laws to competition issues with regional and international dimensions. The AMSs are not reluctant to abandon the principle of the ASEAN Way which focuses on the non-interference of other AMSs' internal affairs and non-conflictual conflict resolution if their vested interests are in jeopardy. In addition, the use of extraterritoriality signifies the AMSs' preparedness to withstand the potential political and legal conflicts and retaliation from concerned AMSs. This stands in stark contrast to commentators' assumptions that the countries are more likely to favour the avoidance of conflicts engendered by the extraterritorial application of national

183. *CCS Fines 10 Freight Forwarders for Price Fixing*, CCS 700/003/11 (2014) (*Freight Forwarders*).
184. *Ibid.*, at paras 524–525.
185. Kurnia Toha, *Extraterritorial Applicability of Indonesia Business Competition Law as an Efforts Dealing ASEAN Single Market*, 15 Jurnal Dinamika Hukum (2015).
186. *KPPU v. PT Pertamina (Persero) et al.*, Putusan Mahkamah Agung Nomor 04K/KPPU/2005 (2005).
187. *Kelompok Usaha Temasek*, KPPU Decision, No. 07/KPPU-L/2007 (2007).
188. Law of the Republic of Indonesia Number 5 Year 1999 Concerning Prohibition of Monopolistic Practices and Unfair Business Competition, Art. 1(5) (1999).
189. *Temasek Holding Limited, dkk. v. KPPU*, Putusan Mahkamah Agung Nomor 496K/PDT.SUS/2008 (2008).

competition law.[190] Moreover, the conflict of jurisdictions regarding competition issues might become a reality for which the ASEAN has not developed a mechanism for the resulting jurisdictional dispute. The implementation of the concept of extraterritoriality directly affects cross-border commerce within the region. Two scenarios might occur: an increase in the cost of complying with requirements for report mergers and an assessment of the same behaviour according to divergent standards.[191] The second scenario was already demonstrated in *Boeing/McDonnell Douglas* and *GE/Honeywell*.

Conscious of the ASEAN's own institutional limitations and in the absence of a relevant mechanism at regional level, it is possible that the *Guidelines I* suggest including a provision for extraterritoriality to deal with intra-regional competition. It is doubtful that extraterritorial application of national competition law is an appropriate answer to problems of regional competition, especially in light of past experiences encountered by more developed jurisdictions. In the interim, the suggestion of extraterritoriality, even without implementation, could further widen the AMSs' disparity. Correspondingly, an AMS with weaker competition jurisdiction will appear less attractive to foreign investment compared with other jurisdictions. Nonetheless, it is inconclusive whether there is a direct correlation between a decrease in the FDI and a weak competition law regime.

[B] Cooperation Agreements in the ASEAN

Cooperation is generally the preferred method for dealing with trans-border competition problems.[192] It is seen as a solution to palliate the conflicts generated by extraterritoriality. Defining cooperation is difficult, not least because it can have various meanings at different levels. Cooperative activities can be formal or informal. The formality in this context is not due to the nature of participating actors but that of the activities involved. Informal cooperation encompasses networking efforts and can take place at the bilateral, regional and multilateral level.

Cooperation can be categorised into two groups: hard cooperation and soft cooperation.[193] In hard cooperation, an authority is requested by its foreign counterpart to take action it might not otherwise have taken, such as positive comity and exchange of confidential information. In contrast, soft cooperation refers to a coordination of competition investigations. Most noteworthy is the absence of network cooperation from this classification. It is plausible that the absence is based on the assumption that only competition authorities can participate in the cooperation. However, cooperation

190. Michael Faure & Xinzhu Zhang, *Towards an Extraterritorial Application of the Chinese Anti-monopoly Law that Avoids Trade Conflicts*, 45 The Geo. Wash. Int'l L. Rev (2013).
191. William E. Kovacic, *Extraterritoriality, Institutions, and Convergence in International Competition Policy*, 97 Am. Soc'y Int'l L. Proc. (2003).
192. *See*, for example, Frédéric Jenny, *International Cooperation on Competition: Myth, Reality and Perspective*, 48 Antitrust Bull. (2003); Eleanor M. Fox, *Can We Solve the Antitrust Problems of Globalization by Extraterritoriality and Cooperation? Sufficiency and Legitimacy*, 48 Antitrust Bulletin (2003).
193. Bruno Zanettin, *Cooperation between Antitrust Agencies at the International Level*, 5 (Hart Publishing 2002).

has exceeded cooperative procedures between national competition authorities and could include private entities, as attested to by the existence of the ICN. Incidentally, the informal form of cooperation is one that has enjoyed the most success.[194] Cooperation can be broadly defined as institutionalised collaboration.[195] Regardless of the variety of forms and levels, the uniting characteristic of cooperation lies in its voluntary approach. Countries are free to choose with whom to cooperate and reserve the right to decide the level of cooperation commitment on a case-by-case basis. Developed economies prefer to enter into a cooperation agreement with partners with the same level of competition law advancement. They fear that by agreeing to cooperate with developing competition law regimes, they might be exposed to an abundance of requests for assistance with little chance of reciprocity. They also fear a negative effect on their trade and/or competition interests. Developing economies without effective competition regimes are also reluctant to enter into such an agreement; they fear unilateral extension of participating countries' competition rules. It follows that voluntary cooperative agreements are more common among developed economies than among developing economies.[196]

The rise of cooperation agreements is attributed to the globalisation of competition restrictions, the internationalisation of competition policies, and the non-viability of united global competition rules.[197] In particular, cooperation is seen as a method to curb aggressive extraterritorial application of national law in favour of the pooling of resources among countries to address common challenges in competition law enforcement.[198]

[1] Various Designs of Cooperation

[a] Bilateral Cooperation

Bilateral cooperation is considered to be the most common form of cooperation and revolves around cooperation between two national competition authorities.[199] The key advantage of bilateral cooperation is that it eliminates conflicts between countries and

194. *See*, e.g., Eleanor M. Fox, *Linked-In: Antitrust and the Virtues of a Virtual Network*, 43 Int'l Law (2009); Hugh M. Hollman & William E. Kovacic, *International Competition Network: Its Past, Current and Future Role*, 20 Minn. J. Int'l L. (2011); Paul Lugard, *The ICN at Ten: Origins, Accomplishments and Aspirations*, *in* The International Competition Network at Ten: Origins, Accomplishments and Aspirations (Paul Lugard ed., Hart Publishing 2011).
195. Jorg Philipp Terhechte, *International Competition Enforcement Law Between Cooperation and Convergence*, 2 (Springer 2011).
196. Alberto Heimler & Frédéric Jenny, *Regional Agreements*, *in* Building New Competition Law Regimes (Lewis ed., Edward Elgar Publishing 2013).
197. Jorg Philipp Terhechte, *International Competition Enforcement Law Between Cooperation and Convergence*, 9 (Springer 2011).
198. Frédéric Jenny, *International Cooperation on Competition: Myth, Reality and Perspective*, 48 Antitrust Bull. (2003).
199. Olga Petrovsky, *International Antitrust Agreement: Premature Proposal and Practical Solutions*, 22 N.Y. Int'l L. Rev (2009).

facilitates convergence and harmonisation between different competition law regimes.[200] In most cases, bilateral cooperation agreements are concluded between two developed economies.[201] This is because the efficiency of such an agreement relies heavily on the principle of reciprocity. Arrangements made between two nations with similar competition laws and converging views on the substantive and procedural competition regulations have a better chance at succeeding in effective enforcement.[202]

Bilateral cooperation is an evolving concept with the degree of cooperation being affected by the level of trust shared by the two parties. Bilateral agreement centres on technical and enforcement assistance, in particular the exchange of information between jurisdictions. The exchange of information between authorities is essential in order to detect anticompetitive conduct with a trans-border reach. In this regard the exchange is crucial since the actions of countries overlap.[203] This measure is particularly useful in merger cases as it helps authorities discern the market definition.[204] However, the information exchanged remains limited. Countries are not allowed to exchange information if it might violate domestic law of privacy or confidentiality, including professional privilege.[205] Therefore, the information shared between competition authorities must be non-confidential. Technical assistance is often included in the rare cases of bilateral agreements between developed and developing economies such as the *EU-Chile Association Agreement*.[206] The purpose of this type of cooperation agreement has shifted slightly from agreements between developed economies since the two parties are not equal. The goal of this agreement is to help strengthen effective competition law enforcement in the weaker competition law regime.[207] It also aims to provide the transfer of skills and techniques in detecting and deterring anticompetitive behaviour.

Generally, bilateral agreements between competition authorities contain six principal components: notification, exchange of information, cooperation, consultation, and comity.[208] This section will focus on comity to highlight its important role in advancing regional cooperation. Comity can exist in both a negative and a positive form.

Negative comity, which seeks to prevent jurisdictional conflicts, was included in the first generation of bilateral cooperation agreements in 1976 when the US signed the

200. Martyn D. Taylor, *International Competition Law: A New Dimension for the WTO?* (Cambridge University Press 2006).
201. Eleanor M. Fox & Daniel A. Crane, *Global Issues in Antitrust and Competition Law* (West 2010).
202. UNCTAD, *Experiences Gained so Far on International Cooperation on Competition Policy Issues and the Mechanisms Used* (1999).
203. Andrew T. Guzman, *Antitrust and International Regulatory Federalism*, 76 NYUL. Rev. (2001).
204. *Ibid.*
205. Brendan Sweeney, *Combatting Foreign Anti-competitive Conduct: What Role for Extraterritoriality?*, 8(1) Melbourne J. Int'l L. (2007).
206. Agreement Establishing an Association between the European Community and its Member States, of the One Part, and the Republic of Chile, of the Other Part (2002).
207. Ana Maria Alvarez & Pierre Horna, *Implementing Competition Law and Policy in Latin America: The Role of Technical Assistance*, 83 Chi.-Kent L. Rev. (2008).
208. Matsuo Matsushita, *International Cooperation in the Enforcement of Competition Policy*, 1 Wash. U. Global Stud. L. Rev. (2002).

Antitrust Accord with Germany.[209] In practice negative comity means that one party will notify the other party when its enforcement of competition law could affect the interests of the latter.[210] This suggests that only one party in the agreement would engage in the enforcement of the competition law while the other party is forced to not engage in any action; hence the term *negative comity*. It is fairly difficult to assess the success of such comity since it is not binding. Countries are not compelled to decline their jurisdiction in favour of another. Moreover, the language used in the agreement is too vague to assess whether it could really prevent conflict of jurisdiction.[211]

Positive comity centres on the idea that one jurisdiction will refer a matter to another with the expectation that the receiving jurisdiction will investigate the claim.[212] This method implies that the referred jurisdiction is better equipped to deal with the competition law issue than the referring country. In contrast to negative comity, positive comity, as indicated by its name, requires positive action. It marks an important development in bilateral agreements in the field of competition law since it requires a high level of trust and confidence on the part of the referring competition authority that the referred competition authority will undertake a serious investigation. However, the referral will not interfere with domestic competition law. This means that if the recipient of the referral is a weak competition authority with an inefficient competition law regime, that authority will not be empowered by virtue of the referral. The referring competition authority will not engage in the investigation. Positive comity appears to work best when countries share similar values in procedural and substantive competition law. The object of positive comity is to allocate the investigation and prosecution of anticompetitive conduct to the country in the best position to carry out functions.[213]

Positive comity has increasingly become more common than negative comity. The exemplar of such an agreement is the agreement between the US and the EU. The cooperation between them is interesting since the two regimes are regarded as the most well developed. In 1991 the EU and the US signed their first bilateral cooperation agreement[214] which contained obligations of reciprocal notification, exchange of information, assistance, positive comity, and negative comity. Unfortunately, the positive comity provision was not sufficiently used. The cause is likely due to the US'

209. Agreement between the United States of America and Germany Relating to Mutual Cooperation Regarding Restrictive Business Practices (1976).
210. OECD, *Cooperation between Member Countries on Anticompetitive Practices Affecting International Trade* (1995).
211. Maher M. Dabbah, *International and Comparative Competition Law* (Cambridge University Press 2010).
212. Merit E. Janow, *Remarks at the ABA Conference on the World Trade Organisation*, http://www.law.georgetown.edu/journals/lpib/symp00/documents/janow.pdf (accessed 11 Nov. 2017). As seen in Joseph M. Moschella, *The Necessity of Active American Involvement in Global Competition Law*, 22 Wis. Int'l L.J. (2004).
213. OECD, *Recommendation Concerning a Consultation and Conciliation Procedure on Restrictive Business Practices Affecting International Trade* (1973); OECD, *Making International Markets More Efficient through Positive Comity in Competition Law Enforcement* (1999).
214. Agreement between the Government of the United States of America and the Commission of the European Community Regarding the Application of Their Competition Law (1991).

tendency to favour the extraterritorial approach.[215] In 1998, the US and the EU concluded their second cooperation agreement.[216] This agreement confirmed the efforts of the two parties to continue applying the principle of positive comity. Most importantly, the agreement includes a presumption that the referring country will defer or suspend its own enforcement activities over a period not exceeding six months when the anticompetitive behaviour occurred principally in or was directed principally to the referred country. It could be said that positive comity provides a tangible commitment to the notion of cooperation.[217]

Nevertheless, the advancement of deeper cooperation between the two authorities was hindered by *GE/Honeywell*. Admittedly, the occurrence of cases like *GE/Honeywell* is rare and thus is more likely to be the exception to the rule. Despite notable drawbacks, the EU-US bilateral cooperation agreement remains the model for several agreements of the same nature.[218]

[b] Multilateral Cooperation

The failure to form a global competition law within the WTO reveals the reluctance of many countries to commit to a legally binding multilateral agreement in the field of competition law. Despite this unwillingness, countries still wish to cooperate in a meaningful way. The attention has thus shifted to an alternative form at the multilateral level, namely non-binding multilateralism which utilises soft harmonisation methods through recommendations, best practices, and guidelines. The benefit of multilateralism over bilateralism is its cover of a broader range of countries. The best-known form of multilateral cooperation is the OECD and the UNCTAD, both offers multilateral cooperation regarding technical assistance provided to countries.

Both organisations publish documents pertaining to the framework of substantive and institutional competition law. Despite the absence of a binding ability, multilateral cooperation has a high level of influence that transcends its membership. Many competition authorities, even non-OECD members, use these works as highly authoritative sources in the field of competition law. The most influential document from the OECD is indubitably the *Recommendation concerning Effective Action against Hard Core Cartels*.[219] Beyond the area of hard core cartels, the OECD also deals with a

215. Olga Petrovsky, *International Antitrust Agreement: Premature Proposal and Practical Solutions*, 22 N.Y. Int'l L. Rev. (2009).
216. Agreement Between the Government of the United States of America and the European Communities on the Application of Positive Comity Principles in the Enforcement of Their Competition Laws (1998).
217. OECD, *Making International Markets More Efficient through Positive Comity in Competition Law Enforcement* (1999).
218. *See*, for example, Agreement between the United States of America and Canada Regarding the Application of Their Competition and Deceptive Marketing Practices Laws (1997); Agreement Between the Government of the United States of America and the Government of Japan Concerning Cooperation on Anticompetitive Activities (1999); Cooperation Agreement between Canada, the EC and the ECSC (1999).
219. OECD, *Recommendation of the Council Concerning Effective Action Against Hard Core Cartels* (1998).

variety of different issues of competition law and policy including mergers and cooperation between competition authorities and Member States.[220] The UNCTAD has also contributed to multilateral cooperation relative to competition law. Its best known work is the *UNCTAD Code*[221] which was adopted unanimously at the UN General Assembly.[222] It contains basic competition law principles generally consistent with the global concept of anticompetitive conduct.[223] Beside the *UNCTAD Code*, the UNCTAD has made other contributions to the field of competition law such as the *Model Law on Competition*[224] which is based on the *UNCTAD Code* to aid members in the adoption of the *UNCTAD Code* into their national legislations. The most efficient mechanism is the peer review system in both the OECD and the UNCTAD. In this system, countries voluntarily submit their competition law regime to be evaluated and recommendations from other regimes as well as from competition law experts are made. Conforming to the nature of multilateral cooperation, the recommendations that emerge from the peer review are not binding; countries are under no obligation to implement the recommendations given in the peer review. While domestic regimes are not required to accept the recommendations, peer reviews succeed in encouraging changes to domestic regimes purely due to peer pressure. The UNCTAD peer review system can be distinguished from that of the OECD by its perspective on development and experience in cooperating with developing economies.

Since the adoption of the *UNCTAD Code*, the UNCTAD has become the primary representative of the interests of lesser developed and transition economies in the area of competition policy as a counterweight to the influence of developed economies in the global setting.[225] The UNCTAD, contrary to the OECD, is truly global considering its composition of countries around the world with different degrees of political and economic progress and its involvement in development issues. By integrating the development factors with the field of competition law, the UNCTAD is preserving the UN's long-standing tradition of advocating for developing and the least developed economies.

[2] The ASEAN's Form of Cooperation

Early on, Ong observed that '[t]he nature and extent of the cooperation arrangements contemplated under the *Blueprint* have not been made publicly known, and any progress on this front will depend very much on the prevailing political climate in each

220. OECD, *Recommendation of the Council concerning Co-operation between Member Countries on Anticompetitive Practices affecting International Trade* (1995).
221. UNCTAD, *The Set of Multilaterally Agreed Equitable Principles and Rules for the Control of Restrictive Business Practices* (1980, 2000, 2015) (*hereinafter* UNCTAD Code).
222. UN, *United Nations General Assembly* (1980).
223. Spencer Weber Waller, *Antitrust and American Business Abroad*, ch. 18 para. 18:4 (3rd ed., West 1997).
224. UNCTAD, *The Model Law on Competition* (2010).
225. Spencer Weber Waller, *Antitrust and American Business Abroad*, ch. 18 para. 18:10A (3rd ed., West 1997).

of these member states'.[226] Once again, the emphasis is on the political connection of the AMSs, reflecting the predominance of the ASEAN way. The *Guidelines I* would later come to define the nature and the extent of cooperation within the ASEAN. According to them, '[t]he overarching or long-term objectives of a cooperative competition policy for the AMSs are the promotion of market integration in the lead up to the establishment of a common market, and the promotion of economic efficiency and growth at a regional level'.[227] The *Guidelines I* are highly educative on how to use regional cooperation to promote a common framework for competition policy to achieve the long-term objective of market integration in 2015. The *Guidelines I* affirm that cooperation can bring about a high degree of consistency in the implementation of competition policy in the ASEAN. Such cooperation can create a dynamic dialogue that serves to build consensus and convergence towards sound competition policy and improve the effectiveness of a national competition enforcement body through the exchange of non-confidential knowledge between the AMSs.[228] The latter two benefits have already been realised by the formation of the AEGC which was established explicitly to secure these benefits. It appears that the *Guidelines I* support the idea that regional cooperation can bring about actual convergence in regional competition law.

However, the *Guidelines I*'s suggestion is limited to formal cooperation between the AMSs' national competition authorities. It envisions cooperation among these authorities that is centred on discussion and exchange of non-confidential information as a secondary activity, with the aim of achieving convergence.[229] Competition agencies generally collect a broad range of information, from industry and market statistics to opinions and analyses done by the agency, involved parties or third parties to the case.[230] Some of this information is confidential and therefore generally requires authorisation from the parties involved before it can be shared.[231] Confidentiality in the context of competition law investigation has to be protected since the information could contain sensitive market or industry information. Private parties have expressed concern that benefits to private parties arising from information sharing and other forms of cooperation often are not substantial or assured and may be outweighed by a variety of perceived disadvantages. These potential disadvantages include exposure to additional legal risks, particularly when substantive laws diverge; significant potential sanctions or private rights of action in the jurisdiction to which the information is disclosed; differences in investigation timetables; the overburdening of competition authorities with so much information that the investigations would be slowed down rather than hastened; and possible misinterpretation when one authority reviews

226. Burton Ong, *Cooperation, Comity and Competition Policy in Singapore, in* Cooperation, Comity, and Competition Policy (Andrew T. Guzman ed., Oxford University Press 2010).
227. ASEAN Secretariat, *ASEAN Regional Guidelines on Competition Policy*, Art. 10.1.1 (2010).
228. *Ibid.*, at Art. 10.2.
229. *Ibid.*, at Art. 10.3.1 read in light of Art. 10.2.
230. Brendan Sweeney, *Combatting Foreign Anti-competitive Conduct: What Role for Extraterritoriality?*, 8(1) Melbourne J. Int'l L. (2007).
231. OECD, *Hard Core Cartels* (2000).

information that has been prepared to address issues under a different legal regime.[232] In response to these concerns, competition authorities have to ensure that any cooperation is within the limit of the confidentiality rules so as to achieve consistent remedies.[233] Moreover, it is in the interest of national competition authorities to preserve anonymity of the source of such information when guaranteed confidentially is often the sole incentive of the acquirement. Waiver of confidentiality is not uncommon especially in merger cases where parties have strong incentives to agree to such exchange.[234] Nonetheless, it is believed that this is not an example of progressive cooperation but merely an expression of the power of a leniency programme.[235] It is thus realistic for the ASEAN to concentrate on a more restricted and informal approach to the exchange of information.

Provisions relating to discussion and exchange of non-confidential information are usually found in bilateral cooperation agreements. In this regard, the ASEAN is narrating a form of regional cooperation which exhibits the characteristics of a bilateral cooperation agreement. Most worrisome is perhaps the *Guidelines I*'s apparent support of the creation of a new platform or agreements, either bilateral or multilateral, between the AMSs or to build upon the existing mechanism of the AEGC.[236] This provision is later reinforced by a requirement presented in the *Guidelines I* that the AMSs develop a regional platform, or understanding, or arrangement, or otherwise build on the AEGC to facilitate cooperation between competition regulatory bodies.[237] The aim of this regional platform is to allow competition regulatory bodies to exchange their experiences, identify best practices, and endeavour to implement cooperative competition policy and competition regulatory body arrangements that provide for harmonisation.[238] Within this framework, working groups may be created to discuss general or specific issues related to the establishment and enforcement of competition policy.[239] However, the regional platform shall not exercise any rule-making function, and no voting rules should be in place within the working groups, as the cooperation is based on consensus building.[240] If the AMSs were to create a regional platform distinct from the AEGC, it is plausible that there would be an overlapping area of competence, rendering the AEGC vulnerable. Another concern resides in the potential of wider disparity in competition cooperation. Only the AMSs that have made similar progress in competition law enforcement would be able to enter into such an agreement, thus inevitably creating, at the very least, a two-tiered level of cooperation

232. Antitrust Division US Department of Justice, *Report of the International Competition Policy Advisory Committee to the Attorney General and Assistant Attorney General for Antitrust*, 182–185 (2000).
233. Robert Pitofsky, *EU and U.S. Approaches to International Mergers-Views from the U.S. Federal Trade Commission* (2000).
234. ICN, *Waivers of Confidentiality in Merger Investigation: Model Confidentiality Waiver* (2007).
235. Brendan Sweeney, *Combatting Foreign Anti-competitive Conduct: What Role for Extraterritoriality?*, 8(1) Melbourne J. Int'l L. (2007).
236. ASEAN Secretariat, *ASEAN Regional Guidelines on Competition Policy*, Art. 10.3.3 (2010).
237. *Ibid.*, at Art. 10.3.1.
238. *Ibid.*, at Art. 10.3.3.
239. *Ibid.*, at Art. 10.3.4.
240. *Ibid.*, at Art. 10.3.5.

within the region. This could ultimately hamper the ASEAN's efforts to harmonise competition law in all the AMSs. At the same time, the suggestion is made in the interest of facilitating better cooperation among similar competition regimes. There is the potential for faster region-wide cooperation in the future by engaging with those who currently have the capability.

[3] The Limit of Cooperation

Cooperation, despite its various forms, is limited by its most obvious advantage: its voluntary approach. The AMSs have the freedom to cooperate but are not obliged to do so. The ASEAN reiterates this position:

> The regional platform shall not exercise any rule-making function and no voting rules should be in place within the working groups, as the cooperation is based on consensus building. Where the platform reaches consensus on recommendations or 'best practices', arising from the projects, each competition regulatory body may decide whether and how to implement the recommendations, through unilateral, bilateral or multilateral arrangements, where appropriate.[241]

It is evident that the continuous reiteration of the voluntary nature of the regional organ is for the benefit of reassuring the AMSs that the platform will not impinge on their sovereignty. Although they will be encouraged to participate, this is entirely dependent on their willingness to do so.

The success of cooperation agreements, particularly bilateral agreements, is indeed impressive and certainly contributes to proving the usefulness of voluntary cooperation agreements between competition authorities.[242] Notwithstanding the progress made in improving relationships between countries in the matter of competition enforcement, the correlation between cooperation and greater harmonisation remains dubious.[243] Simple similarities in competition analysis do not equate to substantive convergence promoted by cooperative activities. Different competition authorities can arrive at the same conclusion regardless of the method used. This is especially true in the case of mergers with no anticompetitive concern where competition authorities would usually approve. Furthermore, it is also difficult to ascertain whether a national competition authority would be able to uncover or investigate anticompetitive behaviour without cooperation. The problem here lies not in the potential benefit of cooperation but in its measurability.

241. *Ibid.*, at Art. 10.3.5.
242. Frédéric Jenny, *Globalization, Competition and Trade Policy: Convergence, Divergence and Cooperation, in* International and Comparative Competition Law and Policies (Yang-Ching Chao, et al. eds., Kluwer Law International 2001).
243. Frédéric Jenny, *International Cooperation on Competition: Myth, Reality and Perspective*, 48 Antitrust Bull. (2003).

Cooperation agreements are not able, in themselves, to address the issue of the interface between trade and competition at the global level:[244] (1) cooperation agreements do little to convince countries which do not have competition law that they should adopt one; (2) cooperation only unites countries with the same level of advancement regarding competition law regime; (3) cooperation is only undertaken when such cooperation is in the mutual interest of the parties to the agreement. Countries that already have similar competition law regimes would be more likely to cooperate with each other. Therefore, cooperation agreements contribute to greater asymmetric disparity in the global scheme. Even among similar competition regimes, the participation of involved countries is still limited by differences in the considerations of competition procedure, fundamental standards, and requirement of transparency. The over-reliance on the voluntary approach could make the benefits of cooperation illusory as evidenced by *Boeing/McDonnell Douglass* and *GE/Honeywell*. There is certainly a possibility that these cases are simply exceptions rather than the rule of ineffectiveness in cooperation.

Perhaps Fox's astute remark made in 2003 remains valid today. She proclaimed that:

> For inbound problems, the combination of extraterritoriality and cooperation works well for nations with well-resourced agencies of large countries addressing matters not encumbered by conflicting national policies. In that set of cases, gaps and illegitimacies are relatively few. For outbound problems, gaps and illegitimacies are significant. For world problems, we are doing remarkably well working with the tools we have, but the tools, alas, are pre-globalisation. In important ways they are not legitimate, and they are not sufficient.[245]

Indeed, there is a 'growing need to elaborate a multilateral framework'.[246] It follows that the tools of extraterritoriality and cooperation handpicked by the ASEAN to assist in its market integration will not be sufficient to resolve the ASEAN regional competition issues.

§5.04 CONCLUSION

In comparison with other regional economic integration efforts, the ASEAN is unique because it is the only regional organisation without a central competition law-related institution capable of monitoring the enforcement of competition law and the AMSs' competition law regimes. It neither has a centralised institution similar to the WAEMU or the COMESA nor a national representative institution comparable to the MERCOSUR's practice. In its pursuit of regional economic integration, the ASEAN has

244. Frédéric Jenny, *Globalization, Competition and Trade Policy: Convergence, Divergence and Cooperation*, *in* International and Comparative Competition Law and Policies (Yang-Ching Chao, et al. eds., Kluwer Law International 2001).
245. Eleanor M. Fox, *Can We Solve the Antitrust Problems of Globalization by Extraterritoriality and Cooperation? Sufficiency and Legitimacy*, 48 Antitrust Bulletin (2003).
246. Frédéric Jenny, *International Cooperation on Competition: Myth, Reality and Perspective*, 48 Antitrust Bull. (2003).

demonstrated a clear reliance on the AMSs national institutional framework of competition enforcement. It falls to the organisation to provide support in the form of necessary information and choices to help the construction of a national competition institution through the *Guidelines I* and *II*.

The sole regional institution dealing with competition law within the ASEAN is the AEGC which is a simple institution capable of providing a platform of discussion to interested AMSs. The AEGC presents similar traits to a voluntary cooperation agreement and opts to resolving regional competition issues through national solutions and bilateral and/or multilateral cooperation. Its support of extraterritoriality helps explain the ASEAN's fixation with national competition institution structures since it chiefly relies on it to resolve its regional issues. The AEGC's limitation is principally caused by the principle of non-interference between the AMSs, or the ASEAN Way, resulting in the absence of a centralised organ. Since this principle is the cherished core value of the organisation, the ASEAN has no other choice but to abide by it and work around it. What it has proposed, no matter how fragile, is undoubtedly the best it can offer. Unfortunately, such institutional design creates a certain dissonance with the harmonisation process of competition law so desired by the ASEAN.

CHAPTER 6

The ASEAN Countries' National Systems

'Designs cannot be conjured in the abstract; they must fit the family that lives in the house, its aspirations, possibilities, and practical limits.'[1] As the architect of the Southeast Asian regional competition law framework, the ASEAN must take into consideration all of the AMSs' aspirations, capabilities, and limitations regarding the enactment and the implementation of competition law. It is crucial that the ASEAN's framework is suitable and compatible with the AMSs' local contexts to avoid disintegration or departure from the regional design. Both scenarios would be detrimental to the ASEAN's economic integration aspiration. The ASEAN presents a peculiar case in that there is an apparent divide between the AMSs who have enacted and enforced competition law before the announcement of the ASEAN initiative in competition law and policy, and the AMSs with no experience in competition law regime. The ASEAN was faced with a difficult task of accommodating existing competition law-related constructions and encouraging individual nations to align their laws with the ASEAN's framework, while at the same time encouraging the enactment of new national competition law regimes.

A quick survey of national competition law landscape in the ASEAN countries reveals that Indonesia[2] and Thailand[3] were the first AMSs to introduce competition law statutes in 1999 followed at a distance by Vietnam[4] and Singapore[5] in 2004. Generally, these enactments were spurred on by a shift in national policy towards a market economy, notably trade liberalisation, the deregulation of the economy, and the privatisation of states' assets, as well as international pressures.[6] Indonesia and

1. Eleanor M. Fox, *Antitrust and Institutions: Design and Change*, 41 Loy. U. Chi. L. J. (2010)., s. 15.
2. Law of the Republic of Indonesia Number 5 Year 1999 Concerning Prohibition of Monopolistic Practices and Unfair Business Competition (1999).
3. Thailand Trade Competition Act (1999).
4. Vietnam Law on Competition, No.27/2004/QH11 (2004).
5. Singapore Competition Act (Ch. 50B) revised on 30 Jan. 2006 (2004).
6. Franz Hepp De Sevelinges, *Snapshot of Competition Laws in ASEAN and China*, 26 AUT Int'l L. Practicum (2013).

Thailand, in their state of 'economic and financial distress',[7] both adopted their first comprehensive competition law in the wake of the Asian Financial Crisis. Indonesia enacted its competition law statute in light of the conditional terms laid down by the IMF in exchange of the latter's financial assistance,[8] while Thailand's competition law was introduced as a part of a financial sector reform package.[9] The enactment of Vietnam competition law was fuelled by the introduction of the *doi moi* policy and was centred around the development of a socialist-oriented market economy. It was reported that a bilateral trade agreement with the US, as well the country's aspirations to join the WTO were the catalyst for its competition legislation.[10] Both internal and external factors contributed to Singapore's comprehensive competition law. The enactment followed its transition to a market economy and the conclusion of a bilateral agreement with the US.[11]

Following the ASEAN's announcement of regional economic integration with competition law as its pillar, Malaysia,[12] Myanmar,[13] Brunei Darussalam,[14] and the Philippines[15] all passed their competition law bills. It is convenient to assume that the imminent arrival of the AEC motivated their enactments in light of the timing. This is especially evident in the case of Brunei Darussalam, Myanmar, and the Philippines whose laws were introduced less than a year prior to the introduction of the AEC even though the ASEAN's contribution and motivation have never been publicly acknowledged by these AMSs. Evidently, not all AMSs could uphold to the commitment of implementing national competition law due to the arrival of the AEC given in the *Blueprint*. Lao PDR and Cambodia were the two AMSs left astray from the ASEAN's vision and direction. The ASEAN thus failed in its basic aspiration. A new *Blueprint*[16] and *An ASEAN Competition Action Plan 2025*[17] were necessarily adopted to chart a continual path for the ASEAN after the establishment of the AEC. In these documents, a new deadline for the implementation of national competition law in all the AMSs is set at before the end of 2016 to demonstrate the region continual commitment to the ASEAN's vision. Yet, even with this new deadline, Cambodia still fails to fulfil the recommitment. However, a new draft competition law, its fifth, which was concluded in March 2016 was scheduled to be submitted to the Council of Ministers by the end of

7. G. Sivalingam, *Competition Policy and Law in ASEAN*, 51 The Singapore Economic Review (2006).
8. Indonesia, *Letter of Intent and Memorandum of Economic and Financial Policies* (29 Jul. 1998).
9. Frank Flatters, *Thailand and the Crisis: Roots, Recovery and Long-Run Competitiveness, in* The Asian Financial Crisis Lessons for a Resilient Asia (Wing Thye Woo, et al. eds., The MIT Press 1997); Thailand, *Letter of Intent* (14 Aug. 1997).
10. Mark Furse, *Antitrust Law in China, Korea and Vietnam*, 26–27 (Oxford University Press 2009).
11. United States-Singapore Free Trade Agreement Art. 12(2)(1) (signed 6 May 2003, ratified 31 Jul. 2003, implemented 1 Jan. 2004).
12. Malaysia Competition Act, Act 712 (2010).
13. The Competition Law, The Pyidaungsu Hluttaw Law No. 9/2015 (2015).
14. *Ibid.*
15. Philippines Competition Act, Republic Act No. 10667 (2015).
16. ASEAN Secretariat, *ASEAN Economic Community Blueprint 2025* (ASEAN Secretariat 2015).
17. ASEAN Secretariat, *ASEAN Competition Action Plan 2025* (ASEAN Secretariat 2015).

the 2017.[18] There is currently no new development on this matter. In the end, Lao PDR was the sole AMS implementing the country's first comprehensive competition law[19] after the establishment of the AEC. A year later, Thailand would finally adopt its modernisation competition law bill after eighteen years without a single enforcement decision. The new *Trade Competition Act of 2017*[20] repealed and replaced the old statute using identical denomination. Because it was the first modernisation competition law statute in the region, it is expected to better align with the ASEAN's vision and direction.

Previous chapters have stated the ASEAN's efforts into the foray of regional competition law both from substantive and institutional perspectives, it is now opportune to turn our regard towards the AMSs. The present chapter offers a comparative approach to the AMSs competition law both substantive and institutional provisions insofar as to offer an assessment on the inter-influence between the ASEAN and its AMSs. In particular, it seeks to understand whether the soft harmonisation at a regional level so desired by the ASEAN could happen under the current direction of the organisation. The process is particularly hard to achieve in light of the ASEAN's over-reliance on the AMSs' willingness to harmonise without the aid of a regional centralised institution.

Using the *Guidelines* as a temporal marker, the chapter is divided into two parts: the AMSs with prior experiences in competition law and the AMSs with competition laws after the ASEAN initiative of regional competition law. Indubitably, the latter's competition statues were implemented under different circumstances from the former. It is necessary to allow sufficient time to pass after the enactment of the law to let the competition law jurisdiction mature and develop its own identity. To conduct an in-depth comparison research between the two categories would be inappropriate in this context without giving them the benefit of maturing and earning experience and expertise from actual enforcement over appropriate period of time.

§6.01 THE AMSs WITH PRIOR EXPERIENCES IN COMPETITION LAW

On the surface, the national competition laws of Indonesia, Thailand, Singapore, and Vietnam include all the core substantive components of competition law, namely, provisions for the prohibition of anticompetitive agreements, abuse of dominant position, and merger control. However, the commonality does not extend beyond this point. Respecting the differences of the regimes established prior to its own initiative, the ASEAN chose to compromise its vision in favour of acceptance by the AMSs to the point of sacrificing the effectiveness of its own regional competition law. In this

18. Khmer Times, *Ministry of Commerce Nears Completion of Competition Law*, http://www.khmertimeskh.com/5088630/ministry-commerce-nears-completion-competition-law/ (accessed 5 Jan. 2018).
19. Law on Business Competition (No. 60/NA) (2015), published in the Lao PDR Official Gazette on January 2016.
20. Thailand Trade Competition Act (2017).

respect, the four AMSs' competition regimes have greatly influenced the ASEAN regional competition law both in its substantive and institutional decisions.

[A] The Goals of Competition Law

Different regimes may have different expectations of competition law and their expectations may change over time as the economies mature and countries gain more experience in the enforcement of competition law. Among the AMSs, opinions on the subject are diverse. Since only a handful of the AMSs has some experiences in competition law enforcement, it is essential that careful attention be paid to the specification of the goals underlying the competition legislation.[21]

All four AMSs have set economic goals as the rationale for national competition laws. The goals of the Indonesian competition law are to improve public welfare and national economic effectiveness and efficiency by creating equal business opportunities for small, medium, and large-scale businesses.[22] Economic efficiency is directed at the firms' level. What stands out in this provision is the emphasis on the protection of business interests regardless of the size of the business, a problem for which Indonesia is known.[23] The language of the statute makes it explicitly clear that SMEs are not singled out as a special interest group. In the case of Thailand, the principal competition-related legislation is the *Trade Competition Act of 1999*.[24] What is unique about this statute is that the goals of competition law cannot be found in any provisions. Instead, they appear in a nota bene at the end of the document. According to the nota bene, the goals of Thailand's competition law are the promotion of free competition and the prevention of unfair competition in business sector.[25] The literature sometimes did not take this nota bene into account and concluded that the *Act* focused on the prohibited practices without explicitly stating the goals sought in preventing these practices.[26] Interestingly, Thailand's competition-related legislations have a habit of camouflaging their objective under the nota bene at the end of the statute. The *Price Fixing and Anti-Monopolies Act of 1979*,[27] which was replaced by the *Act*, also featured the goals 'to control fair price fixing and to prevent monopolies and competition restrictions'[28] in the nota bene. Under Article 4 titled 'Right to business competition'[29] of Vietnam *Competition Law No. 27/2004/QH11*,[30] it would appear that

21. David K. Round & Alec Zuo, *The Welfare Goal of Antitrust Laws in Asia: For Whom Should the Law Toil?*, 22 Asian-Pacific Economic Literature 2 (2008).
22. Law of the Republic of Indonesia Number 5 Year 1999 Concerning Prohibition of Monopolistic Practices and Unfair Business Competition Art. 2 (1999).
23. David K. Round & Alec Zuo, *The Welfare Goal of Antitrust Laws in Asia: For Whom Should the Law Toil?*, 22 Asian-Pacific Economic Literature 2 (2008).
24. Thailand Trade Competition Act (1999).
25. *Ibid.*, at N. B.
26. David K. Round & Alec Zuo, *The Welfare Goal of Antitrust Laws in Asia: For Whom Should the Law Toil?*, 22 Asian-Pacific Economic Literature 2 (2008).
27. The Price Fixing and Anti-Monopolies Act (1979).
28. *Ibid.*, at N. B.
29. Vietnam Law on Competition, No.27/2004/QH11 Art. 4 para. 1 (2004).
30. *Ibid.*

the purpose of the law is the protection of 'freedom to competition within the legal framework'.[31] However, the freedom to competition is decidedly tempered by 'the principles of honesty, non-infringement upon the interests of the state, public interests, legitimate rights and interests of enterprises, consumers and compliance with the provisions of the law'.[32]

Singapore is the only member to state consumer protection as the first order objective of competition law. The *Singapore Competition Act* inscribes the goal 'to protect consumers and businesses from anticompetitive practices of private entities'.[33] This protection is not limited to any national interest group but seems to be offered to both the consumer and businesses of all sizes and of all nationalities. The state's activities in economic sector are explicitly excluded from this statute.

It follows that there are some difficulties in obtaining consensus among the four AMSs on the identity of economic goals. There are various economic goals included in the AMSs' statutes, ranging from economic efficiency, consumer protection, free and fair competition, and economic development. It is noteworthy that Vietnam's definition of free competition is relatively limited. Furthermore, the *Guidelines I* advocate for the general goal of the promotion and protection of competition which do not appear in any of the four AMSs statute.[34]

[B] Substantive Provisions

[1] The Scope of Competition Law

Most AMSs define undertaking according to the functional approach by focusing on the economic activity - specifically on the pecuniary nature of the economic activity - of the subject matter. Indonesia competition law applies to all *business actor* defined as 'individual(s) or business entities, either incorporated as legal entities or not, established and domiciled or conducting business activities within the jurisdiction of the Republic of Indonesia, either independently or jointly based on agreement, conducting various business activities in the economic field'.[35] Therefore, it applies to any business actor doing business in Indonesia, including, amongst other, state-owned enterprises and subsidiaries of foreign enterprises. Vietnam competition law also applies to any business organisations and individuals, referred to as *enterprises*, including enterprises providing public-utility products or services, enterprises operating in State monopoly industries and sectors as well as foreign enterprises and professional associations operating in Vietnam.[36] The scope of the *Singapore Competition Act* is defined in a more generalised and positive manner. It applies to all undertakings, defined as 'any person,

31. *Ibid.*, at Art. 4 para. 1.
32. *Ibid.*, at Art. 4 para. 2.
33. The Competition Commission of Singapore, *Competition Act*, http://www.ccs.gov.sg/content/ccs/en/Legislation/Competition-Act.html (accessed 12 Dec. 2017).
34. ASEAN Secretariat, *ASEAN Regional Guidelines on Competition Policy*, Art. 2.2.1 (2010).
35. Law of the Republic of Indonesia Number 5 Year 1999 Concerning Prohibition of Monopolistic Practices and Unfair Business Competition, Art. 1(5) (1999).
36. Vietnam Law on Competition, No. 27/2004/QH11, Art. 2 (2004).

being an individual, a body corporate, an uncorporated body of persons or any other entity, capable of carrying on commercial or economic activities relating to goods or services'.[37]

Thailand competition law distinguishes itself by utilising the institutional approach focusing on a determined set of commercial activities, namely, distributor, producer, or importer, in the domain of agriculture, industry, commerce, finance, insurance, and services, as well as other undertakings prescribed by ministerial regulations.[38] The *Thai Trade Competition Act of 1999* broadly applies to undertakings in 'agriculture, industry, commerce, finance, insurance, and services and shall include other undertakings prescribed by Ministerial Regulations'.[39] The language used in this statute is highly detailed and specific, demonstrating its intent to clearly and rigidly communicate the scope of the law.

The ASEAN stance on the scope of competition law reflects the stance of the majority of the AMSs since it demonstrates certain preference for the functional approach.[40] Moreover, the ASEAN's confusing view on the inclusion of State-owned enterprises (SOEs) under the purview of comprehensive competition law could mirror the differences witness in the AMSs statutes. State administrations, state-owned enterprises, farmers' groups, and business under a specific regulatory authority are excluded from the application of Thailand competition law[41] whereas the acts or agreements entered into by the government, any statutory body, or any person acting on behalf of the government or that statutory body are exempted from Singapore competition law.[42] Vietnam, on the other hand, State management agencies, State monopolies, and public utilities under a special provision of competition law restricting the scope of their anticompetitive behaviour to only precluding, restricting, or preventing other enterprises from competing in the market.

[2] The Prohibition of Anticompetitive Agreement

The *Guidelines I* employ a broad definition of agreement meaning an occurrence of wills between undertakings regardless of their form or content,[43] reflecting the reality of most of the AMSs. Singapore's *CSS Guidelines on the Section 34 Prohibition* clarify that an agreement occurs when there is a 'consensus on the actions each party [to the agreement] will, or will not, take'.[44] According to the *Singapore Competition Act*, the concept of agreements between undertakings can be expanded to include decisions by associations of undertakings or concerted practices.[45] The language of the *Act* suggests

37. Singapore Competition Act (Ch. 50B) revised on 30 Jan. 2006, Art. 2(1) (2004).
38. Thailand Trade Competition Act, Art. 3 (1999).
39. *Ibid.*, at Art. 3.
40. ASEAN Secretariat, *ASEAN Regional Guidelines on Competition Policy*, Art. 3.2.1.4 (2010).
41. Thailand Trade Competition Act, Art. 4 (1999).
42. Singapore Competition Act (Ch. 50B) revised on 30 Jan. 2006, Art. 31(4) (2004).
43. ASEAN Secretariat, *ASEAN Regional Guidelines on Competition Policy*, Art. 3.2.1.3 (2010).
44. Competition Commission of Singapore, *CCS Guidelines on the s. 34 Prohibition*, para. 2.10 (2007).
45. Singapore Competition Act (Ch. 50B) revised on 30 Jan. 2006, Art. 34 (2004).

that agreement can take any form including an informal one. It covers even mere participation in a meeting with an anticompetitive purpose.

On the other hand, Indonesia competition law uses a more rigid term and identifies a list of agreements, classified according to their object, which are prohibited per se insofar as they result in monopolistic practices or under the rule of reason.[46] Thailand competition law restricts the scope of the term *agreement* to actions on each part to do any act. It follows that a consensus not to act would not fall within the scope of the law. The statute is silent on decisions by associations of undertakings or concerted practices, and block exemptions. It, however, accepts that both form of the concept of agreement, horizontal and vertical agreements, may be subject to the application of the law.[47]

Singapore is the only original AMS whose competition law shall not apply to vertical agreements, unless specifically specified by the Minister of Trade and Industry.[48] In this context, a vertical agreement refers to any agreement entered into between two or more undertakings each of which operates, for the purpose of the agreement, at a different level of the production or distribution chain.[49] The gravity of this exception is considerable considering vertical agreements usually manifest under price (minimum or maximum resale price maintenance) and non-price restraints (exclusive territorial or customer arrangement, exclusive dealings, tie-ins, selective distribution, and quantity forcing).[50] The exemption is on the premise that vertical agreements are generally less detrimental to competition than horizontal agreements.[51] This is in line with the commonly accepted approach which recognises that vertical agreements are generally efficient and thus procompetitive.[52] The ASEAN stance departs from that of Singapore since the *Guidelines I* assert that the 'AMSs should consider prohibiting horizontal and vertical agreements between undertakings that prevent, distort or restrict competition in the AMSs' territory, unless otherwise exempted'.[53]

The AMSs all recognise the division between hard-core cartel and the rule of reason test but differ widely in the method of assessment of anticompetitive agreement. Singapore evaluates the agreement with reference to its object or effect, and the appreciable prevention, distortion or restriction of competition within Singapore.[54] Conversely, an agreement will fall outside of the scope of section 34 when it has an

46. Law of the Republic of Indonesia Number 5 Year 1999 Concerning Prohibition of Monopolistic Practices and Unfair Business Competition, Ch. 3 (1999).
47. Thailand Trade Competition Act, Art. 27 (1999).
48. Singapore Competition Act (Ch. 50B) revised on 30 Jan. 2006, Third Schedule, para. 8(1) (2004).
49. *Ibid.*, at Third Schedule, para. 8(2). The definition corresponds with the general definition of vertical agreement in which it is commonly referred to as 'those between undertakings operating at different levels of the production chain of one same set of goods or services'. *See*, Sandra Marco Colino, *Vertical Agreements and Competition Law: A Comparative Study of the EU and US Regimes*, 1 (Hart Publishing 2010).
50. OECD, *Trade and Competition Policies for Tomorrow*, 43 (OECD Publishing 1999).
51. Competition Commission of Singapore, *CCS Guidelines on the s. 34 Prohibition*, Art. 2.12 (2007).
52. Paul E. Godek, *A Chicago-School Approach to Antitrust for Developing Countries*, 43 The Antitrust Bulletin (1998).
53. ASEAN Secretariat, *ASEAN Regional Guidelines on Competition Policy*, Art. 3.2.1 (2010).
54. Singapore Competition Act (Ch. 50B) revised on 30 Jan. 2006, Art. 34 (2004).

insignificant effect on the market.[55] In this regard, the primary factor considered under the rule of reason test is market share threshold. An agreement involving price-fixing, bid-rigging, market sharing, or output limitations are considered hard-core restriction under the per se rule.[56] Indonesia competition law makes the same distinction, but the agreements are appreciated based on their object.[57] Thailand, on the other hand, evaluates the agreement by reference to its effect.[58] By placing market sharing, and limiting or controlling production under the rule of reason analysis, Thailand's classification of hard-core restrictions appears more restrictive than the Singapore's and the ASEAN *Guidelines I*.[59] This restriction extends to the lack of indication pertaining to the analysis of the rule of reason and the exclusion of agreements with countervailing benefits in the *Thai Trade Competition Act*. It is possible that it is more preoccupied with determining the existence of hard-core cartels under the per se rule.

Generally, the AMSs, with the exception of Thailand, accept countervailing benefits to competition in its appreciation of the rule of reason. In this context, the agreement must present net economic benefit: agreements contributing to improving production or distribution, or promoting technical or economic progress insofar as they do not impose on the undertakings concerning restrictions which are not indispensable to the attainment of those objectives or afford the undertakings concerned the possibility of eliminating competition in respect of a substantial part of the goods or services in question. In addition, Vietnam competition law also grants additional exemption under the rule of reason to certain agreements with countervailing benefits with combined market share equal to or above 30%.[60]

[3] The Prohibition of Abuse of Dominant Position

There is no agreed upon analysis on the definition of dominant position. Thailand competition law operates under a more restrictive analysis by relying exclusively on the criteria of market share threshold in determining market dominance.[61] Indonesia competition law also shares this vision.[62] In comparison, Singapore Competition Commission states that the market share criterion alone may not be sufficiently reliable and suggests other determinants may need to be considered as well. These could

55. This is reminiscent of *Franz Völk v. SPRL. Ets J. Vervaecke*.
56. Competition Commission of Singapore, *CCS Guidelines on the Section 34 Prohibition*, para. 2.20 (2007). Confirmed in *Collusive Tendering (Bid-Rigging) in Electrical and Building Works* (SGCCS 4 2010); *Re Price Fixing of Rates of Modelling Services in Singapore by Modelling Agencies* (2013).
57. Law of the Republic of Indonesia Number 5 Year 1999 Concerning Prohibition of Monopolistic Practices and Unfair Business Competition, Ch. 3 (1999).
58. Office of Thai Trade Competition Commission, *Guidelines on Section 27 of Thailand Trade Competition Act* (2010).
59. ASEAN Secretariat, *ASEAN Regional Guidelines on Competition Policy*, Art. 3.2.2 (2010).
60. Vietnam Law on Competition, No. 27/2004/QH11, Art. 10 (2004).
61. Office of Thai Trade Competition Commission, *Notifications of Trade Competition Commission on Criteria for Business Operator with Market Domination* (2007).
62. Law of the Republic of Indonesia Number 5 Year 1999 Concerning Prohibition of Monopolistic Practices and Unfair Business Competition, Art. 25(2) (1999).

include entry barriers, the degree of innovation, product differentiation, the responsiveness of buyers to price increases, and the price responsiveness of competitors.[63] This position has been sustained by the Competition Appeal Board.[64] Henceforth, the factors that could be considered include the market share of the undertaking, the ability of the undertaking to profitably sustain prices above competitive levels, the undertaking's ability to eliminate or weaken competitors, the existence of countervailing buyer power as well as barriers to entry in the market. However, the primary factor remains the market share and the CCS generally considers market share of above 60% as an indicator of a dominant position in the relevant market.[65] Inspired by the difference exhibited by the AMSs, the ASEAN does not provide any suggestion regarding market dominance assessment. It leaves the decision-making power entirely in the hands of the AMSs.[66]

All the AMSs and the ASEAN make a distinction between two characters of abuse of dominant position: exploitative behaviours of an undertaking which may cause harm to consumer directly and exclusionary conducts which affect the market structure.[67]

[4] Merger Control

Vietnam is the only AMSs not using the term *merger*, preferring instead 'economic concentrations'.[68] Other AMSs as well as the ASEAN employs the term *merger* to cover merger, acquisition, direct and indirect control over the whole or part of an undertaking, and a joint venture to perform on a lasting basis all the functions of an autonomous economic entity.

Most of the AMSs prefer the dominance test focusing on combined market share of the merger in question. Vietnam competition law prohibits economic concentrations where the parties' combined market share exceeds 50%.[69] Thailand uses market share threshold in combination with previous year sale or revenue.[70] In contrast, Singapore selects the SLC test.[71] This means that the focus is on the impact of the merger on the relevant market, in particular changes in market structure and concentrations. The predominant criteria are market share and the concentration ratio. Market share is merely one of the indicators of potential competition concerns – for instance barriers to

63. Competition Commission of Singapore, *CCS Guidelines on the Section 47 Prohibition*, para. 3.7 (2007).
64. *Re Abuse of a Dominant Position by SISTIC.com Pte Ltd*, paras 222–249 (2012).
65. Competition Commission of Singapore, *CCS Guidelines on the Section 47 Prohibition*, para. 3.8 (2007).
66. ASEAN Secretariat, *ASEAN Regional Guidelines on Competition Policy*, Art. 3.3.1.1 (2010).
67. Thailand Trade Competition Act, Art. 25 (1999). Singapore Competition Act (Ch. 50B) revised on 30 Jan. 2006, Art. 47(2) (2004). Vietnam Law on Competition, No. 27/2004/QH11, Art. 13 (2004).
68. Vietnam Law on Competition, No. 27/2004/QH11, Ch. 2. Art. 3 (2004).
69. *Ibid.*, at Art. 18.
70. Resolutions of Trade Competition Commission on Criteria for Business Combination (in Thai) (2013).
71. Singapore Competition Act (Ch. 50B) revised on 30 Jan. 2006, Art. 54 (2004).

entry and expansion and countervailing buyer power.[72] It follows that competition concerns could still be raised even if the market share is below the market share threshold.

The *Guidelines I* follow the example led by Singapore competition law and admit that mergers should be appraised on their economic effect.[73] However, instead of the SLC test, it opts instead for a combining of both the US the SLC test[74] and the EU SIEC test.[75]

The merger notification system adopted by each AMS differ greatly. Thailand adopts the mandatory merger notification regime while Singapore chooses the voluntary notification regime. A voluntary notification system is in place in Singapore and applies to both mergers and anticipated mergers.[76] This is likely a direct transplant of the UK merger control.[77] Consequently, merging undertakings are not required to submit the transaction for review to the competition authority, unless the transaction is likely to pose anticompetitive risk.[78] The CCS firmly believes the choice is most appropriate for Singapore since most mergers are 'unlikely to raise competition concerns'.[79] By not notifying the Singapore Competition Commission, however, undertakings faced the risk of an *ex post facto* investigation by the competition authority. Finally, Indonesia establishes a dual system of voluntary consultation (pre-merger notification) and mandatory post-merger notification.

Conscious of this divide, the *Guidelines I* do not decide between voluntary or mandatory notification, leaving the choice instead to respective AMSs but applies the pre-merger control regimes,[80] following the examples of most competition law jurisdictions in the world.[81]

[C] Institutional Models

Most AMSs follow the integrated institution model. Following the Indonesian competition statute[82] and the Presidential Decree,[83] the Indonesian Competition Commission (KPPU) was established as an independent competition regulatory agency to regulate

72. *Proposed Acquisition by United Parcel Service, Inc. of TNT Express N.V.*, para. 43 (2012).
73. ASEAN Secretariat, *ASEAN Regional Guidelines on Competition Policy*, Art. 3.4.1 (2010).
74. The Clayton Act, 15 U.S.C. §§ 12–27, 29 U.S.C. §§52–53 (2006).
75. Council Regulation (EC) No. 139/2004 on the Control of Concentrations between Undertakings, Art. 2(2) (2004). The previous criterion of dominant position has been reduced to a mere example of significant impedance of effective competition. However, dominant position has not completely been erased from the *EUMR*. It still appears on the regulation as a prime indication of concentration between undertakings incompatible with the common market. *See* Art. 2(3) of the *EUMR*.
76. Singapore Competition Act (Ch. 50B) revised on 30 Jan. 2006, Arts 56–58 (2004).
77. *See*, Enterprise Act [2002] c.40, Art. 96.
78. Paas-Mohando, *Choice of Merger Notification System for Small Economies*, 34 E.C.L.R. (2013).
79. Competition Commission of Singapore, *Public Consultation on Proposed Merger Regime* (2006).
80. ASEAN Secretariat, *ASEAN Regional Guidelines on Competition Policy*, Art. 3.4.4 (2010).
81. Paas-Mohando, *Choice of Merger Notification System for Small Economies*, 34 E.C.L.R. (2013).
82. Law of the Republic of Indonesia Number 5 Year 1999 Concerning Prohibition of Monopolistic Practices and Unfair Business Competition Art. 30 (1999).
83. Presidential Decree No. 75/1999 Komisi Pengawas Persaingan Usaha (1999).

competition, enforce competition law, and provide recommendations to the government regarding competition-related policies. It is accountable to only the President and the House Representatives. Singapore also created a single national competition authority named the Competition Commission of Singapore[84] assuming the roles of investigation, enforcement, and adjudication.

In the same year as the establishment of the KPPU, Thailand established its Trade Competition Commission based on provisions of the *Thai Trade Competition Act*,[85] which would assume the bifurcated judicial model where the investigative and enforcement authorities are separated.[86]

Vietnam is the only AMS with two institutional arrangements: the Vietnam Competition Administration Department established in 2004 under the Ministry of Trade and the Vietnam Competition Council established in 2006 as an independent agency. Both organs were established on the basis of the same competition statute.[87] Vietnam follows this model with the Vietnam Competition Authority undertaking the investigation role of competition restriction conducts, application for exemptions for agreements and mergers, and unfair competition practices,[88] while the Vietnam Competition Council is responsible for the enforcement and adjudication of competition law cases.[89]

With these different configurations, the ASEAN has no other choice but to support all three models, with demonstrated slight preference for the integrated model.[90]

§6.02 THE AMSs WITH COMPETITION LAWS AFTER THE ASEAN INITIATIVE

Following the ASEAN's initiative of regional economic integration with competition policy as its pillar, Malaysia,[91] Myanmar,[92] Brunei Darussalam,[93] and the Philippines[94] all passed their national competition law statute. Lao PDR adopted its first comprehensive competition law[95] after the establishment of the AEC when the original deadline has long passed. The enactment of the Lao PDR competition law replaced the Prime Minister's *Decree No. 15 on Trade Competition* which was adopted on 4 February

84. Singapore Competition Act (Ch. 50B) revised on 30 Jan. 2006, Part 2 (2004).
85. Thailand Trade Competition Act, Ch. 1 (1999).
86. Michael J. Trebilcock & Edward M. Iacobucci, *Designing Competition Law Institutions*, 25 World Competition (2002).
87. Vietnam Law on Competition, No. 27/2004/QH11, Ch. 4 (2004).
88. *Ibid.*, at Art. 49.
89. *Ibid.*, at Art. 53.
90. ASEAN Secretariat, *Guidelines on Developing Core Competencies in Competition Policy and Law for ASEAN*, 31 (2012).
91. Malaysia Competition Act, Act 712 (2010).
92. The Competition Law, The Pyidaungsu Hluttaw Law No. 9/2015 (2015).
93. *Ibid.*
94. Philippines Competition Act, Republic Act No. 10667 (2015).
95. Law on Business Competition (No. 60/NA) (2015).

2004.[96] It is a non-comprehensive competition law statute since it only applies to monopolies and unfair competition. The *Decree* has never been enforced because the Trade Competition Commission, the authority in charge of its implementation and enforcement,[97] has never been created.[98] A year later, Thailand finally adopted its modernisation competition law bill[99] which came to replace the old statute with the principal aim to transform the competition commission institution.

Despite the concretisation of the ASEAN initiative in regional competition law, denoted by the adoption of *the Guidelines I*, the ASEAN influence on the AMSs national competition law still remains limited. Naturally, it is expected that the AMS whose competition law was enacted after the realisation of the ASEAN initiative in light of their commitment to enact national competition law statute before the arrival of the AEC would follow the direction of the ASEAN. However, this was not the case. At the most fundamental level, not all the AMSs competition law contain the three core competition law provisions: prohibition of anticompetitive agreement, prohibition of abuse of dominant position, and merger control. Malaysia, in particular, does not have a merger control regime despite it being highlighted in the *Guidelines I* as one of the most important competition law rules. This absence is inexplicable and deprives the Malaysian Competition Commission of considerable power and influence in exercising its functions and duties.[100] Furthermore, merger control is especially important for developing economies which typically have small market economies. As mergers reduce the number of competitors and increase the market share of the merged entities, the result will be to increase any concentration already present in the market.[101]

[A] The Goals of Competition Law

Most of the AMSs neglect the *Guidelines I* general goal of the promotion and protection of competition.[102] However, all the AMSs in possession of comprehensive competition law related statutes have set economic goals as the rationale for their national competition laws. *Malaysia Competition Act*, which was enacted in 2010 and became effective in January 2012, states the purpose of the law as 'to promote economic development by promoting and protecting the process of competition, thereby protecting the interests of consumers'.[103] The language of the law suggests that there is a hierarchical order of the goals. The primary objectives of the economic goals are the promotion of economic development and the promotion and protection of the process of competition while the secondary objective is the protection of consumer welfare.

96. Decree No. 15/PMO on Trade Competition [2004].
97. *Ibid.*, at Art. 16.
98. Terence Lim & Abigail Kway, *ASEAN Competition Law*, Ch. IV s. 1 (2nd ed., LexisNexis 2012).
99. Thailand Trade Competition Act (2017).
100. Cassey Lee, *Competition Law Enforcement in Malaysia: Some Recent Developments* (ERIA Discussion Paper Series 2014).
101. Jurgita Malinauskaite, *Efficiency Tests in the Merger Control Regimes of the Baltic Countries: Myth or Reality*, 18 International Company and Commercial Law Review (2007).
102. ASEAN Secretariat, *ASEAN Regional Guidelines on Competition Policy*, Art. 2.2.1 (2010).
103. Malaysia Competition Act, Act 712 (2010).

Similarly, Brunei Darussalam's competition law goal is to promote economic efficiency, economic development, and consumer welfare.[104] The Philippines statute recognises economic efficiency and the promotion of free and fair competition, the prevention of economic concentration, the protection of consumer welfare, the advancement of domestic and international trade, as well as economic development as the goals of competition law.[105] In line with a long established tradition, Thailand modernised *Trade Competition Act of 2017* referred to the goal of competition law in the nota bene which is the protection and promotion of free and fair competition while referencing the old statute it came to repeal.[106]

The Myanmar competition law stands out for its omission of economic efficiency among its economic goals. It follows that there are some difficulties in obtaining consensus on the identity of economic goals among the AMSs. The Myanmar competition law aims to 'prevent the public interests from being harmful', control unfair competition, prevent abuse of market power, and control agreements and plans that cause limitations on competition.[107] The statute makes no attempt to identify public interests. Myanmar competition law is the only regime that highlights protection of public interest without defining it.

In addition, none of the AMSs have included regional integration in their goals of competition law. The blatant disregard of the common reference guide published by the ASEAN Secretariat meaningfully suggests that the AMSs are operating independently from the ASEAN and its ambition.

[B] Substantive Provisions

[1] The Scope of Competition Law

Some AMSs follow the ASEAN stance on the scope of competition law.[108] The Philippines employ the functional approach by stating that the law shall apply to any person or entity engaged in any trade, industry, and commerce in the borders of the country and international trade with direct, substantial, and reasonable foreseeable effects in trade, industry, and commerce in the Philippines.[109] Malaysia competition law applies to *enterprises* defined as any entities carrying on commercial activities relating to goods or services, both within and outside Malaysia, provided that the commercial activity has an effect on competition in any market in Malaysia.[110] In comparison, the scope of Lao PDR competition law extends to domestic and foreign

104. Brunei Competition Order, Art. 1(3) (2015).
105. Philippines Competition Act, Republic Act No. 10667, Art. 2 (2015).
106. Thailand Trade Competition Act, nota bene, p. 26 (2017).
107. The Pyidaungsu Hluttaw Law No. 9, Art. 3 (2015).
108. ASEAN Secretariat, *ASEAN Regional Guidelines on Competition Policy*, Art. 3.2.1.4 (2010).
109. Philippines Competition Act, Republic Act No. 10667, Art. 3 (2015).
110. Malaysia Competition Act, Act 712, Art. 3 (2010).

individuals, legal entities, and organisations with a business presence in Lao PDR (including SOEs)[111,112] focusing on the institutional approach.

[2] The Prohibition of Anticompetitive Agreement

All the AMSs follow the example set in the *Guidelines I* and employ a broad definition of agreement, which describe an agreement as an occurrence of wills between undertakings regardless of their form or content.[113] In addition, both forms of horizontal and vertical agreements are accepted.

All of the AMSs include provisions recognising the per se rule and rule of reason with countervailing benefit exception. Interestingly, Lao PDR exempts anticompetitive agreements where such agreements promote technological and academic progress, improve the quality of goods and services or enhance the competitiveness of SMEs.[114] Similarly, the Myanmar competition law shall not apply to anticompetitive agreements dedicated to promoting technological advance, improve the quality of good and service, raise competitiveness of SME, raise competitiveness of Myanmar in the international market.[115] The latter sacrifices the support for the ASEAN single market structure for the benefit of local undertakings.

[3] The Prohibition of Abuse of Dominant Position

Not all of the AMSs competition laws use the term *dominant position* since Myanmar competition law prefers the term 'monopolisation on market in competition'.[116] In particular, Lao PDR makes a distinction between market control and monopolisation.[117] The former is considered a unilateral or joint market share exceeding the thresholds established by the Commission; whereas the latter is considered to include both single and groups of companies that solely supply a market.

All the AMSs and the ASEAN make a distinction between two characters of abuse of dominant position: exploitative behaviours of an undertaking which may cause harm to consumer directly and exclusionary conducts which affect the market structure.[118]

111. Khouanchay Iemsouthi, *Competition Law and Policy in Lao PDR, The 12th East Asia Top Level Officials' Meeting on Competition Policy 9 September 2016, Seoul, Korea*, http://www.mycc.gov.my/sites/default/files/1-5%28Mr.Khouanchay%20Iemsouthi%29%20Laos%20MoIC.pdf (accessed 12 Dec. 2017).
112. *Lao PDR Lays Foundation for Competition Regime*, https://www.dfdl.com/resources/legal-and-tax-updates/lao-pdr-lays-foundation-for-its-competition-regime/ (accessed 18 Feb. 2018).
113. ASEAN Secretariat, *ASEAN Regional Guidelines on Competition Policy*, Art. 3.2.1.3 (2010).
114. Law on Business Competition (No. 60/NA), Art. 45 (2015).
115. The Pyidaungsu Hluttaw Law No. 9, Art. 14 (2015).
116. *Ibid.*, at Art. 15.
117. Law on Business Competition (No. 60/NA), Art. 30 (2015).
118. Thailand Trade Competition Act s. 25 (1999). Singapore Competition Act (Ch. 50B) revised on 30 Jan. 2006 Art. 47(2) (2004). Vietnam Law on Competition, No. 27/2004/QH11, Art. 13 (2004).

[4] Merger Control

The ASEAN employs the term *merger* to cover merger, acquisition, direct and indirect control over the whole or part of an undertaking, and a joint venture to perform on a lasting basis all the functions of an autonomous economic entity. While most states adopt identical denomination, on the other hand, Myanmar prefers using the term 'collaboration among business'[119] to include merger, consolidation, acquisition, joint venture, or any other collaboration.

The *Guidelines I* admit that mergers should be appraised on their economic effect[120] through a combination of both the US SLC test[121] and the EU SIEC test.[122] Brunei Darussalam evaluates merger based on the SLC test for both actual and potential consequences.[123] Myanmar competition law forbids merger with extreme dominance or which decreases competition through acquisition of sole or minority shares of the business.[124] It further states that market share criterion shall be used in the economic evaluation.[125] In comparison, the Philippines competition law is the only regime to employ the criterion of transaction value,[126] however it leaves the possibility for the Philippines Competition Commission to add other appropriate criteria such as market share threshold in the future. The inclusion of transaction size threshold is considered innovative and beneficial to new competition law jurisdiction because it is subject to a lesser degree of manipulation than the calculation of undertakings' market share.[127] Lao PDR defines anticompetitive merger as business mergers that result in: a market share over the determined level; an effect on access to the market or that limit technological development; and an effect on consumers, other businesses, and the development of national socio-economy.[128] In this regard, it recognised both the market share and other anticompetitive criterion. It is noteworthy that all of the AMSs opt for a balancing approach which includes an efficiency defence in its evaluation of merger despite awareness of the difficulties in analysing efficiency gains as a new competition law jurisdiction with crippling lack of necessary resources.

The ASEAN does not express preference between voluntary and mandatory merger notification, leaving the choice instead to respective AMSs[129] resulting in a

119. The Pyidaungsu Hluttaw Law No. 9, Art. 30 (2015).
120. ASEAN Secretariat, *ASEAN Regional Guidelines on Competition Policy*, Art. 3.4.1 (2010).
121. The Clayton Act, 15 U.S.C. §§ 12–27, 29 U.S.C. §§52–53 (2006).
122. Council Regulation (EC) No. 139/2004 on the Control of Concentrations between Undertakings, Art. 2(2) (2004). The previous criterion of dominant position has been reduced to a mere example of significant impedance of effective competition. However, dominant position has not completely been erased from the *EUMR*. It still appears on the regulation as a prime indication of concentration between undertakings incompatible with the common market. *See* Art. 2(3) of the *EUMR*.
123. Brunei Competition Order, Art. 23 (2015).
124. The Pyidaungsu Hluttaw Law No. 9, Art. 31 (2015).
125. *Ibid.*, at Art. 32.
126. Philippines Competition Act, Republic Act No. 10667, Art. 17 (2015).
127. A. E. Rodriguez & Ashok Menon, *The Limits of Competition Policy: The Shortcomings of Antitrust in Developing and Reforming Economies*, 90 (Kluwer Law International 2010).
128. Law on Business Competition (No. 60/NA), Art. 38 (2015).
129. ASEAN Secretariat, *ASEAN Regional Guidelines on Competition Policy*, Art. 3.4.4 (2010).

widened diversity in terms of merger notification regime. The majority of the AMS, not unlike Myanmar and the Philippines, opt for a mandatory regime of pre-merger notification.[130] Some AMSs, notably Brunei Darussalam and Lao PDR, choose a dual regime of both pre-merger and post-merger notification.[131] Lao PDR requires all undertakings to file a voluntary pre-merger notification to the Commission unless the businesses are SMEs. Mergers between SMEs are subject to a mandatory notification post-merger. Brunei Darussalam competition law regime, on the other hand, prefers voluntary notification for both pre- and post-merger notification.

[C] Institutional Models

The ASEAN supports all three institutional models: bifurcated judicial model, bifurcated agency model, and integrated agency model, with ostensible preference in favour of the integrated model.[132] The Malaysian Competition Commission[133] was established entrusted with both enforcement and implementation powers.[134] The Myanmar competition law which became effective on February 2017 envisages the establishment of the Competition Commission of Myanmar.[135] It is believed that the Competition Policy Division of Ministry of Commerce is still in the process of preparing the formation of the Commission whose independent status is dubious since members of the Commission can come from Union Ministers or government Departments background. The Laos Competition Commission is also poised to soon be established.[136] It will be chaired by Vice Minister of Industry and Commerce and its members will comprised of representatives from line ministries and representative from Laos National Chamber of Commerce and Industry and the Bar Association. The Commission primary responsibility is to investigate and enforce substantive competition violations. Finally, the Competition Commission of Brunei Darussalam with the power to both investigate and enforce competition law promises no independence since it shall receive direction from the Minister.[137]

The Philippines is the only AMS with a bifurcated judicial model.[138] The Philippine Competition Commission is an independent quasi-judicial agency attached to the Office of the President. The country still retains the old organisation named the Office for Competition under the Department of Justice who still conducts preliminary investigation and prosecute all criminal offence.[139]

130. Philippines Competition Act, Republic Act No. 10667, Art. 17 (2015).
131. Brunei Competition Order, Arts 26 & 27 (2015).
132. ASEAN Secretariat, *Guidelines on Developing Core Competencies in Competition Policy and Law for ASEAN*, 31 (2012).
133. Malaysia Competition Commission Act, Act 713, Art. 3 (2010).
134. Malaysia Competition Act, Act 712, Art. 16 (2010).
135. The Pyidaungsu Hluttaw Law No. 9, Art. 5 (2015).
136. *Lao PDR Lays Foundation for Competition Regime*, https://www.dfdl.com/resources/legal-and-tax-updates/lao-pdr-lays-foundation-for-its-competition-regime/ (accessed 18 Feb. 2018).
137. Brunei Competition Order, Part 2, Art. 3 (2015).
138. Philippines Competition Act, Republic Act No. 10667, Art. 5 (2015).
139. *Ibid.*, at Art. 13.

Major institutional reform in the new *Thailand Trade Competition Act of 2017* points towards a sincere inclination to align with the ASEAN's vision regarding competition law. Henceforth, the Trade Competition Commission shall be reformed and transformed into an independent entity under the Constitution.[140] It is precisely this change in the institutional design that most reflected the anti-corruption context surrounding the adoption of the new statute. The new *Act* attempts to grant independence to the Commission by extracting them from the Ministry of Commerce. Despite the effort in making the Commission independent, the new Commission formation is unlikely to be devoid of interference. Indeed, the *Act* insists that the Commissioners are appointed by the Prime Minister from a list selected and nominated by a Committee composing of high level bureaucrats, representatives of big business association, and a consumer representative.[141]

§6.03 CONCLUSION

The ASEAN's approach towards regional competition law appears more receptive to the AMSs' experiences, especially the experiences of Indonesia, Thailand, Singapore, and Vietnam whose competition law regimes were firmly in place before the ASEAN's announced vision of a regional competition law. The *Guidelines I* certainly admit so in their formulation.[142] In contrast, the ASEAN only has limited influence on the formulation of new competition law regimes.

Examining the AMSs' competition law regimes reveal some superficial commonalities, chiefly in the core areas of competition law. Malaysia, however, strays from this pattern as it does not have a merger control regime in its comprehensive competition law. The AMSs regimes differ widely in details especially in the areas of the scope of competition law and the economic analysis of anticompetitive behaviours. The cause of this situation could be the differences in the origin of the law, namely different socio-political contexts conducive to their enactments. To accommodate these differences, the ASEAN, through both *Guidelines*, opt for a neutral stance neither forcing nor directing the AMSs to adopt a certain shape of competition law.

With regards to the competition law institution, all AMSs have established at least one dedicated regulatory body in charge of enforcing competition law. This is perhaps the area where the discrepancy between the AMSs and the ASEAN is most obvious. The majority of the AMSs echoes the ASEAN's preference for an integrated model.[143] Only a few of the AMSs established dedicated national competition law authorities under the bifurcated judicial and bifurcated agency model. However, the ASEAN should still be disappointed that the only strong suggestion it has made with respect to competition law has been ignored by the AMSs. Indeed, the principle of independence of the

140. Thailand Trade Competition Act, Art. 27 (2017).
141. *Ibid.*, at Art. 11.
142. ASEAN Secretariat, *ASEAN Regional Guidelines on Competition Policy*, Foreword (2010).
143. ASEAN Secretariat, *Guidelines on Developing Core Competencies in Competition Policy and Law for ASEAN*, 32 (2012).

competition law institution, which is highly regarded by the ASEAN,[144] is not held in the same regard by the AMSs competition law authorities.

Despite the ASEAN's effort in establishing a regional competition law that is compatible with the AMSs local contexts, many differences still persist. Furthermore, the AMSs have not shown any interest or progress in adapting their competition laws to more closely resemble the vision of the ASEAN. The willingness to undertake soft harmonisation does not seem to be present within the AMSs. This departure from the regional design can be detrimental to the ASEAN's economic integration aspiration.

144. ASEAN Secretariat, *ASEAN Regional Guidelines on Competition Policy*, Art. 4.1.3 (2010).

CHAPTER 7

Epilogue and Encore

There is admiration to be found in the ASEAN's ambition in creating a regional competition law, if not in the execution.

As is often the case when pursuing regional competition law in developing jurisdictions, the ASEAN is faced with various challenges such as differences in socio-political situations, uneven economic development, resource restrictions, and lack of a competition culture. Some obstacles are decidedly ASEAN-specific: the AMSs' diversity in the area of economics and politics, and the principle of non-interference or the ASEAN Way. However, it became evident that rather than overcoming the obstacles the ASEAN's approach to regional competition law is instead defined by these fundamental limitations.

To attain regional competition law so desired, the ASEAN opted for a soft harmonisation approach which is a non-binding multilateralism offering more flexibility and practicality than binding commitments. The primary flaw of the soft harmonisation approach is its over-reliance on participating states' voluntary commitment and willingness to follow the regional approach. Most of the ASEAN's contributions regarding substantive competition policy concentrate on supporting the enactment of the AMSs' domestic competition law statutes. The ASEAN has never proposed a framework unique or conducive to its vision. Instead, it is content with presenting known best practices in the field of competition law and policy to the AMSs. The AMSs are free and even encouraged to neglect the ASEAN's assembled efforts in favour of their own particular needs, situations, or preferences. Giving the AMSs such a large margin of flexibility leads to a regional organisation that is a vehicle for economic, social, and political divergence on various issues rather than compelling the AMSs to move towards regional economic integration.

For a regional organisation characterised by its constant evolution, the ASEAN's institutional structure has never evolved beyond its original conception which is the informal cooperation. The ASEAN has long operated under a decentralised structure with no supranational institution. While the ASEAN Secretariat is the main regional institutional body, it does not possess decision-making power. Decisions are made through consultation and consensus at the ASEAN Summit in accordance with the ASEAN Way. Consequently, the ASEAN lacks adequate regional institutional structure to uphold its lofty ambition. The ASEAN has neither established a supranational institution nor a representative institution composed of national representatives at regional level. In their stead, it has created an expert competition organ called the AEGC which is composed of national competition authorities or related governmental officials in the case of the AMSs without relevant competition law authorities. If a regional competition issue emerges, the ASEAN opts to resolve such an issue through national extraterritorial solutions, and bilateral and multilateral cooperation. The ASEAN is thus forced to rely on the AMSs national systems to uphold its regional competition law.

The ASEAN's choice of harmonised regional competition law without a central institution is a mixture of the MERCOSUR's harmonisation approach, which focuses on encouraging Member States to enact and enforce national competition law, and the NAFTA's free trade area agreement's lack of a dispute resolution system. The ASEAN departs from conventional wisdom where harmonisation, whether soft or hard, could only happen with the inclusion of a central organ competent of enforcing regional competition law and monitoring Member States' compliance with the regional framework. The ASEAN charts a new road towards regional competition law that is distinctive from other regional models.

The ASEAN regional competition law failed to resonate with the AMSs. This is possibly due to the AMSs' levity in commitment. The ASEAN expresses its preference for a spontaneous move towards harmonisation by the AMSs through increased contact among competition authorities and relevant officials with the help of the information provided and facilitated by the ASEAN. However, an examination of the AMSs' competition law regimes has revealed that the spontaneous harmonisation of national competition laws as envisioned by the ASEAN is unlikely to occur. Despite sharing some similarities in the broad principles of competition law across jurisdictions, the AMSs' domestic competition laws are not harmonised. For instance, Malaysia's competition law does not contain provisions on merger control. Further discrepancies are observed between the scope of competition law and the actual competition assessment in the enforcement of the law. While all the AMSs with competition law statutes have established national competition authorities, different models have been adopted. It appears that the AMSs continue to largely ignore the path charted by the ASEAN. Nonetheless, it should not be ignored that the ASEAN has succeeded in convincing the AMSs of the importance of enacting a comprehensive competition law, even if it could not make its own preference heard.

Early prognosis of the ASEAN regional competition law since the arrival of the AEC at the end of 2015 points towards a sentiment of disappointment. In defiance of the pledge to introduce national competition law before the institution of the AEC, the AMSs have not unanimously followed through with this basic commitment; Cambodia is still in the process of drafting its first national competition law statute. The AMSs' failure to fulfil the minimal expectation is instrumental to the lack of credibility of the ASEAN regional framework of competition law. Consequently, the ASEAN is in danger of joining many other developing jurisdictions' experience with regional competition law in that they only exist in the text. The ASEAN is likely to replicate the COMESA's unimpactful experience caused by the fact that some of its Member States, notably Malawi, could not meet the domestic enforcement obligations.[1] In recognition of the state of the ASEAN regional competition law, it has been suggested that '[m]ore time may be needed for ASEAN to have a systematic harmonisation of competition law'.[2] However, it is plausible that temporal extension could only serve to prolong the problematic state of the ASEAN regional competition law.

When the AEC was formally introduced on the 31 December 2015, it was accompanied by a regional competition law framework that aims to inform rather than create a common approach and without a regional institution capable of enforcement or monitoring duty. The path of the ASEAN regional competition law does a disservice to the AEC and directly contribute to its current stagnant state, neither thriving nor crumbling. The AEC's predicament, in turn, directly affects the state of the ASEAN Community since the AEC is its important supporting pillar. The AEC is currently operating as a single market, in name, devoid of an effective regional competition law, despite being previously hailed as the most feasible pillar of the ASEAN Community. In the end, although the ASEAN has made significant progress, incontestably, it has not yet achieved its primary objective of constructing a single market.

Despite past disappointment, the ASEAN is still committed to carry on the burden of the past with renewed determination. The ASEAN formally recognises the necessity of establishing common core elements with respect to the legal frameworks on competition law and policy amongst the AMSs,[3] in the form of an *acquis communautaire*. The new *Blueprint*[4] acknowledges past failure and seems committed to strengthening the ASEAN Community with more emphasis on deeply integrated and highly cohesive ASEAN economy. There are now new priorities which are the development and promotion of micro, small, and medium enterprises in its economic integration efforts, as well as embracing the digital economy. The *ASEAN Competition Action Plan*[5] was enacted to aid in the concrete realisation of the *Blueprint* and details strategic goals, initiatives, and outcomes on competition policy and law in ASEAN over the next ten years after the entry of the AEC. The measures indicate the ASEAN's wish to improve on existing mechanism and harmonisation approach by improving on their efficiency. To help achieve this renewed ambition, the *ASEAN Competition Action Plan* suggests five strategic goals which are:

I. Effective competition regimes are established in all ASEAN Member States (AMS);

1. George K. Lipimile & Elizabeth Gachuiri, *Allocation of Competences Between National and Regional Competition Authorities: The Case of COMESA*, *in* Competition Provisions in Regional Trade Agreements: How to Assure Development Gains (Philippe Brusick, et al. eds., UNCTAD/DITC/CLP/2005/1 2005).
2. De Sevelinges, *Snapshot of Competition Laws in ASEAN and China*, 26 AUT Int'l L. Practicum (2013).
3. ASEAN Secretariat, *ASEAN Discusses Approach to Effective Competition Enforcement*, http://www.asean.org/news/asean-secretariat-news/item/asean-discusses-approach-to-effective-competition-enforcement (accessed 13 Nov. 2017).
4. Secretariat, *ASEAN Economic Community Blueprint 2025* (ASEAN Secretariat 2015).
5. Secretariat, *ASEAN Competition Action Plan 2025* (ASEAN Secretariat 2015).

II. The capacities of competition-related agencies in AMS are strengthened to effectively implement [competition law and policy];
III. Regional cooperation arrangements on [competition law and policy] are in place;
IV. Fostering a competition-aware ASEAN region; and
V. Moving towards greater harmonization of competition policy and law in ASEAN.[6]

To date, there is no apparent and concrete execution of these five strategic goals. It is likely that the most realistic and achievable measure is to enhance the responsibilities of the AEGC. This could be done through the inclusion of new tools such as the peer review of the AMSs' domestic competition policies in comparison with the approaches of the ASEAN, the installation of deeper cooperation and coordination efforts, and concrete communication between national competition authorities concerning the enforcement and development of domestic competition law regimes. The peer review system, in particular, corresponds well to the nature of the ASEAN organisation which relies on good relationship and mutual respect between members without infringing on their sovereignty. While it is understandable that establishing a centre of merger notification for mergers with regional dimension within the ASEAN will be challenging, the AEGC could considerably benefit from acting as an information centre for merger notification filings on a regular basis.

There is genuine admiration to be found in the ASEAN's ambition in creating regional competition law. The ASEAN current harmonisation approach is best perceived as the first step towards the realisation of such an ambition. This first step suitably takes into account the current stage of the ASEAN integration as well as the tools and mechanisms at the ASEAN disposal. As the ASEAN moves towards further integration, an increasing number of binding agreements would soon follow. As the level of integration grows, the binding character of liberalising agreements becomes more important, and as the levels of legal obligation and the precision of the rules increase, delegation of rule interpretation and dispute adjudication is often observed.[7] The introduction of the AEC and subsequent documents in the form of the *Blueprint* and the *ASEAN Competition Action Plan* all stand testament to this recent ASEAN growth.

6. *Ibid.*
7. Miles Kahler, *Legalization as Strategy: The Asia-Pacific Case*, 54 International Organization (2000).

Bibliography

Books and Book Sections

Anthony Amunategui Abad, *Competition Law and Policy in the Framework of ASEAN in Competition Policy and Regional Integration, in Competition Policy and Regional Integration in Developing Countries* (Josef Drexl, et al. eds., Edward Elgar Publishing 2012).

Amitav Acharya, *Europe and Asia: Reflections on a Tale of Two Regionalisms, in Regional Integration in East Asia and Europe: Convergence or Divergence?* (Bertrand Fort & Douglas Webber eds., Routledge 2006).

Giuliano Amato, *Antitrust and the Bounds of Power* (Hart Publishing 1997).

Mary L. Azcuenaga, *The Evolution of International Competition Policy: A Federal Trade Commission Perspective* (1992).

Mor Bakhoum, *Reflections on the Concepts of 'Economic Freedom', 'Free Competition' and 'Efficiency' from the Perspective of Developing Countries, in* The Goals of Competition Law (Daniel Zimmer ed. Edward Elgar Publishing 2012).

Mor Bakhoum & Julia Molestina, *Institutional Coherence and Effectiveness of a Regional Competition Policy: the Case of the West African Economic and Monetary Union (WAEMU), in Competition Policy and Regional Integration in Developing Countries* (Josef Drexl, et al. eds., Edward Elgar Publishing 2012).

Delroy S. Beckford, *Implementing Effective Competition Policy through Regional Trade Agreements: the Case of CARICOM, in Competition Policy and Regional Integration in Developing Countries* (Josef Drexl, et al. eds., Edward Elgar Publishing 2012).

Simon Bishop & Mike Walker, *The Economics of EC Competition Law: Concepts, Application and Measurement* (3rd ed., Sweet & Maxwell 2010).

Thérèse Blanchet, et al., *The Agreement on the European Economic Area (EEA): A Guide to the Free Movement of Goods and Competition Rules* (Clarendon Press 1994).

Robert H. Bork, *The Antitrust Paradox: A Policy at War with Itself* (Free Press 1978).

Robert H. Bork, *The Tempting of America* (Touchstone 1990).

Marco Botta, *Competition Policy: The EU and Global Networks, in EU Policies in a Global Perspective: Shaping or Taking International Regimes?* (Gerda Falkner & Patrick Müller eds., Routledge 2014).

Marco Botta, *Competition Policy: the EU and Global Networks, in EU Policies in a Global Perspective: Shaping or Taking International Regimes?* (Gerda Falkner & Patrick Müller eds., Routledge, Taylor & Francis Group 2014).

Lucian Cernat, *Eager to Ink, But Ready to Act? RTA Proliferation and International Cooperation on Competition Policy, in Competition Provisions in Regional Trade Agreements: How to Assure Development Gains* (Philippe Brusick, et al. eds., UNCTAD/DITC/CLP/2005/1 2005).

May Fong Cheong & Yin Harn Lee, *Malaysia and Singapore, in The Political Economy of Competition Law in Asia* (Mark Williams ed. Edward Elgar Publishing 2013).

Siow Yue Chia & Michael G. Plummer, *ASEAN Economic Cooperation and Integration: Progress, Challenges and Future Directions* (Cambridge University Press 2015).

Jones Clifford, *Competition Dimensions of NAFTA and the European Union: Semi-Common Competition Policy, Uncommon Rules, and No Common Institutions* (2006).

Malcolm B. Coate, *Theory Meets Practice: Barriers to Entry in Merger Analysis* (2008).

Sandra Marco Colino, *Vertical Agreements and Competition Law: A Comparative Study of the EU and US Regimes* (Hart Publishing 2010).

Maher M. Dabbah, *The Internationalisation of Antitrust Policy* (Cambridge University Press 2003).

Maher M. Dabbah, *International and Comparative Competition Law* (Cambridge University Press 2010).

Sanchita Basu Das, *The ASEAN Economic Community and Beyond: Myths and Realities* (ISEAS 2016).

Paul J. Davidson, *ASEAN: The Evolving Legal Framework for Economic Cooperation* (Times Academic Press 2002).

Martin J. Dedman, *The Origins and Development of the European Union 1945–2008* (2nd ed., Routledge 2009).

Melaku Geboye Desta, *Exemptions from Competition Law in Regional Trade Agreements: A Study Based on Experiences in the Agriculture and Energy Sectors, in Competition Provisions in Regional Trade Agreements: How to Assure Development Gains* (Philippe Brusick, et al. eds., UNCTAD/DITC/CLP/2005/1 2005).

G. Bruce Doern & Stephen Wilks, *Comparative Competition Policy: National Institutions in a Global Market* (Oxford University Press 1996).

Jörn Dosch, *The ASEAN Economic Community: The Status of Implementation, Challenges and Bottlenecks* (CARI 2013).

Josef Drexl, *Economic Integration and Competition Law in Developing Countries, in Competition Policy and Regional Integration in Developing Countries* (Josef Drexl, et al. eds., Edward Elgar Publishing 2012).

Michael G. Egge, *The New EC Merger Regulation: Recipe for Profound Change or More of the Same?* (2004).

Claus Dieter Ehlermann & Laraine L. Laudati, *Panel Discussion: Competition Policy Objectives, in European Competition Law Annual 1997: Objectives of Competition Policy* (Claus Dieter Ehlermann & Laraine L. Laudati eds., Hart Publishing 1998).

Simon J. Evenett, *What Can We Really Learn from the Competition Provision of RTAs?, in Competition Provisions in Regional Trade Agreements: How to Assure Development Gains* (Philippe Brusick, et al. eds., UNCTAD/DITC/CLP/2005/1 2005).

Russel H. Fifield, *National and Regional Interests in ASEAN: Competition and Cooperation in International Politics* (ISEAS 1979).

Harry First, et al., *The United States: The Competition Law System and the Country's Norm, in The Design of Competition Law Institutions: Global Norms, Local Choices* (Eleanor M. Fox & Michael J. Trebilcock eds., Oxford University Press 2012).

Frank Flatters, *Thailand and the Crisis: Roots, Recovery and Long-Run Competitiveness, in The Asian Financial Crisis Lessons for a Resilient Asia* (Wing Thye Woo, et al. eds., The MIT Press 1997).

Eleanor M. Fox, *GE/Honeywell the U.S. Merger that Europe Stopped-A Story of the Politics of Convergence, in Antitrust Stories* (Eleanor M. Fox & Daniel A. Crane eds., Foundation Press 2007).

Eleanor M. Fox, *Competition, Development and Regional Integration: In Search of a Competition Law Fit for Developing Countries, in Competition Policy and Regional Integration in Developing Countries* (Josef Drexl, et al. eds., Edward Elgar Publishing 2012).

Eleanor M. Fox & Daniel A. Crane, *Global Issues in Antitrust and Competition Law* (West 2010).

Eleanor M. Fox, et al., *The Past and Future of International Antitrust: Gaps, Overlaps and the Institutional Challenge, in Building New Competition Law Regime* (David Lewis ed. Edward Elgar 2012).

Eleanor M. Fox & Michal S. Gal, *Drafting Competition Law for Developing Jurisdictions: Learning from Experience, in The Economic Characteristics of Developing Jurisdictions: Their Implications for Competition Law* (Michal S. Gal, et al. eds., Edward Elgar Publishing 2015).

Eleanor M. Fox, et al., *Cases and Materials on United States Antitrust in Global Context* (2nd ed., West 2004).

David Fruitman, *Vietnam, in The Political Economy of Competition Law in Asia* (Mark Williams ed. Edward Elgar Publishing 2013).

Andreas Fuchs, *Characteristic Aspects of Competition and Their Consequences for the Objectives of Competition Law – Comment on Stucke, in The Goals of Competition Law* (Daniel Zimmer ed. Edward Elgar Publishing 2012).

Mark Furse, *Antitrust Law in China, Korea and Vietnam* (Oxford University Press 2009).

Michal S. Gal, *Competition Policy for Small Market Economies* (Harvard University Press 2003).

Michal S. Gal, *The Ecology of Antitrust: Precondition of Competition Law Enforcement in Developing Countries, in Competition, Competitiveness and Development: Lessons from Developing Countries* (UNCTAD ed. UNCTAD/DITC/CLP/2004/1 2004).

Michal S. Gal, *Extra-territorial Application of Antitrust – The Case of a Small Economy (Israel), in Cooperation, Comity, and Competition Policy* (Andrew T. Guzman ed. Oxford University Press 2010).

Michal S. Gal & Inbal Faibish Wassmer, *Regional Agreements of Developing Jurisdictions: Unleashing the Potential, in Competition Policy and Regional Integration in Developing Countries* (Josef Drexl, et al. eds., Edward Elgar Publishing 2012).

Damien Geradin, et al., *Extraterritoriality, Comity and Cooperation in EU Competition Law, in Cooperation, Comity, and Competition Policy* (Andrew T. Guzman ed. Oxford University Press 2010).

David J. Gerber, *Law and Competition in the Twentieth Century Europe* (Oxford University Press 1998).

David J. Gerber, *Law and Competition in Twentieth-Century Europe: Protecting Prometheus* (Oxford University Press 2001).

David J. Gerber, *Global Competition: Law, Markets and Globalisation* (Oxford University Press 2010).

David J. Gerber, *Asia and Global Competition Law Convergence, in* Asian Capitalism and the Regulation of Competition (Michael W. Dowdle, et al. eds., Cambridge University Press 2013).

D. G. Goyder, *EC Competition Law* (4th ed., Oxford University Press 2003).

D. G. Goyder, et al., *Goyder's EC Competition Law* (5th ed., Oxford University Press 2009).

Jürgen Haacke, *ASEAN's Diplomatic and Security Culture: Origins, Development and Prospects* (Routledge 2005).

Alberto Heimler & Frédéric Jenny, *Regional Agreements, in Building New Competition Law Regimes* (David Lewis ed. Edward Elgar Publishing 2013).

High Authority, *Memorandum on the Anti-Trust Policy of the High Authority* (European Coal and Steel Community 1964).

Herbert Hovenkamp, *Federal Antitrust Policy: The Law of Competition and Its Practices* (Thomson West 2005).

Pearl Imada, et al., *A Free Trade Area: Implications for ASEAN* (ISEAS 1991).

Stefano Inama & Edmund W. Sim, *The Foundation of the ASEAN Economic Community: An Institutional and Legal Profile* (Cambridge University Press 2015).

Roger Irvine, *The Formative Years of ASEAN: 1967-1975, in Understanding ASEAN* (Allison Broinowski ed. Macmillan 1982).

Nathalie Jalabert-Doury, Les Instruments de Coopération Plurilatéraux et Multilatéraux de Soft Law Élaborés par l'OCDE (2007).

Frédéric Jenny, *Globalization, Competition and Trade Policy: Convergence, Divergence and Cooperation, in International and Comparative Competition Law and Policies* (Yang-Ching Chao, et al. eds., Kluwer Law International 2001).

Frédéric Jenny, *Competition Enforcement in Testing Times: Beyond National Level* (2009).

Frédéric Jenny & Pierre M. Horna, *Modernization of the European System of Competition Law Enforcement: Lessons for Other Regional Groupings, in Competition Provisions in Regional Trade Agreements: How to Assure Development Gains* (Philippe Brusick, et al. eds., UNCTAD/DITC/CLP/2005/1 2005).

Alison Jones & Brenda Sufrin, *EU Competition Law: Text, Cases, and Materials* (4th ed., Oxford University Press 2011).

Alison Jones & Brenda Sufrin, *EU Competition Law: Text, Cases, and Materials* (5th ed., Oxford University Press 2014).

R. Shyam Khemani & Mark A. Dutz, *The Instruments of Competition Policy and Their Relevance for Economic Development, in Regularities Policies and Reform: A Comparative Perspective* (Claudio R. Frischtak ed. World Bank 1995).

Thanat Khoman, *ASEAN Conception and Evolution, in The ASEAN Reader* (K.S. Sandhu, et al. eds., ISEAS 1992).

Ioannis Kokkoris & Rodrigo Olivares-Caminal, *Antitrust Law amidst Financial Crises* (Cambridge University Press 2010).

Neelie Kroes, *European Competition Policy – Delivering Better Markets and Better Choices, European Consumer and Competition Day* (2005).

Robert Z. Lawrence & Robert E. Litan, *Saving Free Trade: A Pragmatic Approach* (Brookings Institution 1986).

Cassey Lee, *Model Competition Laws, in Competitive Advantage and Competition Policy in Developing Countries* (Paul Cook, et al. eds., Edward Elgar 2007).

Cassey Lee, *Competition Law Enforcement in Malaysia: Some Recent Developments* (ERIA Discussion Paper Series 2014).

Cassey Lee & Yoshifumi Fukunaga, *Competition Policy Challenges of Single Market and Production Base* (ERIA 2013).

Michael Leifer, *ASEAN and the Security of Southeast Asia* (Routledge 1989).

Ioannis Lianos & Arianna Andreangeli, *The European Union: The Competition Law System and the Country's Norm, in The Design of Competition Law Institutions: Global Norms, Local Choices* (Eleanor M. Fox & Michael J. Trebilcock eds., Oxford University Press 2012).

Terence Lim & Abigail Kway, *ASEAN Competition Law* (2nd ed., LexisNexis 2012).

George K. Lipimile, *The COMESA Regional Competition Regulations, in Competition Policy and Regional Integration in Developing Countries* (Josef Drexl, et al. eds., Edward Elgar Publishing 2012).

George K. Lipimile & Elizabeth Gachuiri, *Allocation of Competences Between National and Regional Competition Authorities: The Case of COMESA, in Competition Provisions in Regional Trade Agreements: How to Assure Development Gains* (Philippe Brusick, et al. eds., UNCTAD/DITC/CLP/2005/1 2005).

Philip Lowe, *The Substantive Standard for Merger Control, and the Treatment of Efficiencies in Merger Analysis: an EU Perspective* (2002).

Paul Lugard, *The ICN at Ten: Origins, Accomplishments and Aspirations, in The International Competition Network at Ten: Origins, Accomplishments and Aspirations* (Paul Lugard ed. Hart Publishing 2011).

Frederick A. Mann, *The Doctrine of Jurisdiction in International Law* (Académie de Droit International, Receuil des Cours 1964).

Francisco Marcos, *Do Developing Countries Need Competition Laws and Policy?* (EALE Conference, Madrid 2006).

Francisco Marcos, *Downloading Competition Law from a Regional Trade Agreement: A Strategy to Introduce Competition Law in Bolivia and Ecuador, in Competition*

Law and Policy in Latin America (Eleanor M. Fox & D. Daniel Sokol eds., Hart Publishing 2009).

Philip Marsden, *Acta Non Verba: 'Talking Shop', Don't Become Another Talking Shop, in The International Competition Network at Ten: Origins, Accomplishments and Aspirations* (Paul Lugard ed. Hart Publishing 2011).

Pradeep S. Mehta & Nitya Nanda, *The Role of Civil Society in Promoting Competition Culture at the Regional Level, in Competition Provisions in Regional Trade Agreements: How to Assure Development Gains* (Philippe Brusick, et al. eds., UNCTAD/DITC/CLP/2005/1 2005).

Massimo Motta, *Competition Policy: Theory and Practice* (Cambridge University Press 2004).

Shaun Narine, *Explaining ASEAN: Regionalism in Southeast Asia* (Lynne Rienner Publishers 2002).

Natasya Sirait Ningrum, *Indonesia, in* The Political Economy of Competition Law in Asia (Mark Williams ed. Edward Elgar Publishing 2013).

Okeoghene Odudu, *The Boundaries of EC Competition Law: The Scope of Article 81* (Oxford University Press 2006).

Burton Ong, *Cooperation, Comity and Competition Policy in Singapore, in Cooperation, Comity, and Competition Policy* (Andrew T. Guzman ed. Oxford University Press 2010).

Anestis S. Papadopoulos, *The International Dimension of EU Competition Law and Policy* (Cambridge University Press 2010).

Laura Perret, *The Multiple Personalities of EU Competition Law: Time for a Comprehensive Debate on Its Objectives, in The Goals of Competition Law* (Daniel Zimmer ed. Edward Elgar Publishing 2012).

Robert Pitofsky, *EU and U.S. Approaches to International Mergers-Views from the U.S. Federal Trade Commission* (2000).

Richard A. Posner, *Antitrust Law* (2nd ed., University of Chicago Press 2001).

Christopher B. Roberts, *ASEAN Regionalism: Cooperation, Values and Institutionalisation* (Routledge 2012).

Barry J. Rodger, *Competition Law and Policy in the EC and UK* (3rd ed., Cavendish 2004).

A. E. Rodriguez & Ashok Menon, *The Limits of Competition Policy: The Shortcomings of Antitrust in Developing and Reforming Economies* (Wolters Kluwer 2010).

Heba Shahein, *Designing Competition Laws in New Jurisdictions: Three Models to Follow, in New Competition Jurisdiction: Shaping Policies and Building Institutions* (Richard Whish & Christopher Townley eds., Edward Elgar Publishing 2012).

Udin Silalahi, *The Necessity of ASEAN Competition Law: An Idea* (2007).

Ajit Singh, *Competition and Competition Policy in Emerging Markets: International and Developmental Dimensions* (2002).

Oliver Solano & Andreas Sennekamp, *Competition Provisions in Regional Trade Agreements* (OECD, COM/DAF/TD(2005)3/FINAL 2006).

Janet D. Steiger, *Harmonization of the United States and Mexican Antitrust Law under NAFTA* (1995).

Taimoon Stewart, et al., *Competition Law in Action: Experiences from Developing Countries* (IDRC 2007).
Simon S. C. Tay, et al., *Reinventing ASEAN* (ISEAS 2001).
Martyn D. Taylor, *International Competition Law: A New Dimension for the WTO?* (Cambridge University Press 2006).
Chadwick Teo, *Competition Policy and Economic Growth* (2003).
Jorg Philipp Terhechte, *International Competition Enforcement Law Between Cooperation and Convergence* (Springer 2011).
Thailand, *Letter of Intent* (14 August 1997).
Lawan Thanadsillapakul, *The Harmonization of ASEAN: Competition Laws and Policy from an Economic Integration Perspective, in Competition Policy and Regional Integration in Developing Countries* (Josef Drexl, et al. eds., Edward Elgar 2012).
Sakda Thanitcul & R. Ian McEwin, *Thailand, in The Political Economy of Competition Law in Asia* (Mark Williams ed. Edward Elgar Publishing 2013).
Khin Ohn Thant, *Competition Policy and Economic Growth in ASEAN Countries: A Myanmar's Perspective* (The ASEAN Conference on Fair Competition Law and Policy 2003).
Le Danh Vinh, *Building Competition Law in Vietnam to meet the Need of Regulating Market Economy and in the Light of Trade Liberalisation and International Economic Integration* (2003).
Spencer Weber Waller, *Antitrust and American Business Abroad* (3rd ed., West 1997).
Richard Whish & David Bailey, *Competition Law* (7th ed., Oxford University Press 2012).
Mark Williams & Ruby Ann S. Jalit, *The Philippines, in The Political Economy of Competition Law in Asia* (Mark Williams ed. Edward Elgar Publishing 2013).
Noboyuki Yasuda, *The Evolution of Competition Law in Southeast Asian Countries* (2003).
Siripol Yodmuangchareon, *The Urgency of Competition Law* (2003).
Bruno Zanettin, *Cooperation between Antitrust Agencies at the International Level* (Hart Publishing 2002).

Journal Articles

Draft International Antitrust Code as a GATT-MTO-Plurilateral Trade Agreement (reprint), 64 Antitrust & Trade Reg. Rep. (1993).
EEA Competition Law, 14 E.C.L.R. Supp. 1 (1993).
Interview with Anne K. Bingaman, 8 Antitrust (1993).
Amitav Acharya, *Transnational Production and Security: Southeast Asia's 'Growth Triangles'*, 17 Contemporary Southeast Asia (1995).
Chris Allen, et al., *The Competition Effects of the Single Market in Europe*, 13 Economic Policy 441 (1998).
Ana Maria Alvarez & Pierre Horna, *Implementing Competition Law and Policy in Latin America: The Role of Technical Assistance*, 83 Chi.-Kent L. Rev. (2008).
Jonathan B. Baker & Timothy F. Bresnahan, *Estimating the Residual Demand Curve Facing a Single Firm*, 6 International Journal of Industrial Organization (1988).

Mark Beeson, *ASEAN's Ways: Still Fit for Purpose?*, 22 Cambridge Review of International Affairs (2009).

Christopher Bellamy, *Some Reflections on Competition Law in the Global Market*, 34 New Eng. L. Rev. (1999).

Robert H. Bork, *Legislative Intent and the Policy of Sherman Act*, 9 J. of L. & Eco. (1966).

Gary B. Born, *A Reappraisal of Extraterritorial Reach of U.S. Law*, 24 Law & Pol'y Int'l Bus (1992).

Marco Botta, *The Cooperation between the Competition Authorities of the Developing Countries: Why Does It Not Work? Case Study on Argentina and Brazil*, 5 Comp. L. Rev. (2009).

Marco Botta, *Fostering Competition Culture in the Emerging Economies: The Brazilian Experience*, 32 World Competition (2009).

Dean Brockbank, *The 1995 International Antitrust Guidelines: The Reach of U.S. Antitrust Law Continues to Expand*, 2 J. Int'l Legal Stud. (1996).

Joseph F. Brodley, *The Economic Goals of Antitrust: Efficiency, Consumer Welfare, and Technological Progress*, 60 N.Y.U. L. Rev. (1987).

Jeremy Brown & Gavin Robert, *The European Economic Area: How Important Is It?*, 14 E.I.P.R. 379 (1992).

Leszek Buszynski, *ASEAN's New Challenges*, 70 Pacific Affairs (1997).

Thomas K. Cheng, *Convergence and Its Discontents: A Reconsideration of the Merits of Convergence of Global Competition Law*, 12 Chi. J. Int'l L 433 (2012).

Simon Chesterman, *Does ASEAN Exist? The Association of Southeast Asian Nations as an International Legal Person*, 12 S.Y.B.I. L. (2008).

David Cox & Richard Harris, *Trade Liberalisation and Industrial Organisation: Some Estimates for Canada*, 93 Journal of Political Economy 115 (1985).

O. Richard Cunningham & Anthony J LaRocca, *Harmonisation of Competition Policies in a Regional Economic Integration*, 27 Law & Pol'y Int'l Bus. (1995).

Maher M. Dabbah, *Competition Law and Policy in Developing Countries: A Critical Assessment of the Challenges to Establishing an Effective Competition Law Regime*, 33 World Competition (2010).

Russell W. Damtoft & Ronan Flanagan, *The Development of International Networks in Antitrust*, 43 The International Lawyer (2009).

Carl Davidson, *Cartel Stability and Tariff Policy*, 17 Journal of International Economics 219 (1984).

Paul J. Davidson, *The ASEAN Way and the Role of Law in ASEAN Economic Cooperation*, 8 S.Y.B.I. L. (2004).

José Tavares De Araújo, Jr. & Louis Tineo, *Harmonization of Competition Policies among MERCOSUR Countries*, 24 Brook. J. Int'l L. (1998).

André Filipe Zago De Azevedo, *MERCOSUR: Ambitious Policies, Poor Practices*, 24 Brazilian J. of Pol. Econ. (2004).

Franz Hepp De Sevelinges, *Snapshot of Competition Laws in ASEAN and China*, 26 AUT Int'l L. Practicum (2013).

Makan Delrahim, *The Long and Winding Road: Convergence in the Application of Antitrust to Intellectual Property*, 13 Geo. Mason L. Rev. (2005).

Diane A. Desierto, *Postcolonial International Law Discourses on Regional Developments in South and Southeast Asia*, 36 Int'l J. Legal Info. (2008).

Andreas Diem, *EEA Competition Law*, 15 E.C.L.R. 268 (1994).

Michael C. Dorf, *Legal Indeterminacy and Institutional Design*, 78 N.Y.U. L. Rev. (2003).

S. N. Eisenstadt & Louis Roniger, *Patron-Client Relations as a Model of Structuring Social Exchange*, 22 Comparative Studies in Society and History (1980).

Kenneth G. Elzinga, *The Goals of Antitrust: Other Than Competition and Efficiency, What Else Counts?*, 125 U. Pa. L. Rev. (1977).

Andrew Evans, *Voluntary Harmonisation in Integration between the European Community and Eastern Europe*, 22 E.L. Rev. 201 (1997).

Michael Ewing-Chow, *Culture Club or Chameleon: Should ASEAN Adopt Legalization for Economic Integration?*, 12 S.Y.B.I. L. (2008).

Michael Faure & Xinzhu Zhang, *Towards an Extraterritorial Application of the Chinese Anti-monopoly Law that Avoids Trade Conflicts*, 45 The Geo. Wash. Int'l L. Rev (2013).

Christine Federlin, *Enforcement of the European Economic Area Competition Rules (EEA): Division of Competence and Co-operation between the European Commission*, 4 Int'l Bus. L.J. (1994).

John J. Flynn, *The Raegan Administration's Antitrust Policy, 'Original Intent' and the Legislative History of the Sherman Act*, 33 Antitrust Bull. (1988).

Ian Forrester & Christopher Norall, *The Laicization of Community Law: Self-Help and the Rule of Reason: How Competition Law Is and Could Be Applied*, 21 Common Market L. Rev. (1984).

Eleanor M. Fox, *Can We Solve the Antitrust Problems of Globalization by Extraterritoriality and Cooperation? Sufficiency and Legitimacy*, 48 Antitrust Bulletin (2003).

Eleanor M. Fox, *Economic Development, Poverty and Antitrust: The Other Path*, 13 Sw. J. L. & Trade Am. (2007).

Eleanor M. Fox, *Linked-In: Antitrust and the Virtues of a Virtual Network*, 43 Int'l Law (2009).

Eleanor M. Fox, *Antitrust and Institutions: Design and Change*, 41 Loy. U. Chi. L. J. (2010).

Eleanor M. Fox & Janusz A. Ordover, *Internationalising Competition Law to Limit Parochial State and Private Action: Moving towards the Vision of World Welfare*, 24 Int'l Bus. Law. (1996).

Eleanor M. Fox & A. Jorge Padilla, *The Follower Phenomenon: Implications for the Design of Monopolization Rules in a Global Economy*, 76 Antitrust L.J. (2010).

Eleanor M. Fox & Lawrence A. Sullivan, *Antitrust – Retrospective and Prospective: Where Are We Coming From? Where Are We Going?*, 62 N.Y.U. L. Rev. (1987).

James J. Friedberg, *The Convergence of Law in an Era of Political Integration: The Wood Pulp Case and the Alcoa Effects Doctrine*, 52 U. Pitt. L. Rev. (1991).

K. C. Fung, *Economic Integration as Competitive Discipline*, 33 International Economic Review 837 (1992).

Michal S. Gal, *Size Does Matter: the Effects of Market Size on Optimal Competition Policy*, 74 S. Cal. L. Rev. (2001).

Michal S. Gal, *The 'Cut and Paste' of Article 82 of the EC Treaty in Israel: Conditions for a Successful Transplant*, 9 European Journal of Law Reform (2007).

Michal S. Gal, *Antitrust in a Globalized Economy: The Unique Enforcement Challenges Faced by Small and Developing Jurisdictions*, 33 Fordham Int'l L.J. (2009).

Michal S. Gal, *Regional Competition Law Agreements: An Important Step for Antitrust Enforcement*, 60 U. Toronto L.J. (2010).

Barbara C. George, et al., *Increasing Extraterritorial Intrusion of European Union Authority into U.S. Business Mergers and Competition Practices: U.S. Multinational Businesses Underestimate the Strength of the European Commission from GE/Honeywell to Microsoft*, 19 Conn. J. Int'l L. 571 (2004).

Damien Geradin, *The Perils of Antitrust Proliferation: The Globalisation of Antitrust and the Risks of Overregulation of Competitive Behavior*, 10 Chi. J. Int'l L (2009).

David Gerber, *The Extraterritorial Application of German Antitrust Law*, 77 American Journal of International Law 756 (1983).

Paul E. Godek, *One U.S. Export Eastern Europe Does Not Need*, 15 Regulation (1992).

Paul E. Godek, *A Chicago-School Approach to Antirust for Developing Countries*, 43 The Antitrust Bulletin (1998).

Joseph P. Griffin, *Foreign Governmental Reactions to U.S. Assertions of Extraterritorial Jurisdiction*, 6 Geo. Mason L. Rev. (1997).

Andrew T. Guzman, *Is International Antitrust Possible?*, 73 N.Y.U. L. Rev. 1501 (1998).

Andrew T. Guzman, *Antitrust and International Regulatory Federalism*, 76 N.Y.U. L. Rev. (2001).

Andrew T. Guzman, *The Case for International Antitrust*, 22 Berkeley J. Int'l Law (2004).

Deborah A. Haas, *Out of Others' Shadows: ASEAN Moves Toward Greater Regional Cooperation in the Face of the EC and NAFTA*, 9 Am. U. J. Int'l L. & Pol'y (1994).

George Winthrop Haight, *International Law and Extraterritorial Application of the Antitrust Laws*, 63 Yale L. J. (1954).

John O. Haley, *Competition Law for the Asia-Pacific Economic Cooperation Community: Designing Shoes for Many Sizes*, 1 Wash. U. Global Stud. L. Rev. (2002).

George A. Hay, *Market Power in Antitrust*, 60 Antitrust L.J (1991).

Anna-Louise Hinds, *The New EC Merger Regulation – The More Things Change the More They Stay the Same?*, 17 European Business Law Review (2006).

Hugh M. Hollman & William E. Kovacic, *International Competition Network: Its Past, Current and Future Role*, 20 Minn. J. Int'l L. (2011).

Lin Chun Hung, *ASEAN Charter: Deeper Regional Integration under International Law?*, 9 Chinese J. of Int'l L 821 (2010).

Frédéric Jenny, *International Cooperation on Competition: Myth, Reality and Perspective*, 48 Antitrust Bull. (2003).

Miles Kahler, *Legalization as Strategy: The Asia-Pacific Case*, 54 International Organization (2000).

Nicholas de BelleVille Katzenbach, *Conflicts on an Unruly Horse: Reciprocal Claims and Tolerances in Interstate and International Law*, 65 Yale L. J. (1956).

Peter Kenevan & Andrew Winden, *Flexible Free Trade Area: The ASEAN Free Trade Area*, 34 Harv. Int'l L.J. (1993).

William E. Kovacic, *Designing and Implementing Competition and Consumer Protection Reforms in Transitional Economies: Perspectives from Mongolia, Nepal, Ukraine, and Zimbabwe*, 44 DePaul L. Rev. (1995).
William E. Kovacic, *Getting Started: Creating New Competition Policy Institutions in Transition Economies*, 23 Brook. J. Int'l L. (1997).
William E. Kovacic, *Merger Enforcement in Transition: Antitrust Controls on Acquisitions in Emerging Economies*, 66 U. Cin. L. Rev. (1998).
William E. Kovacic, *Extraterritoriality, Institutions, and Convergence in International Competition Policy*, 97 Am. Soc'y Int'l L. Proc. (2003).
William E. Kovacic, *Achieving Better Practices in the Design of Competition Policy Institutions*, 50 The Antitrust Bulletin (2005).
William E. Kovacic, *The Institutions of Antitrust Law: How Structure Shapes Substance*, 110 Mich. L. Rev. (2012).
William E. Kovacic & David A. Hyman, *Competition Agency Design: What's on the Menu?*, 8 European Competition Journal (2012).
Margaret Levenstein & Valerie Y. Suslow, *Contemporary International Cartels and Developing Countries: Economic Effects and Implications for Competition Policy*, 71 Antitrust L.J. (2004).
Lee Leviter, *The ASEAN Charter: ASEAN Failure or Member Failure?*, 43 N.Y.U. J. Int'l L. & Pol. 159 (2010).
Ioannis Lianos, *The Contribution of the United Nations to the Emergence of Global Antitrust Law*, 15 Tul. J. Int'l & Comp. L. (2007).
Kjell Erik Lommerud & Lars Sorgard, *Trade Liberalization and Cartel Stability*, 9 Review of International Economics 343 (2001).
Carolina Alberto Lopez & Jacint Soler Matutes, *Open Regionalism Versus Discriminatory Trading Agreements: Institutional and Empirical Analysis*, 14 ASEAN Econ. Bull. (1998).
Luu Huong Ly, *Regional Harmonization of Competition Law and Policy: An ASEAN Approach*, 2 Asian J. Int. Law (2012).
Tay-Cheng Ma, *Competition Authority Independence, Antitrust Effectiveness, and Institutions*, 30 Int'l Rev. L. & Econ. (2010).
Neil Macfarquhar, *U.N. Doubts Fairness of Election in Myanmar*, THE NEW YORK TIMES, 21 Oct. 2010.
Jurgita Malinauskaite, *Efficiency Tests in the Merger Control Regimes of the Baltic Countries: Myth or Reality*, 18 International Company and Commercial Law Review (2007).
Matsuo Matsushita, *International Cooperation in the Enforcement of Competition Policy*, 1 Wash. U. Global Stud. L. Rev. (2002).
Lee McGowan & Stephen Wilks, *The First Supranational Policy in the European Union: Competition Policy*, 28 European Journal of Political Research (1995).
Salil K. Mehrar, *More is Less: A Law-and-Economics Approach to the International Scope of Private Antitrust Enforcement*, 77 Temp. L. Rev. (2004).
Joseph M. Moschella, *The Necessity of Active American Involvement in Global Competition Law*, 22 Wis. Int'l L.J. (2004).

John M. Nannes, *Transparency in Federal Antitrust Enforcement Decisions: A Reaction to Professor Grimes*, 51 Buff. L. Rev. (2003).

Joseph E. Neuhas, *Power to Reverse Foreign Judgments: The British Clawback Stature under International Law*, 81 Colum. L. Rev. (1981).

Gesner Oliveira, *Competition Policy in Brazil and MERCOSUR: Aspect of the Recent Experience*, 24 Brook. J. Int'l L. (1998).

Burton Ong, *The Origins, Objectives and Structure of Competition Law in Singapore*, 29 World Competition (2006).

Katri Paas-Mohando, *Choice of Merger Notification System for Small Economies*, 34 E.C.L.R. (2013).

Raju Parakkal, *Political Characteristics and Competition Law Enactment: A Cross-Country Empirical Analysis*, 56 The Antitrust Bulletin (2011).

Ernst-Ulrich Petersmann, *Legal, Economic and Political Objectives of National and International Competition Policies: Constitutional Functions of WTO, 'Linking Principles' for Trade and Competition*, 34 New Eng. L. Rev. (1999).

Olga Petrovsky, *International Antitrust Agreement: Premature Proposal and Practical Solutions*, 22 N.Y. Int'l L. Rev (2009).

Deepa Rishikesh, *Extraterritoriality Versus Sovereignty in International Antitrust Jurisdiction*, 14 World Competition (1991).

A. E. Rodriguez & Mark D. Williams, *The Effectiveness of Proposed Antitrust Programs for Developing Countries*, 19 N.C.J. Int'l L. & Com. Reg. 209 (1994).

David K. Round & Alec Zuo, *The Welfare Goal of Antitrust Laws in Asia: For Whom Should the Law Toil?*, 22 Asian-Pacific Economic Literature 2 (2008).

Faaez Samadi, *Convergence Issues Loom Large for ASEAN*, Global Competition Review (2013).

Philipp J. H. Schroder, *Cartel Stability and Economic Integration*, 15(2) Review of International Economics 313 (2007).

Peter H. Schuck, *Is a Competent Federal Government Becoming Oxymoronic?*, 77 George Washington L. Rev. (2009).

Louis B. Schwartz, *'Justice' and Other Non-Economic Goals of Antitrust*, 127 U. Pa. L. Rev. (1979).

Vijay S.V. Selvam, *The EC Merger Control Impasse: Is there a Solution to this Predicament*, 25 E.C.L.R. (2004).

George T. L. Shenoy, *The Emergence of a Legal Framework for Economic Policy in ASEAN*, 29 Malaya Law Review (1987).

Manisha M. Sheth, *Formulating Antitrust Policy in Emerging Economies*, 86 Geo. L. J. (1997).

G. Sivalingam, *Competition Policy and Law in ASEAN*, 51 The Singapore Economic Review (2006).

Alasdair Smith & Anthony J. Venables, *Completing the Internal Market in the European Community: Some Industry Simulations*, 32 European Economic Review 1501 (1988).

Daniel D. Sokol, *Order Without (Enforceable) Law: Why Countries Enter into Non-enforceable Competition Policy Chapters in Free Trade Agreements*, 83 Chi.-Kent L. Rev. (2008).

D. Daniel Sokol, *Designing Antitrust Agencies for More Effective Outcomes: What Antitrust Can Learn from Restaurant Guides*, 41 Loyola University Chicago Law Journal (2010).

Richard M. Steuer, *The Simplicity of Antitrust Law*, 14 U. Pa. J. Bus. L. (2012).

Maurice E. Stucke, *Antitrust 2025*, CPI Antitrust Journal (2010).

Maurice E. Stucke, *Reconsidering Competition*, 81 Miss. L.J. (2011).

Maurice E. Stucke, *Reconsidering Antitrust's Goals*, 53 B.C. L. Rev. (2012).

Lawrence A. Sullivan, *Economics and More Humanistic Disciplines: What Are the Sources of Wisdom for Antitrust*, 125 U. Pa. L. Rev. (1977).

Alastair Sutton, *'Extraterritoriality' in Competition Law from a European Perspective*, 16 AUT Int'l L. Practicum (2003).

Alexandr Svetlicinii & Külliki Lugenberg, *Merger Remedies in a Small Market Economy: The Estonian Experience*, E.C.L.R. (2012).

Brendan Sweeney, *Combatting Foreign Anti-competitive Conduct: What Role for Extraterritoriality?*, 8(1) Melbourne J. Int'l L. (2007).

Kevin Y.L. Tan, *The Making and Remaking of Constitutions in Southeast Asia: An Overview*, 6 Sing. J. Int'l & Comp. L. (2002).

Simon S. C. Tay, *The ASEAN Charter: Between National Sovereignty and the Region's Constitutional Moment*, 12 S.Y.B.I. L. (2008).

Lawan Thanadsillapakul, A New Direction for ASEAN Regionalisation in the Changing Global Legal and Economic Environment (2000) (PhD Thesis, Lancaster University).

Kurnia Toha, *Extraterritorial Applicability of Indonesia Business Competition Law as an Efforts Dealing ASEAN Single Market*, 15 Jurnal Dinamika Hukum (2015).

Michael J. Trebilcock & Edward M. Iacobucci, *Designing Competition Law Institutions*, 25 World Competition (2002).

Michael J. Trebilcock & Edward M. Iacobucci, *Designing Competition Law Institutions: Values, Structure, and Mandate*, 41 Loy. U. Chi. L.J. (2010).

Jarrod Tudor, *A Comparison of the Jurisprudence of the ECJ and the EFTA Court on the Free Movement of Goods in the EEA: Is There an Intolerable Separation of Article 34 of the TFEU and Article 11 of the EEA?*, 17 San Diego Int'l L.J. 75 (2015).

Donald F. Turner, *Application of Competition Laws to Foreign Conduct: Appropriate Resolution of Jurisdictional Issues*, 10 World Competition (1986).

John Vickers, *Market Power in Competition Case*, 2 European Law Journal (2006).

John Vickers, *Competition Law and Economics: A Mid-Atlantic Viewpoint*, ECJ 1 (2007).

Sven B. Volcker, *Mind the Gap: Unilateral Effects Analysis Arrives in EC Merger Control*, 25 E.C.L.R. (2004).

Spencer Weber Waller, *The Internationalization of Antitrust Enforcement*, 77 B.U. L. Rev. (2002).

Daniel P. Weick, *Competition Law and Policy in Senegal: A Cautionary Tale for Regional Integration?*, 33 World Competition (2010).

George O. III White, *From Snowplows to Siopao—Trying to compete in a Global Marketplace: The ASEAN Free Trade Area*, 8 Tulsa J. Comp. & Int'l L. (2000).

Mark Williams, *Competition Law in Thailand: Seeds of Success or Fated to Fail?*, 27 World Competition (2004).

Mark Williams, *The Lion City and the Fragrant Harbor: The Political Economy of Competition Policy in Singapore and Hong Kong Compared*, 54 Antitrust Bulletin (2009).

Megan R. Williams, *ASEAN: Do Progress and Effectiveness Require a Judiciary?*, 30 Suffolk Transnat'l L. Rev. 433 (2007).

Diane P. Wood, *International Harmonization of Antitrust Law: The Tortoise or the Hare*, 3 Chi. J. Int'l L. (2002).

Stéphanie Yon-Courtin, *ASEAN: L'ASEAN Publie des Lignes Directrices en Matière de Concurrence*, 4 Revue Concurrences (2010).

Table of Cases

Andean Community

Decision 285 Concerning Rules and Regulations for Preventing or Correcting Distortions in Competition Caused by Practices that Restrict Free Competition (1991), **45, 46**

Decision 608 Concerning Regulations for the Protection and Promotion of Competition in the Andean Community (2005), **45, 46**

European Free Trade Association

L'Oréal Norge AS v. Aarskog Per AS and Others and Smart Club Norge, Cases E-9/07 and E-10/07, EFTA Ct. Rep. 258 (2008), **31**

European Union

Court of Justice

Ahlström Osakeyhtiö v. Commission, Case 89/85, ECR I-1307 (1993), **121**

Albany International BV v. Stichting Bedrijfspensioenfonds Textielindustrie, Case 67/96, ECR I-5751, Jacobs AG (1999), **83**

Commission v. Italy, Case 118/85, ECR 2599 (1987), **83**

Établissements Consten S.à.R.L. and Grundig-Verkaufs-GmbH v. Commission, Cases 56/64, 58/64, ECR 299 (1966), **56, 57**

Europemballage Corporation and Continental Can Company Inc. v. Commission of the European Communities, Case 6/72, ECR 215 (1973), **89, 90**

Fédération Française des Sociétés d'Assurance v. Ministry of Agriculture and Fisheries, Case 244/94, ECR I-4013 (1995), **82**

Franz Völk v. S.P.R.L. Ets J. Vervaecke, Case 5/69, ECR 295 (1969) CMLR 273 (1969), **144**

GlaxoSmithKline Services Unlimited v. Commission, Cases 501/06 P, 513/06 P, 515/06 P, 519/06 P, I-09291 (2009), 4 CMLR 2 (2009), **56, 57**

Hoffmann-La Roche & Co. AG v. Commission, Case 85/76, ECR 461 (1979), **89**

General Court

Commission Decisions and Notices

European Free Trade Association Court

Indonesia

MERCOSUR

Permanent Court of International Justice

United States

Supreme Court

Circuit Courts

District Courts

Singapore

Competition Commission of Singapore

Competition Appeal Board

West African Economic and Monetary Union Court of Justice

Table of Legislation

Indonesia

Lao PDR

Malaysia

Mexico

Myanmar

New Zealand

Philippines

Singapore

South Africa

Thailand

United Kingdom

United States

Vietnam

Table of Regulations

Andean Community

ASEAN

Caribbean Community and Common Market

Common Market for Eastern and Southern Africa

Economic Community of West African States

European Economic Area

European Free Trade Association

European Union

MERSOCUR

Thailand

Thailand Ministerial Regulations under Thailand Trade Competition Act of 1999 (1999), **142**

West African Economic and Monetary Union

Traité de l'Union Monétaire Ouest-Africaine (1973), **40**

Table of Treaties

Index

O

P

R

S

T

U

W

INTERNATIONAL COMPETITION LAW SERIES

1. Ignacio De Leon, *Latin American Competition Law and Policy: A Policy in Search of Identity*, 2001 (ISBN 90-411-1542-0).
2. Wim Dejonghe & Wouter Van de Voorde (eds), *M & A in Belgium*, 2001 (ISBN 90-411-1594-3).
3. Yang-Ching Chao, Gee San, Changfa Lo & Jiming Ho (eds), *International and Comparative Competition Law and Policies*, 2001 (ISBN 90-411-1643-5).
4. Martin Mendelsohn & Stephen Rose, *Guide to the EC Block Exemption for Vertical Agreements*, 2002 (ISBN 90-411-9813-X).
5. Clifford A. Jones & Mitsuo Matsushita (eds), *Competition Policy in the Global Trading System: Perspectives from the EU, Japan and the USA*, 2002 (ISBN 90-411-1758-X).
6. Christian Koenig, Andreas Bartosch, Jens-Daniel Braun & Marion Romes (eds), *EC Competition and Telecommunications Law*. Second Edition, 2009 (ISBN 978-90-411-2564-4).
7. Jürgen Basedow (ed.), *Limits and Control of Competition with a View to International Harmonization*, 2002 (ISBN 90-411-1967-1).
8. Maureen Brunt, Economic Essays on Australian and New Zealand Competition Law, 2003 (ISBN 90-411-1991-4).
9. Ky P. Ewing, Jr., *Competition Rules for the 21st Century: Principles from America's Experience*, Second Edition, 2006 (ISBN 90-411-2477-2).
10. Joseph Wilson, *Globalization and the Limits of National Merger Control Laws*, 2003 (ISBN 90-411-1996-5).
11. Peter Verloop & Valérie Landes (eds), *Merger Control in Europe: EU, Member States and Accession States*, Fourth Edition, 2003 (ISBN 90-411-2056-4).
12. Themistoklis K. Giannakopoulos, *Safeguarding Companies' Rights in Competition and Anti-dumping/Anti-subsidies Proceedings*, Second Edition, 2011 (ISBN 978-90-411-3404-2).
13. Marjorie Holmes & Lesley Davey (eds), *A Practical Guide to National Competition Rules across Europe*, Second Edition, 2007 (ISBN 978-90- 411-2607-8).
14. Sigrid Stroux, *US and EU Oligopoly Control*, 2004 (ISBN 90-411-2296-6).
15. Tzong-Leh Hwang and Chiyuan Chen (eds), *The Future Development of Competition Framework*, 2004 (ISBN 90-411-2305-9).

16. Phedon Nicolaides, Mihalis Kekelekis and Maria Kleis, *State Aid Policy in the European Community: Principles and Practice,* Second Edition, 2008 (ISBN 978-90-411-2754-9).
17. Doris Hildebrand, *Economic Analyses of Vertical Agreements: A Self- Assessment*, 2005 (ISBN 90-411-2328-8).
18. Frauke Henning-Bodewig, *Unfair Competition Law: European Union and Member States*, 2005 (ISBN 90-411-2329-6).
19. Duarte Brito & Margarida Catalão-Lopes, *Mergers and Acquisitions: The Industrial Organization Perspective,* 2006 (ISBN 90-411-2451-9).
20. Nikos Th. Nikolinakos, *EU Competition Law and Regulation in the Converging Telecommunications, Media and IT Sectors*, 2006 (ISBN 90-411- 2469-1).
21. Mihalis Kekelekis, *The EC Merger Control Regulation: Rights of Defence. A Critical Analysis of DG COMP Practice and Community Courts' Jurisprudence*, 2006 (ISBN 90-411-2553-1).
22. Mark R. Joelson, *An International Antitrust Primer: A Guide to the Operation of United States, European Union and Other Key Competition Laws in the Global Economy*, Third Edition, 2006 (ISBN 90-411-2468-3).
23. Themistoklis K. Giannakopoulos, *A Concise Guide to the EU Anti-dumping/ Anti-subsidies Procedures*, 2006 (ISBN 90-411-2464-0).
24. George Cumming, Brad Spitz & Ruth Janal, *Civil Procedure Used for Enforcement of EC Competition Law by the English, French and German Civil Courts*, 2007 (ISBN 978-90-411-2471-5).
25. Jürgen Basedow (ed.), *Private Enforcement of EC Competition Law,* 2007 (ISBN 978-90-411-2613-9).
26. Jung Wook Cho, *Innovation and Competition in the Digital Network Economy: A Legal and Economic Assessment on Multi-tying Practices and Network Effects*, 2007 (ISBN 978-90-411-2574-3).
27. Akira Inoue, *Japanese Antitrust Law Manual: Law, Cases and Interpretation of the Japanese Antimonopoly Act*, 2007 (ISBN 978-90-411-2627-6).
28. René Barents, *Directory of EC Case Law on Competition,* 2007 (ISBN 978-90-411-2656-6).
29. Paul F. Nemitz (ed.), *The Effective Application of EU State Aid Procedures: The Role of National Law and Practice*, 2007 (ISBN 978-90-411-2657-3).
30. Jurian Langer, *Tying and Bundling as a Leveraging Concern under EC Competition Law,* 2007 (ISBN 978-90-411-2575-0).
31. Abel M. Mateus & Teresa Moreira (eds), *Competition Law and Economics – Advances in Competition Policy and Antitrust Enforcement*, 2007 (ISBN 978-90-411-2632-0).
32. Alberto Santa Maria, *Competition and State Aid: An Analysis of the EC Practice*, 2007 (ISBN 978-90-411-2617-7).
33. Barry J. Rodger (ed.), *Article 234 and Competition Law: An Analysis,* 2007 (ISBN 978-90-411-2605-4).

34. Alla Pozdnakova, *Liner Shipping and EU Competition Law,* 2008 (ISBN 978-90-411-2717-4).
35. Milena Stoyanova, *Competition Problems in Liberalized Telecommunications: Regulatory Solutions to Promote Effective Competition*, 2008 (ISBN 978-90-411-2736-5).
36. *EC State Aid Law/Le Droit des Aides d'Etat dans la CE. Liber Amicorum Francisco Santaolalla Gadea*, 2008 (ISBN 978-90-411-2774-7).
37. René Barents, *Directory of EC Case Law on State Aids,* 2008 (ISBN 978- 90-411-2732-7).
38. Ignacio De Leon, *An Institutional Assessment of Antitrust Policy: The Latin American Experience*, 2009 (ISBN 978-90-411-2478-4).
39. Doris Hildebrand, *The Role of Economic Analysis in EU Competition Law: TheEuropean School*, Fourth Edition, 2016 (ISBN 978-90-411-6245-8).
40. Eugène Buttigieg, *Competition Law: Safeguarding the Consumer Interest. A Comparative Analysis of US Antitrust Law and EC Competition Law,* 2009 (ISBN 978-90-411-3119-5).
41. Ioannis Lianos & Ioannis Kokkoris (eds), *The Reform of EC Competition Law: New Challenges,* 2010 (ISBN 978-90-411-2692-4).
42. George Cumming & Mirjam Freudenthal, *Civil Procedure in EU Competition Cases before the English and Dutch Courts*, 2010 (ISBN 978-90-411-3192-8).
43. A.E. Rodriguez & Ashok Menon, *The Limits of Competition Policy: The Shortcomings of Antitrust in Developing and Reforming Economies*, 2010 (ISBN 978-90-411-3177-5).
44. Mika Oinonen, *Does EU Merger Control Discriminate against Small Market Companies? Diagnosing the Argument with Conclusions*, 2010 (ISBN 978-90-411-3261-1).
45. Eirik Østerud, *Identifying Exclusionary Abuses by Dominant Undertakings under EU Competition Law: The Spectrum of Tests*, 2010 (ISBN 978-90-411-3271-0).
46. Marco Botta, *Merger Control Regimes in Emerging Economies: A Case Study on Brazil and Argentina*, 2011 (ISBN 978-90-411-3402-8).
47. Jürgen Basedow & Wolfgang Wurmnest (eds), *Structure and Effects in EU Competition Law: Studies on Exclusionary Conduct and State Aid*, 2011 (ISBN 978-90-411-3174-4).
48. George Cumming (ed.), *Merger Decisions and the Rules of Procedure of the European Community Courts*, 2012 (ISBN 978-90-411-3671-8).
49. Eduardo Molan Gaban & Juliana Oliveira Domingues (eds), *Antitrust Law in Brazil: Fighting Cartels,* 2012 (ISBN 978-90-411-3670-1).
50. Giandonato Caggiano, Gabriella Muscolo & Marina Tavassi (eds), *Competition Law and Intellectual Property: A European Perspective,* 2012 (ISBN 978-90-411-3447-9).
51. Ben Van Rompuy, *Economic Efficiency: The Sole Concern of Modern Antitrust Policy? Non-efficiency Considerations under Article 101 TFEU*, 2012 (ISBN 978-90-411-3870-5).

52. Liyang Hou, *Competition Law and Regulation of the EU Electronic Communications Sector: A Comparative Legal Approach*, 2012 (ISBN 978-90-411-4047-0).
53. Barry Rodger, *Landmark Cases in Competition Law: Around the World in Fourteen Stories*, 2012 (ISBN 978-90-411-3843-9).
54. Andreas Scordamaglia-Tousis, *EU Cartel Enforcement: Reconciling Effective Public Enforcement with Fundamental Rights*, 2013 (ISBN 978-90-411-4758-5).
55. Bernardo Cortese (ed.), *EU Competition Law: Between Public and Private Enforcement*, 2014 (ISBN 978-90-411-4677-9).
56. Barry Rodger (ed.), *Competition Law: Comparative Private Enforcement and Collective Redress across the EU*, 2014 (ISBN 978-90-411-4559-8).
57. Nada Ina Pauer, *The Single Economic Entity Doctrine and Corporate Group Responsibility in European Antitrust Law*, 2014 (ISBN 978-90-411-5262-6).
58. Urška Petrovčič, *Competition Law and Standard Essential Patents: A Transatlantic Perspective*, 2014 (ISBN 978-90-411-4960-2).
59. David Telyas, *The Interface between Competition Law, Patents and Technical Standards*, 2014 (ISBN 978-90-411-5418-7).
60. Katerina Maniadaki, *EU Competition Law, Regulation and the Internet: The Case of Net Neutrality*, 2014 (ISBN 978-90-411-4140-8).
61. Horacio Vedia Jerez, *Competition Law Enforcement and Compliance across the World: A Comparative Review*, 2015 (ISBN 978-90-411-5815-4).
62. Kadir Ba, *The Substantive Appraisal of Joint Ventures under the EU Merger Control Regime*, 2015 (ISBN 978-90-411-5816-1).
63. Alberto Santa Maria, *Competition and State Aid: An Analysis of the EU Practice*, Second Edition, 2015 (ISBN 978-90-411-5818-5).
64. Lúcio Tomé Feteira, *The Interplay between European and National Competition Law after Regulation 1/2003: "United (Should) We Stand?"*, 2016 (ISBN 978-90-411-5663-1).
65. Giovanni Pitruzzella & Gabriella Muscolo(eds), *Competition and Patent Law in the Pharmaceutical Sector: An International Perspective*, 2016 (ISBN 978-90-411-5927-4).
66. Małgorzata Cyndecka, *The Market Economy Investor Test in EU State Aid Law: Applicability and Application*, 2016 (ISBN 978-90-411-6102-4).
67. Damiano Canapa, *Trademarks and Brands in Merger Control: An Analysis of the European and Swiss Legal Orders*, 2016 (ISBN 978-90-411-6717-0).
68. Inge Graef, *EU Competition Law, Data Protection and Online Platforms: Data as Essential Facility*, 2016 (ISBN 978-90-411-8324-8).
69. Anders Jessen, *Exclusionary Abuse after the* Post Danmark I *Case: The Role of the Effects-Based Approach under Article 102 TFEU*, 2017 (ISBN 978-90-411-8996-7).
70. Baskaran Balasingham, *The EU Leniency Policy: Reconciling Effectiveness and Fairness*, 2017 (ISBN 978-90-411-8479-5).
71. Eugene Stuart & Iana Roginska-Green, *Sixty Years of EU State Aid Law and Policy: Analysis and Assessment*, 2018 (ISBN 978-90-411-8869-4).

72. Anna Renata Pisarkiewicz, *Margin Squeeze in the Electronic Communications Sector: Critical Analysis of the Decisional Practice and Case Law*, 2018 (ISBN 978-90-411-6246-5).
73. Ploykaew Porananond, *Competition Law in the ASEAN Countries: Regional Law and National Systems*, 2018 (ISBN 978-90-411-9102-1).

www.ingramcontent.com/pod-product-compliance
Ingram Content Group UK Ltd.
Pitfield, Milton Keynes, MK11 3LW, UK
UKHW020815290926
15470UKWH00003B/1168

9 789041 191021